Perils of Protection

Children's Literature
Association Series

Perils of Protection

Shipwrecks, Orphans, and Children's Rights

Susan Honeyman

UNIVERSITY PRESS OF MISSISSIPPI / JACKSON

The University Press of Mississippi is the scholarly publishing agency of the Mississippi Institutions of Higher Learning: Alcorn State University, Delta State University, Jackson State University, Mississippi State University, Mississippi University for Women, Mississippi Valley State University, University of Mississippi, and University of Southern Mississippi.

www.upress.state.ms.us

The University Press of Mississippi is a member of the Association of University Presses.

Copyright © 2019 by University Press of Mississippi
All rights reserved

First printing 2019

∞

Library of Congress Cataloging-in-Publication Data available
ISBN 978-1-4968-1989-5 (cloth)
ISBN 978-1-4968-2111-9 (paper)
ISBN 978-1-4968-1990-1 (epub single)
ISBN 978-1-4968-1991-8 (epub institutional)
ISBN 978-1-4968-1992-5 (pdf single)
ISBN978-1-4968-1993-2 (pdf institutional)

British Library Cataloging-in-Publication Data available

Contents

ACKNOWLEDGMENTS vii

INTRODUCTION
Familial Fallacies 3

1   WOMEN AND CHILDREN FIRST
Shipwreck, Sentiment, Property, and Survival 15

2   NO CHILD IS AN ISLAND
Robinsonades, Islanding, and the Right to Roam 45

3   BABIES IN BOXES
Finding and Loving Other People's Children 75

4   THE PRISON HOUSE OF COMICS CENSORSHIP
AND PARTICIPATORY RESISTANCE 124

5   THE PRICE OF PROTECTIONIST PRETENSE 157

CONCLUSION
A Last Note on the Nuclear Family 184

Notes 191

Works Cited 201

Index 217

Acknowledgments

My deepest gratitude goes to Bonnie Bing Honeyman for modeling how we can and should care for other people's children. Her commitment to community, especially service to children, continues to inspire me. Thanks to my students, with whom I've honed this material for more than a decade; colleagues Michelle Beissel Heath, Lorna Bracewell, Megan Hartman, and Jessica Isaac for source tips; Anna Wagemann for my index; and Sam Umland for much-needed and patient advice throughout my comics collecting. It was an honor to interview Nell Rose Kottal Wall for her generous insights as a former "funny book" fan and favorite of Sheldon Mayer during the 1950s. Thanks also to Erin Weinman and Special Collections staff at Harvard's Schlesinger Library, Katie Keene at the University Press of Mississippi, and the Research Services Council at the University of Nebraska at Kearney for a course release that enabled fuller focus on research. Lara Saguisag, as editor and conference panel organizer, was crucial in motivating my initial drafts of chapters 4 and 5, and as reviewer, she encouraged and generously critiqued my work, stimulating further questioning and helping to smooth many of my very rough edges. My gratitude to *Children's Literature Association Quarterly* (39, no. 2), *The Lion and the Unicorn* (40, no. 2), and *Children's Literature* (45) for permission to reprint sections of earlier work published there, which reappear here briefly or in expanded form as case studies.

I am indebted to Marguerite Tassi, my longtime mentor and model of sage, politic grace. Thank you to Heidi Eichbauer for your healing influence, unflinching honesty, seaworthy vocabulary, and ability to make me howl with laughter. To Kate Benzel, who has the spirit of a hawk but the heart of a sailor, thank you for keeping me afloat. And I am always indebted to William Avilés, my partner in crime and everyday adventures.

Perils of Protection

Introduction

Familial Fallacies

In Louise Fitzhugh's *Nobody's Family Is Going to Change* (1974), eleven-year-old Emancipation (Emma) Sheridan "found a book on children's rights.... It seemed to go on and on about how there weren't any. Of course, if children didn't have any rights, then naturally it would be hard to write a book about those rights. All you could write about was the absence of them" (156). Emma's commentary aptly describes the situation many of us find ourselves in when we try to talk about children's rights in the US context, where protectionism reigns, and concepts like "self-determination" and "participation" are less recognized as human rights that might equitably extend to minors in any practical application. By investigating cultural reflections of this situation, I aim to reveal subtle (and not so subtle) impulses in adult rhetoric that can confuse child rights issues, especially surrounding what might seem to be the best of our intentions—protecting children.

For the past fifteen years, I've been implicitly coaxing awareness of child rights in my writing and explicitly doing the same in my classes. In both efforts, I've been surprised at how repeatedly I'm confronted with a common but usually unacknowledged factor in violations of children's liberties: case after case reveals that confusion of child participatory rights for an encroachment on parental rights willfully overlooks that invoking the rights of children for protection without participation results in less of both. This problem is particularly extreme in the United States, where a range of experiences represented in cases like Savana Redding's strip search for two ibuprofen, Matthew Limon's incarceration, Trayvon Martin's shooting, Kaitlyn Hunt's relationship with a younger girlfriend whose right to consent was not protected, and Achmed Mohammed's clock are relatively commonplace in media coverage that nonetheless rarely mentions the minors' human rights. Legal approaches to the issue rarely enter into or inform humanities discourse. As a specialist in children's literature, a former court-appointed special advocate (CASA) for children in foster care familiar with the bureaucracy of child protection, and an amateur folklorist/ethnographer, I've eagerly awaited a source that addresses this dearth in connectivity. I'm equally surprised that it remains unwritten. In an effort to redress the oversight, I will utilize literary parallels and rhetorical analysis to identify a deeper structure of protectionism that, through a history of privatizing childhood, has in fact left minors increasingly isolated in dwindling (and sometimes nonexistent) social units such as "nuclear family," vulnerable to multiple injustices made possible by eroded or unrecognized participatory rights.

From the vantage point of legalistic expertise, many have written about the failure of the United States to ratify the UN Convention on the Rights of the Child, the most globally adopted human rights treaty in history, and most make a noble stab at speculation, and we need to follow their lead toward explaining this inertia on the level of popular beliefs and narratives (Archard, Walker, Woodhouse). Legal human rights discourse will always be as flawed as our biases. John Wall points out, for example, that "rights" reflect their scribes: "If indeed it turns out that cultures are completely diverse, then it becomes difficult to see in exactly what sense one may speak any more of 'human rights,' except perhaps as expressions of a particular set of Western historical values" (32). Interdisciplinary approaches within the humanities can apply insights about child rights in a lay context that is more broadly accessible and might suggest why common reactions against child participation stubbornly persist with or without structural support. My contribution to such efforts will be to expose the faulty reasoning in a consistent undergirding rhetorical paradox that strips children of supposed birthrights in Western ideologies through narratives of development, empire, industry, and progress. For popular and legal audiences, my analysis will provide closer consideration of the hidden premises we rely upon to justify encroaching on unprotected youth liberties at a narrative level. Within literary and cultural childhood studies, I also hope to encourage greater appreciation for how important material consideration of "real" children is to what we do.

One of the most fascinating scholarly advances in children's literature in the past three decades has been the effort to understand its unique position as a genre written for an audience with a contested identity, written predominantly by persons outside of that category of social subjectivity. Many of us have invested much time and effort dealing with the politics of identity, power, and subjectivity for those defined as children. We've debated definitions of that subjectivity, tested the limits of constructivism, and swung back into various extremes of embodiment, essentialism, or technically avoiding the subject (in both senses of the term). Multiple "impossibilities" of the genre have required a whole lot of theorizing that sometimes, in its broader strokes, misses the concrete reality of children's actual experiences. Judith Butler has seen such inquiry as a broader trend in the humanities, asking of the reputed demise of humanities publications, "Have the humanities undermined themselves, with all their relativism and questioning and 'critique,' or have the humanities been undermined by all those who *oppose* all that relativism and questioning and critique?" (129). However we answer this question, it is clear that the rise of theory, which traded in problematizing first the individual and then the subject, destabilized assumptions about how scholars should approach human relationships to literary texts. Valentine Cunningham suggests that "if there is one feature of what reading should do and engage with, and yes, theorize, 'after' Theory, it is the presence, the rights, the needs of the human subject, in texts, in the originations of texts, in the reception of texts" (142). Literature scholars can refocus on the human subjects always implicitly at the center of our study but rarely included in our theorizing, without overstepping the limits of our discursive expertise. Reading stories for and by children as potential rights-respecting narratives,[1] we can consider the consequential impact of narratives without generalizing about those addressed and represented by such discourse. We can stop *avoiding the subject* and acknowledge the "human" in the "humanities."

But, as Emancipation Sheridan so aptly frames it in my introductory paragraph, avoiding the subject of child rights is a historically engrained practice in popular discourse. Finding it hidden in disparate literary locations will require some eclectic leaps and bounds. Karen Sánchez-Eppler models in her work the rigorous and necessarily creative sourcework required of childhood studies that aim to focus on child-authored or child-authentic evidence, which can result in "archival" work in "the more elastic sense of the term as a repository for stuff of the past" (2013a, 215–17, 218). In this sense I will also grasp where possible for "bit(s) of childhood flotsam" selectively or haphazardly preserved, often at cross-purposes (219). Where possible, I privilege direct sources[2]—historic accounts by minors, archival letters, comics letter columns, and popular publications by young writers. I will also use literary sources, not simply as objects of study, but as reflecting communal perspectives toward child protection and participation. I am not speaking for actual children or intending to present all accounts as equally authentic but trying to identify rights-oriented rhetoric and contradictions created by unchecked protectionism. Following a roughly chronological and selectively topical organization, I will consider the following protections and infringements in corresponding narratives: from prioritized rescue to property status in heroic narratives and maritime history, geographic freedom to islanding in the robinsonade tradition and sailing narratives, abandonment and adoption in foundling lore and cultural practices, access to knowledge and literary choice in the case of 1950s comics censorship, and medical (non)disclosure in healthcare and illness narratives for children.

Another organizing principle will be suggested in the economic processes of capitalism. Frederick Engels recognized that the industrial isolation of community into smaller units and the resulting privatization of family matters (marriage, paternity, child rearing) directly conceptualized women and children as property, codified from the beginning of primitive accumulation. Child rights, as a result, have been connected, at least within capitalist cultures, to matters of ownership, but "intensive parenting" of middle-class consumerist society, wherein the child is the center that defines the nuclearized family, motivates a narrative erasure of the economic and legal tethers restricting children unfairly. These, too, are obscured by protectionist narratives, which redirect attention to idealized or overburdened parents by mythologizing the supposed innocence, victimization, and vulnerability of children rather than potential agency.

Applying the terminology of child-rights scholar David Archard, Michael Grossberg writes, "In the United States, liberation and caretaking aptly label the poles around which contests over children's rights have been fought for over a century" (20). I prefer the more internationally utilized terms of "participation" versus "protection" rights, as they decenter the adult-authorizing implications of *liberating* or *granting* care for children by instead focusing on their rights as innate, to be *taken* and *exercised*. Youth as rights holders are never consistently recognized as having both, because as one matures into self-determining thought and behavior, the need for protective rights gradually recedes, in a completely individual, relative, contextually shifting, and idiosyncratic way. More importantly, this gradual process can imperceptibly cloak what protectionist policy makers overlook and want the rest of us to overlook, which is that imposing protection when and where the youth in question no longer requires or wants it is in direct violation of their participatory rights to survival, freedom, privacy, consumer choice, access to information, and consent. Unrecognized in the United States and resisted in many wealthy, industrialized nations, children's participatory needs and self-determination are easily disregarded in the name of protection, seemingly shielding children while actually curtailing their participation and choice.

The UN Convention on the Rights of the Child recommends "that the child, for the full and harmonious development of his or her personality, should grow up in a family environment, in an atmosphere of happiness, love and understanding" (further codified in articles 8 and 9). When we generalize about children, we often are also implicitly generalizing about a model family, from a hegemonic "middle-class" view of "nuclearized" households consisting of "conjugal," and, implicitly, two heterosexual, biological parents. Such projections reify a norm that few of us actually fit. Yet it is very difficult to generalize "the child" outside of such an assumed structural support in the private domestic sphere. D. W. Winnicott famously claimed, "There is no such thing as an infant," by which he "meant, of course, that whenever one finds an infant one finds maternal care, and without maternal care there would be no infant" (1). Although we no longer necessarily gender primary caregiving, we recognize as a truism that a newborn is entirely dependent upon others for care. But does that care have to be maternal, paternal, or even familial? We know that although often prioritized, this arrangement is not always possible or safe, and it certainly not been globally or historically absolute. Even so, Stephanie Coontz has written, "[P]eople *conceive of* the family as a natural phenomenon, even where the fiction is blatantly obvious" (1988, 13). And as the dependence of infants slowly gives way to increased mobility and self-care for children and then teens, we continue to struggle to recognize them in their limited but always eventual public identities. Take, for example, Hannah Arendt's baffling critique of racial desegregation in 1959:

> [O]verlapping of rights and interests becomes apparent when we examine the issue of education in the light of the three realms of human life—the political, the social, and the private. Children are first of all part of family and home, and this means that they are, or should be, brought up in that atmosphere of idiosyncratic exclusiveness which alone makes a home a home, strong and secure enough to shield its young against the demands of the social and the responsibilities of the political realm. (55)

We relegate our conceptualizations of "shielding" homes to the private sphere so that we don't even see when and where they do not exist for particular children. Arendt is imposing a privileged bias in her assumption that the private is somehow not political and social. But children are just as socially and politically determined as any other humans—and many need recourse to public, not private, protections. Arendt's dismissive assumption is a common one and perhaps a primary reason it is too easy for so many to rally in defense of parents when child rights come up—there is a dominant assumption that all children have loving and capable parents and that those who support child rights are infringing on the rights of these parents. But it is the children *without such support* who even more desperately need explicitly recognized protective *and* participatory rights in the public sphere.

As we often cannot see outside of an idealized caretaking context, and we continue to project as a child tries to grow within and against both their real and imagined family confines, my analysis of protective and participatory rights will attempt frequent contextualization within the demographically shifting concepts of family and economic developments that are thought to contribute to such shifts. Following decades and dozens of studies that characterize the rise of industrialization and consumer capitalism as causing the privatization and nuclearizing of families, surrounding children within increasingly insular domestic boundaries, I will to some degree necessarily rely on the broad strokes of a "middle-class" model, in spite of its exclusionary indefinability. Materialist history demonstrates that the middle class doesn't really exist as a definable absolute—other than being what most of us think we are and are not. Rather, it is an illusory norm representing the hegemonic status quo (Coontz 1988, 2016). Dominant depictions of the middle-class family and childhood serve merely as a historicizing backdrop to my more specific focus on narratives of protection and participation.

Historical studies of family tend to focus on proving or disproving the relevance of the middle-class nuclearized model, popular representations concretize it, and my analysis will rely on it for setting a context that hopefully will keep social structure in mind. Such methods allow us to detect some broader changes that, whether realistic or not, are certainly consequential to how we perceive, treat, and unintentionally affect young people. Two particularly documentable and often-repeated premises are of the privatization of family (Parsons, Talcott, Donzelot, Sennett, Coontz) and the increased sentimental valuing of childhood (Zelizer, Cross, Cook), both of which are generally seen as results of economic change (industrial capitalism, globalization, and consumerism). More recently, such developments have been inflected by scholars with attention to the power of emotionalism and its affective results. Courtney Weilke-Mills describes the "affectionate citizenship" expected of nineteenth-century children, Lauren Berlant investigates heightened bourgeois misrecognition at the beginning of the twenty-first century, Sara Ahmed resuscitates the buried concept of "will," and Eva Illouz casts our current economic stage as one of emotional capitalism, in which

> the conventional division between an a-emotional public sphere and the private sphere saturated with emotions begins to dissolve, as it becomes apparent that throughout the twentieth century middle-class men and women were made to focus intensely on their emotional life, both in the workplace and in the family.... Never has the private self been so publicly performed and harnessed to the discourses and values of the economic and political spheres. (Illouz 4)

These developments help to explain how and why we can be capable of such repetitive yet unjust protectionist impositions infringing on child participation without experiencing ideological dissonance.

How can protection, which sounds so comforting, do harm? Like the children we imagine are helpless, we simply don't know any better. Our emotions get the better of us, and our stories do little to challenge our misguided consciences. But, as Jonathan Todres and Sarah Higinbotham describe this obstacle, "[m]oving from viewing children as objects of love and charity to seeing them also as subjects of rights is a significant shift" (197). For the children who don't even benefit from the protections accorded by sentiment, this shift is especially imperative. In this book I will trace ideologies rationalizing protective encroachment on child participation to a deeper structure inherent in industrial modernization implicit in public discourse and literary narratives. Each chapter centers on the same pattern of oppressive logic, but I hope that the pervasive evidence of this process will be all the more convincing as demonstrated in the disparate contexts of survival hierarchies, geographic restriction, abandonment, domestic containment, censorship, and pretense.

In *What's Wrong with Children's Rights*, Martin Guggenheim writes, "For some, the Convention on the Rights of the Child is regarded as the camel's nose in the tent.... Yet this country's refusal to sign the convention has very little to do with children's rights" (10). By way of explanation, he offers some important grounding in American history, showing that we've come a long way. But he also explains our legal inertia, or why we don't go further: "In the United States, rights tend to be 'negative' (freedom from government oppression). Many countries have a dramatically broader conception of rights that incorporates 'positive' rights (obligations owed to them by government). The international community is far more likely to regard rights as including positive claims than is the United States" (6, 14). Protective rights—from domestic abuse, sexual predation, exploitation—are negative rights, and important ones; participatory rights—to education, self-determination, healthcare—are positive rights. The latter will indicate the tricky issue Guggenheim illuminates. American children do have the right to education, although a family can opt for home schooling and fill their children's heads with an astounding amount of damaging antiscientific nonsense that further perpetuates a culture in which grown adults with impressive college credentials can claim that global warming is a hoax drummed up by intellectual "elites." And as for universal healthcare for children, good luck (I hope you see my point). For other positive rights, American child advocates tend to mention international law for at least a codified example—we simply don't have an accessible popular vocabulary for greater enforceable participatory rights in our own ideological systems (12). I can only speak for myself, but where I turn to the Convention on the Rights of the Child (CRC), I do so only as an example of the type of stipulation that might give children recourse to justice in specific uncovered circumstances, not as a simplified panacea. The problem is much deeper than what goes on in our courts.

Guggenheim provides a totalizing reason for the tricky business of child advocacy in the United States: "For better or worse, the law's treatment of children began from the bottom up, starting with infants and young children. To be a young child means to be completely dependent upon another for the most basic needs of survival. For this reason, young children and their caregivers are inextricably linked" (17). Fears of diminishing the socially sacred bond of parenthood are mistaken but powerful factors preventing any significant revision. In contrast, he claims, "Regrettably, a leading characteristic of the children's rights movement is its propensity to separate children's interests from their parents.' It is also its most egregious error" (13). This is where Guggenheim commits the fallacy of throwing out the baby with the bathwater. To assume that supporting children's rights is necessarily against their parents' rights hits the same reductionist and emotional chord that sometimes prompts claims that all child rights advocates are trying to let kids "divorce" from their parents (yes, I know the term is "emancipation," but detractors tend not to). The only time I can imagine, albeit in my far less legally knowledgeable little brain, children's and parents' rights actually being in conflict is in cases where the child needs protection from *them*, which is just another way of pointing out where participatory rights are most crucial for children to have. I can't imagine that preserving the link between an abused child and a life-threateningly abusive parent would trump protecting the child in such cases. And I might add that in my time as a court-appointed child advocate, I have not known a judge or attorney to actually visit foster children in their placements or the homes of their biological parents, other than *guardian ad litem*s, who, Guggenheim argues, are not necessary (159–67).

I am trying to stress subtler levels on which adult interests do not always selflessly serve the young. Overprotection is one way protectionism unbalanced by participation can go very much awry, but the main examples I want to keep foremost in readers' minds are the kids who need protection from crisis situations that threaten lasting trauma or worse, where participation must also play a part. The hegemonic view often commits erasure of such crises by falling back on familialism—blaming parents or imagining that having parents is the only solution to all child rights violation. Parents can be the problem, but we aren't even acknowledging the many ways in which kinless children also need help, or we assume parents are in the equation and have necessary supports when we blame them. Runaways, even foster kids, sound to some automatically like "problem children," when it is, in fact, their parents who almost always are the reason[3] for their kids being homeless or in care as wards of the state (not that I agree with most reasons for removal, but that's for another time and better legal mind). Abuse of parental rights in unjust removals, Guggenheim reveals, is also a more recent problem: "Although there has been a foster care system in place in the United States for well over 150 years, for much of that period—up to the 1970s—most children in foster care had been placed there by parents who were temporarily unable to care for them" (181). In contrast, the chaotic triage of public and private agencies that pass for a foster care program today in this country has certainly abused parents as well as children *in the name of protection*, especially in poorer pockets of our population. Where the system breaks down, it functions more as a pipeline to prison for many parents and children caught up in the process. But that doesn't mean that something like Child Protective Services (hopefully much improved and well funded) shouldn't exist.

How one feels about the courts or government being involved in family crisis is probably more a matter of political ideology than a necessary splitting of hairs over human-rights rhetoric. One of Guggenheim's reviewers, Richard J. Gelles, perhaps put it most succinctly: "[O]ne of the reasons the United States has such a large children welfare system and spends nearly $20 billion annually on out-of-home care is that there are so few universalistic social support programs for children." He concludes, cheekily encapsulating the *differend* that is the fallout of American party politics: "The cost of keeping government out of child rearing is that government stays out of child rearing. With rights, come responsibilities" (44).[4] Right- and left-leaning disagreements about children are often, as Guggenheim says, "about more than children themselves" (3). Some look at a larger picture and see the privatization of community services, even the economy based on private enterprise and unregulated profit, as a primary cause of fragmentation and isolation of children. For example, Henry Giroux blames free-market fundamentalism for the "devalued landscape of public schooling" in which "disciplining young people seems to be far more important than educating them" (3). In contrast, John O'Neill feels more optimistic about the possibilities for "sustainable childhoods" and greater "family capital" working within the existing system:

> [F]amily resources are a crucial factor. Thus, the capital value of children will vary according to the shifting contexts of family authority, subsistence, and state benefits. Once the feudal family had lost its subsistence base in the shift to industrial production, its traditional authority over its children was lost to the factory system. The material desperation of parents in turn fed into the

raw exploitation of child labor, which early industrialists regarded as a quasi-natural demand of competitive capitalism. Once industrialism had worked its full effects upon family relations, however, the overall effect on the family was to open up possibilities for the expression of individual personality in both sexes, adult or child. (21)

O'Neill assumes that with material support and reclaiming parental authority, family and child desperation will recede. I absolutely agree that families and children require far greater priority in social programing and funding. But the nostalgic appeal to bring back traditional parental authority taps some pretty fuzzy logic that only serves the privileged, considering that it depended entirely upon the subjugation of women and the entire household to a patriarch-provider. This is one reason I focus on the middle-class model in what follows—to demonstrate that the problem is not one of financial means alone. "Traditional authority" over children is deeply imbalanced by protectionism and requires stabilization through recognizing children as potential rights holders through public participation, to be exercised as their capacities for self-determination emerge.

This book is meant to follow the historic material roots of protectionism but also subtler instances of child participation in the midst of its evolution. At its most basic and cliché level, protectionism requires lip service to "putting children first," while obscuring just exactly what that means or how it can be done. Beginning with "Women and Children First: Shipwreck, Sentiment, Property, and Survival," I focus on the harsher hierarchies of survival usually hidden by sentimental romance and heroic narrative. Such hierarchies were enabled by eighteenth- and nineteenth-century principles of property and ownership, in which children were far from first and often dead last. Although the chivalrous echo "women and children first" would become a dominant sentiment in fictionalized modern survival narratives, maritime histories tell a different story about protective measures for children at sea, which I will highlight through historic accounts of rescue practice during famous shipwrecks, the legal predicament of *Amistad* "orphans," and even customs of survival cannibalism. Protection, where present, is highly selective, and even where seemingly fairly applied can impede participation.

For centuries, sea work, leisure travel, and migration were presented as standard opportunities open for youth to explore and seek education through adventure—just think of the American frontier, the European tradition of the gentleman's tour, or the humble example of Herman Melville's Ishmael, who calls the whaling ship "my Yale College and my Harvard" (159). Sailing experience in particular could grant youth voices credibility as global citizens, as with the *Amistad*'s Ka'le and the *Medusa*'s Charlotte-Adélaïde Picard, but by the twenty-first century when Izzy Skenazy rode the subway alone at age nine, his mother was branded "America's worst mom." Jay Griffiths has demonstrated that our geographic restriction of the young was initially tied to the privatization of property, but the Free-Range parenting movement today blames US media and a culture of fear. In chapter 2, "No Child Is an Island: Robinsonades, Islanding, and the Right to Roam" I turn my attention to this shrinking territory young people are permitted to roam in the twentieth and twenty-first centuries, due to protectionist eliding of participation. Literary illustrations of "islanding" in popular and literary depictions from the twentieth century are contextualized within my analysis of protections. By the twenty-first century, the sentimentalized suppression of youth was fascinatingly demonstrated by the popularity and corporate sponsorship of teen sailors, as well as a corresponding protectionist backlash. Competitions for "youngest" status in breaking records lowered conspicuous sailing ages to such an extent that sailing organizations had to stop recognizing age-related records to avoid liability for increasingly younger attempts. In the failure of Abby Sunderland's global venture (with much parent blaming) and Laura Dekker's success (in spite of immense persecution from child protectionists), I will fully consider these subtler consequences of protectionist premises.

In chapter 3, "Babies in Boxes: Finding and Loving Other People's Children," I will set up a temporal contrast for twenty-first-century tendencies by reaching further into a generalized past, beginning with folklore and traditions of child abandonment, to connect and compare them with familiar modern parallels like baby boxes and foster care, reflected more lightly in 1920's comic strips like Frank King's *Gasoline Alley* (1918–59), Elzie Segar's *Thimble Theatre* (1919–38), and Harold Gray's *Little Orphan Annie* (1924–68). Woven in with "real-world" examples will be representations from popular narratives like Pullman's *Golden Compass* (1995), McGraw's *The Moorchild* (1996), and Lo's *The Huntress* (2011). Although a discussion of child rights in the context of ancient and medieval practices may seem anachronistic, my motivation is to show that tensions between the needs for child participation and child protection have been entrenched in our narrative traditions long before there was any talk of child liberation. In fact, this chapter should set up recognition of ways in which participation was actually greater for some children before industrialization peaked, revealing through contrast a dominant modern motif of child containment.

Chapter 4, "The Prison House of Comics Censorship and Participatory Resistance" centers on child rights to access knowledge and entertainment of their choosing with the example of comics censorship in the 1940s and 1950s in particular, and a case study of resistance in Sheldon Mayer's comic book series, *Sugar and Spike*, which was conceived at the height of this controversy. Favoring evidence in letter columns, fan mail, and letters to the Senate Subcommittee on Juvenile Delinquency protesting against censorship, I demonstrate how protests for participation were for the most part ignored in the name of protecting minors. By utilizing archival material as an indication of the reciprocity between comics creators and readers, I hope to also demonstrate the capacity of many minors for democratic participation demonstrated within the medium and industry of comic books.

Looking more intimately at "The Price of Protectionist Pretense" for my fifth chapter, I propose reading children's books about illness as potential rights-bearing, or rights-suppressive, discourses, through the lens of anthropological findings about actual children facing potentially life-threatening disease or inoculation to protect against it. Jonathan Todres and Sarah Higinbotham write that "children's literature [has] been ignored as a rights-bearing discourse," yet "literature is a source of law for children" (1). By looking closely at the spirit of that "law" in literary depictions for children, I hope, again, to clearly demonstrate perils of protectionist sentiment systemic in our culture. Adults often actively withhold the truth from dying child patients, denying their ethical rights to medical honesty, awareness, and agency. Children's books about cancer enact the same denial and dishonesty about terminal illness by establishing a common pretense for politely avoiding the touchy subject, demonstrating the pervasiveness of a protectionism that in fact impinges upon children's participatory rights to full knowledge and self-determination about their bodies. Ultimately "cancer books" tend to "protect" parents during their emotional struggle to support children rather than respecting young patients and readers by acknowledging their right to be informed and participate as knowing medical subjects.

Each chapter will expose and expound on how child participation is often infringed by so-called protective measures, which, ironically, become oppressive rather than nurturing. In this effort I weave in motifs of chivalry, fragility, and manipulation through containment: ships in bottles, enclosures, islands, babies in boxes, baskets, playpens, and the "prison houses" of language and pretense. Against confining practices, young persons have always demonstrated a democratic capacity that needs not only to be *expressed* but *exercised* at *will*. Ending on a positive note with one fictional model of a radical peer public, I will conclude with a recap of the history of the nuclearized family and reassert that children should have the right to a public and participatory identity and can form fair, self-governing youth publics when given the chance. We, as the public, need to step up in providing community connections as well as greater collective support for child care.

1

Women and Children First

Shipwreck, Sentiment, Property, and Survival

So we made women with their children go,
The oars ply back again, and yet again;
Whilst, inch by inch, the drowning ship sank low,
Still under steadfast men.
   —"The Loss of the *Birkenhead*," Francis Hastings Doyle

"Good skipper," use him truly,
For he is ill and sad
"Hush! Hush!" He cried, then cruelly
He kill'd the little lad.
   —Ballad of Richard Parker, traditional

To shake them out of their sentimental grooves about kids, I often ask my students a question that should be simple for anyone who has traveled on commercial airlines to answer: "What do you do if a plane depressurizes and oxygen masks come down over your seat and your child's?" Each time, a surprising number get it wrong or don't know. "Put it on your child first?" No. Again an obvious question, "Why not?" Even more fumble on this one—because you have to override the nurturing instinct (a murky concept at best) to instead get your mask on first so that you'll be conscious enough to help your child.

I'm fascinated by how completely our sentiments about "putting children first" can suppress our fears about child vulnerability and dependence to the point of actually putting them at greater risk. We are so ideologically oriented toward prioritizing protection of "women and children first" that overriding the sentiment requires abstract concentration. And yet, when the plane lands, and you walk through a crowded airport with your kids, you don't let your young child out of your sight, especially to use a bathroom. You may consider leashing them to some conglomeration of suitcases or see someone else do this. Protective measures like these require much less reflection. But history does not read like a scene from *Titanic*. Women and children have certainly not always been first.

Sure, it's a nice sentiment, and it even may have been a progressive step when first used as the HMS *Birkenhead* hit Pinnacle Rock in 1852 and flooded quickly, killing "a hundred or more passengers" in their sleep (445 would drown or be eaten by sharks once in the water). Captain Salmond reportedly sounded the alarm with "Abandon ship! Every man for himself!" But Lieutenant Colonel Seton stood firm: "Stand fast the ranks—women and children first!" (Blackmore 8). One *Birkenhead* survivor, Marian Parkinson, who was only three years and eight months old when it wrecked, recalled the resulting procedure:

> I can remember quite well my mother taking me in her arms on deck in our night clothes and giving me to a cabin boy to hold whilst she went again down below to fetch a cloak, and they lowered me into the boat. When she got back she could not find me and all the boats had pushed off. Two officers swung mother from the side of the vessel as she was sinking and she just caught the side of the boat and fell amongst the people. If she had fallen the other way they must have left her as the boat was being drawn by the sinking vessel. (Phillips 61)

Once all women and children had secured seats, "[t]he places in the remaining serviceable lifeboats were filled using the system the Army has always called 'Funeral Order'—youngest first—and these too were lowered into the sea and rowed clear of the ship" (Oliver 210). The event has since epitomized a sacrificial valuation of vulnerable passengers and crew that nonetheless reaffirms their helplessness. According to once teen-sailor Robin Lee Graham,

> The *Birkenhead* disaster is remembered because every woman and child was saved. The men stood on the deck in line, knowing that most of them were going to drown, while the women and children filled the boats. Copies of Thomas Hemy's famous *Birkenhead* picture of a boy drummer beating a final salute to his comrades was hung in the nurseries of Victorian England and children were told that this was the discipline and courage which had created the British Empire. (Graham 118)

There is disagreement on how exactly Seton phrased the policy, but "women and children first" would become well known in maritime and military custom as the "*Birkenhead* drill" and a legendary model for masculine heroism in sea tales for boys and sailors. Rudyard Kipling immortalized the event in his "Soldier an' Sailor Too" (1896), emphasizing the youth of those who perished: "Their work was done when it 'adn't begun; they was younger nor me an' you; / Their choice it was plain between drownin' in 'eaps an' bein' mopped by the screw, / So they stood an' was still to the *Birken'ead* drill, soldier an' sailor too!" (315). Although famous as an expression about the necessity of protecting the young and female, it became an important doctrine in the cult of manhood socializing boys. Douglas Phillips considers the *Birkenhead* drill a paramount example of "Christian chivalry" (16). Apparently, the rest of us don't care about children?

But decades before Seton's policy, even literary representations reveal a crack in the sentimental facade. The shipwreck in *Swiss Family Robinson* (1812) left the title family stranded as the crew abandoned them without a second thought: "The sailors forbore from swearing, and were now employed in prayers, or in making the absurdest vows as the condition of their release from danger. Each recommended his soul to God, but at the same moment thought of contriving the best means for preserving his life" (11). In contrast, the pastor patriarch of the family prays for his children: "Heaven will surely have pity on them, thought I, and will save their parents to guard their tender years" (12). Child survival in such cases is cast in terms showing that it is entirely dependent upon parental survival.

Even so, a more sentimental subtext is what sticks accessibly in our public memory. Women, sailors were reminded, needed the help and protection of men just as children do of their parents—they could not be expected or even trusted to save themselves. The most ludicrous and lasting example of this comes from a fictionalized account of the 1744 wreck of the *Saint-Géran* from Jacques-Henri Bernadin de Saint-Pierre's 1788 pastoral, *Paul and Virginia*. In it the author capitalizes (unsuccessfully for a contemporary audience) upon the particularly tragic fact that the ship was anchored very near port when it sank. Virginia, Saint-Pierre's heroine, is aboard the sinking ship: "Only one of the sailors had remained on deck, all the others having cast them to themselves into the sea. He was completely naked and muscular as Hercules. We saw him approach Virginia with respect, throw himself down before her and even do what he could to remove her clothes; but she, turning away her eyes, rejected with dignity his attempts to help her" (120). Unwilling to part with the heavy clothing that would surely drown her in the storm-swept waves, she "kept one hand on her billowing clothes, placed the other on her heart, and raising upwards eyes shining with serenity, seemed an angel taking flight for heaven" (121).[1] Later, Paul consoles his grief for Virginia with the recognition that she "preferred to lose [her] life rather than violate modesty" (132). Clearly, self-preservation is not as strong an instinct for a proper lady appropriately attired.

Virginia's death has been immortalized in a multitude of illustrations featuring it as the climax of the novel (see figure 1.1). And those soaked, billowy skirts and, more importantly, her dead body still in them, represent an even larger genre of postshipwreck images of ladies drowned and washed up at shore in the eighteenth- and nineteenth-century equivalent of wet t-shirt contests—a full display of women's most desirable assets, which do not, apparently, include breathing. Kathleen Foster recounts a few reasons for this iconography in her gorgeous reconstruction of Winslow Homer's process for his rescue masterpiece, *The Life Line* (1884), explaining that whereas the "women-and-children" theme was in vogue decades earlier, "[s]implifying his focus, Homer also streamlined the narrative by eliminating the child that so frequently added a sentimental and wholesome note to midcentury images.... The departure of the family story also opens the door to romance between these two strangers [rescuee and rescuer]" (64–65). Classic examples of family-focused "female shipwreck" art that included a "wholesome" motivation of child-saving are Henry Edward Dawe's *My Child! My Child!* and *They're Saved! They're Saved!* (1832), which together as a diptych read rather like adventure comic panels. Like them, Winslow Homer's *Life Line* allows the woman to survive for a happier and heroic resolution (see figures 1.2 and 1.3). Yet, Foster explains that the specter of Virginia's death is present even in this choice. Homer knew that by not including a child, he could tap "the viewer's recollection of the forlorn motif of the drowned maiden on the shore ... where a woman lies dead, betrayed by men and overwhelmed by the sea" in the "horrifying accounts of female shipwreck victims and myriad representations of *Paul and Virginia*" (65). Just as women are often mutilated in comics to represent man pain through the "women-in-refrigerators" trope, the threat of any damsel in distress actually dying apparently heightens the erotic charge.

Even in an image that glorifies the rush of risk and spirit of adventure, like Winslow Homer's *Yachting Girl* (1880) shown on this book's cover, the girl subject is "[d]ressed more for the parlor than the open sea, she sits back, reaches up to grab a rope, and jauntily crosses her ankles as she turns to watch the course of the other yachts.... [S]he is something of a pinup, artfully posed to represent a modern type of adventuresome and (notwithstanding corset and petticoats) athletic American womanhood" (Foster 3). Her high-heeled shoes also poorly fit her for any athletic activity, let alone any safety in resting her feet so casually while balanced on the headrails. She represents the perils of sailing but offers also a sexually charged but conveniently dispensable body for the dramas of the sea. The fact that Homer chose a girl on the precipice of womanhood to capture the live action does not cancel out awareness of her future function.

Figure 1.1. "Le Naufrage de Virginie," etching and engraving, by F. Bellavitis. Public Domain.

The opportunity to sexually charge rescue images is not the only reason for dropping the child figure from shorter-lived woman-and-child shipwreck iconography. The sentiment of "women and children first" burrowed into popular consciousness was always really about the availability of women, not protecting kids, who were more likely part of the scene as pity props. Robin Miskolcze provides such an example from "a mother aboard the *Home* in 1837" whose "infant was in her arms, pressed close to her bosom ... [A] wave wrested the infant from her grasp and hurled it into the foaming waters ... [B]efore the relentless surge could hide her lost one for ever, she sprang into the breakers and perished" (qtd. in Miskolcze 2007, 39–40). The dying child represents mother pain to promote empathy for women, who are in turn more valuable to men as protectors of their young. The extent to which the phrase "women and children first" is really just another expression for "mothers first—we need them to do the hard work of parenting" was especially apparent to me when I found that most scholarly sources on the trope and practice had little to no focus on actual children in anything but the title. If women and children are first in actual history, the kids are a bit more like a precious carry-on bag in the bargain.

Figure 1.2. Henry Edward Dawe, My Child! My Child! (1832). Philadelphia Museum of Art. Purchased with the E. Moran Endowment Fund for American Art, 2011-179-1.

So, the self-sacrificing women of history and fiction who die trying to rescue their young (or petticoats) demonstrate the true functionality of women and children first—to reinforce the importance of proper ladies as breeders and nurturers, not to evoke compassion for vulnerable children. The swings of seeming illogic—from brutalizing dispensable children to denying their vulnerability through stubborn parental projections, make more sense if we can identify a common premise. Sharon M. Meagher and Patrice Diquinzio explain that these contradictions "uncover a logic of paternalistic treatment of women and children that purports to protect them but almost always also disempowers them and sometimes harms them" (1). Protective measures don't necessarily counter oppression, and in some cases the sentimentality that results can make matters worse. For example, on the *Titanic*, following the procedure of women and children first saved young and female lives at a much greater proportion to other shipwrecks, but "men were denied entry into boats with ample place for additional passengers," so many needlessly died for a manly ideal. Some women also resisted separating from husbands or erringly thought evacuation to be more dangerous than the ship because *Titanic* wasn't listing yet (Koldau 14). Narratives surrounding this most famous shipwreck confirmed a prejudicial

Figure 1.3. Henry Edward Dawe, They're Saved! They're Saved! (1832). Philadelphia Museum of Art. Purchased with the E. Moran Endowment Fund for American Art, 2011-179-2.

view of women more in keeping with the mood of *Paul and Virginia* than any nautical verisimilitude—eclipsing primal struggles in the icy depths with attention to the civility of an orchestral send-off that probably only first-class passengers could even hear.

Some *Titanic* survivors, especially those who'd been children at the time of the wreck, were particularly vexed by constant media intrusiveness and confused about why the *Titanic* in particular roused so much public interest (notably, Millvina Dean, who'd been less than two months old, and Eleanor Johnson, a toddler; see Geller 157, 168). Often considered the worst maritime disaster by affluent westerners who would have trouble naming any other sunken ships, the 1912 sinking of the "unsinkable" luxury ship has been mythologized completely out of proportion. Linda Maria Koldau writes, "We have a notorious disaster whose details offer a unique blending of fact and fiction; we have an historical event that right at the time it occurred began to be turned into myth" even though the "*Titanic* was not really special—until the ship went down" (9). In her analysis, Koldau attempts to explain: "Why does hardly anybody remember the 9,000 victims of the *Wilhelm Gustoff* sinking on January 30, 1945, or, using a peacetime comparison, the almost 4,400 causalities when the Philippine ferry *Doña Paz* collided with an oil tanker and sank on December 20, 1987?" (10). Clearly it is not sheer number of lives lost (*Titanic*'s toll was 1,500) but the "who" that matters. And why not more lasting international attention to the *Sewol* ferry disaster of 2014, due to gross misconduct and negligence (with a captain charged and convicted of murder), in which 250 of the 304 fatalities were teenagers? It is certainly not because of the age of victims either.

Of course the standard biases of class and nationalism were at play (even Cameron's film demonstrates that), but Koldau offers more precise reasons for the cultural obsession about *Titanic*: it was the largest man-made moving object in the world at the time it sailed, the arrogance of calling it "unsinkable" led to irony worthy of a great tragedy of ancient Greek or Shakespearean proportions, it sank slowly enough for matters of honor to be thought out and so at stake, it made the *Birkenhead* drill of "women and children first" an internationally recognizable principle in spite of its rarity of use and not being a law, and the ship itself was mythologized as youthful virgin on her "maiden voyage" (10–11). These last three reasons are most relevant to the context of my argument.

Certainly, timing is an issue: the *Titanic* took two hours and forty minutes to sink. Comparing data from the *Titanic* (1912) and *Lusitania* (1915) disasters, Bruno S. Frey, David A. Savage, and Benno Torgler have hypothesized that "survival instinct" takes over in ships that sink quickly, giving no time for protocol or higher reasoning (4863). This would certainly explain why so much melodrama and sentimentality surround the event. But the *Birkenhead* sank in only twenty minutes, although with less than a tenth the number of people, more successfully evacuating "vulnerable" travelers. Mikael Elinder and Oscar Erixson indicate that "[u]nlike other types of catastrophes, e.g., earthquakes, tsunamis, and terrorist attacks, a maritime disaster is characterized by the presence of a well-defined leader. On board a ship, the captain is the commanding officer with the supreme power to give and enforce orders. In the evacuation of the *Titanic* (1912), the captain ordered WCF [women and children first] and officers were reported to have shot at men who disobeyed the order" (13221). There were clear structural incentives to follow a protocol that conformed to dominant ethics and heroic sentiment.

But inequities of power are also made clear in such reasoning, especially in the larger context of shipwrecks in general. Elinder and Erixson give a complex and convincing account of rescue hierarchies and other determining factors in life-saving practice: age, gender, class, nationality, and proportionality of groups. Comparing the *Titanic* with sixteen other maritime disasters since the *Birkenhead*, where the protocol of women and children first was recorded in use for the first time, they find that, contrary to popular belief, "women have a large survival disadvantage compared with men" (13223), which increases inversely with proportionality (13220), "that compliance with the WCF norm is *exceptional* in maritime disasters," and "prime aged *adults have a survival advantage over children*" (my emphasis, 13222–23). The captain's authority and use of the protocol can improve child survival, but that is simply not the norm (see figure 1.4). Elinder and Erixson conclude: "On the basis of our analysis, it becomes evident that the sinking of the *Titanic* seems to have spurred misconceptions about human behavior in disasters" (13224). These misconceptions have as much of a pattern as sea customs do.

Because the ship's crew knew there weren't enough lifeboats, explicitly prioritizing who would get seats was imperative. They were sinking slowly enough to institute a plan—in fact, so much so that many felt the ship was safer than the lifeboats. There was time to strategize and even enforce evacuation. Even so, the rescue of women and children first was not such a success on *Titanic* as it had been on the *Birkenhead*: "All five of the children in first class and all 24 of the children in second class were saved. Third class children were not so lucky: Only 23 of the 76 children escaped the icy waters" (qtd. in Prince and Howard 27). But, of course, it wasn't just a matter of luck. The sentiment, not the reality, dominates representations of *Titanic*'s "maiden" and final voyage. As a sentiment, not a legally enforced policy, women and children first created some order but also confusion that decided the fate of many passengers, especially as "many children were grabbed willy-nilly and thrown into boats" by their clothing (Geller 168). The two officers in charge of getting passengers on lifeboats interpreted the command differently, demonstrating the difficulty of universally applying protections to a relative and so culturally undefinable group of persons. First Officer William Murdoch (starboard) understood the command to mean that women and children "had first priority when a boat was being loaded. But when there were no women forthcoming,[2] or those who were at hand refused to leave their husbands, he would relent and allow husbands and wives to go together into the boats. When there were no more married couples standing by, a handful of single men were given permission to climb into the lifeboats" (Butler 2009, 71). Second Officer C. H. Lightoller (portside) took a different approach, interpreting the women-and-children-first command as "women and children only. And sometimes he would be the one to decide where the line between child and adult was to be drawn" (71). This grim and imperfect process resulted in grim and imperfect interpretations. Rosa Abbott Smith had the misfortune of evacuating portside: "Rosa knew that she would be turned back if she attempted to enter with her sons. Aged 14 and 16, Eugene and Rossmore were children to her, but men to Second Officer Lightoller" (Geller 142). She chose to stay with her sons, who perished in the water from hypothermia, and was herself saved by chance from the water by a lifeboat.

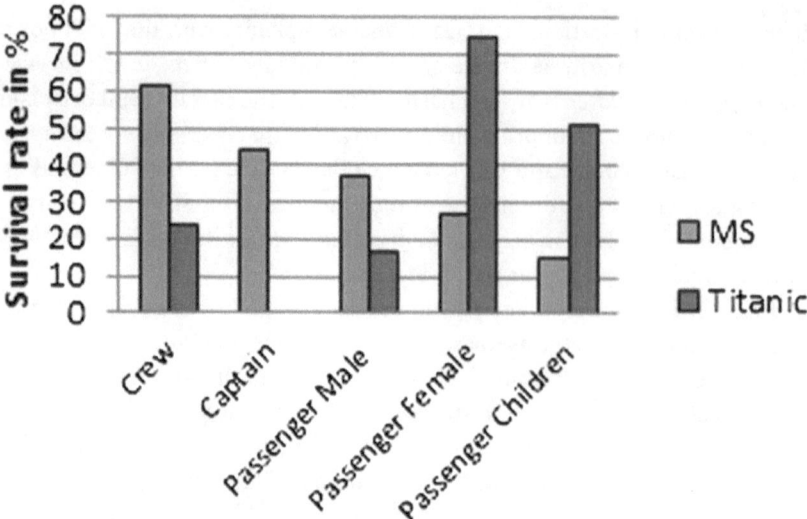

Figure 1.4. Mikael Elinder and Oscar Erixson, "Gender, Social Norms, and Survival in Maritime Disasters." Proceedings of the National Academy of Sciences of the United States of America 109, no. 33. (August 14, 2012): 13220–24. Reprinted with permission of PNAS.

Daniel Allen Butler writes that at one point, Lightoller "suddenly spotted a teenage boy, Jack Ryerson, climbing over the gunwale, and called out, 'That boy can't go!' Jack's father, Arthur Ryerson bristled. Placing his arm around Jack's shoulders he said, 'Of course the boy goes with his mother—he's only thirteen.' Lightoller relented, but was heard to mutter, 'No more boys'" (71). The inexperience of youth and cult of masculinity doomed fifteen-year-old Alfred Rush, who was looking forward to his sixteenth birthday when "he could then discard his infantile knee-breeches for the long trousers and the grown-up activities of a man.... When the women were separated from the men and sent to the boats, Alfred, who might have been spared due to his small stature, chose to stay behind. Proud of his newly acquired manhood he said, 'No, I'm staying here with the men!'" (Geller 139). Such a precarious intersection of age and gender bias makes it into children's fiction as well. In Eve Bunting's *SOS Titanic* (1996), 15-year-old Barry O'Neill is advised by other passengers to "say you're only thirteen." Instead he thinks "he'd look like a terrible fool, or a coward, or both," and so watches as "the first lifeboat began its slow creak downward. Barry counted seventeen in the boat, which was supposed to hold fifty-four" (193).

Although it may sound like blaming the victims, Molly Brown pointed out that this overeager heroism motivated by sentiment rather than pragmatic policy was self-destructive for many on the *Titanic*: "many men went down with the ship who should have saved themselves for their family's sakes. I do not condemn the men utterly for doing what by education and training they had been made to consider themselves irrevocably to do, but I say it is a false standard of conduct they adhere to" (qtd. in Miskolcze 2014, 179). Adult male survivors were in a double-bind of masculinity whereby, ironically, like *Paul and Virginia*'s title maiden, they had the rigidly false dilemma of dying for honor or surviving in shame. There is also the distinct possibility that, from the perspective of those who knew the history of doomed shipwreck aftermaths like that of the *Medusa*, to err on the side of underfilled lifeboats was much safer than overloading them.

Not only did the men and boys die in greater proportion as a result, but men who survived were at times shamed by the cult of masculinity associated with women and children first. Linda Maria Koldau writes that "This does not only confirm women's traditional role in western society (a woman receives gallant protection, but in turn has to subordinate to man, who yields this protection), but also the definition of 'true manhood.' Woe to the men who entered a lifeboat without the explicit command of an officer, without a conspicuous heroic feat" (18). Even eight-year old Marshall Drew understood, during the harrowing experience of being lowered in the lifeboat watching "row after row of portholes go black," that different behaviors were expected of boys, girls, and women: "This was 1912. Little boys didn't cry. You were a little man. You kept a stiff upper lip. I went to sleep on the life preservers. I woke up in daylight and 360 degrees there were icebergs" (Geller 116). One of the *Titanic* sources I bought used came with some marginal graffiti left by the previous reader. As I rushed, red-faced, to erase these lovely little tokens I noticed a pattern. Every time the testimony cited was from an adult male *survivor* of the shipwreck my precursor had written, "notorious homosexual."

Perhaps it was this cult of masculinity and protectionism, as well as the "virginal" status of the ship, that influenced other curious age-related decisions made during evacuation: priority to newlyweds. Survivor Helen Walton Bishop, who was nineteen on the voyage, recalled "Someone said, 'Put in the brides and grooms first.' There were three newly married couples who went into that boat. Altogether, there were 28 who went in our boat. There might as well have been 40 or 50, but the half hundred men on deck refused to leave even though there was room for them" (Geller 43). Yet, this sentiment broke down in cases judged in conflict with the infantilizing directive—women and children trumped newlyweds when the bride was much younger than the groom: "There was Daniel Marvin, reassuring his eighteen-year-old bride of two weeks, 'It's all right, little girl,' as he helped her into the lifeboat" (Butler 125). These separations were not always favored, even if they meant survival, seen most sensationally in the experience of Celiney Yasbeck, who'd been married less than two months when she became the subject of the *Detroit News Tribune* headline, "Girl Bride Torn from Husband at Pistol Point" (qtd. in Geller 179). Yasbeck said, "They held me down and said he would go in another boat and join me afterwards. But I never saw him again" (181). Needless to say, these young brides lost their new husbands to the disaster due to age differences, and because females were more infantilized than males of the same age.

Like literary depictions of women in shipwreck, there is a nauseating tendency in *Titanic* narratives to focus on linens, fashion, and the finery of first-class passenger experiences to suggest that the real tragedy was the loss of property. One thing that is often missing from such stories is the awareness and sometimes resistance of women and children to the "protected" and passive role they are expected to adopt. When Emma Ward Bucknell found herself in Lifeboat 8, she "soon learned that the assigned crew had no idea how to row. She herself took to the oars to teach them, together with other resourceful women. Emma was always proud to claim that she and her maid rowed the long night through" (Geller 40). The most famous of women to be hailed as *Titanic* heroes is Molly Brown, who would also become redefined in contemporary retellings like the musical and Cameron's film: "Immediately after her heroism in 1912, she seemed destined to become the antithesis of the pitiful shipwrecked girl.... Molly Brown emerged as a physically assertive and politically progressive woman during the wreck and in its aftermath. However, we can see that the musical's depiction of Brown minimizes her heroism in deference to the gender, race, and class politics of the early 1960s, whilst the 1997 film continues this distortion by minimizing her heroism again, this time in deference to an early-nineteenth-century vision of the shipwrecked woman" (Miskolcze 2014, 184). Within the larger ideological mold that shaped women and children first, women (and younger females) were damned either way by potential media spin.

A lighter way of thinking about the perils of sentimentalizing survival through protectionist tropes (erasing the politics in the romance of "heroism") is suggested in "Ladies First," adapted from Shel Silverstein by Mary Rodgers and performed by Marlo Thomas for *Free to Be . . . You and Me* (1972). In it, a "tender, sweet young thing" and "little lady" always has to be first, requiring special attention to be "careful of my lovely dress and my nice white socks and my shiny, shiny shoes and my curly, curly locks" (Rodgers). But when trapped in the jungle by "a bunch of hungry tigers," she gets indignant about not having her customary special treatment, demanding, "untie me this instant!" One tiger replies, "we were all just ... uh ... trying to decide who to untie first," and of course she insists, "'Ladies first! Ladies first!' And so she was. And mighty tasty, too" (Rodgers). Of course, the equity-feminist message here is not to fall for the appeasing trap of "special rights," which can be used to keep persons "in their place," but instead to fight for "equal rights." No one who rode the "special" bus in school felt all that special. Being "first" isn't all it's cracked up to be within the double-binds of binarized gender, and the grisly fate of this "tender, sweet young thing" will be more relevant than you might expect below.

Sentimentality, like romance, chivalry, and heroism that truck heavily in it, is ideologically potent. The *Birkenhead* drill (women and children first) could counter and comfort male anxieties about the rise of maternal centrality in the family sphere. Rather than resting on disingenuous apologist claims of cherishing or idolizing women and children, protective measures can also be used in service of glorifying male power and sacrifice. In the dedication to his masculinist, jingoistic, Islamophobic, antifeminist drivel titled *The Birkenhead Drill*, Douglas Phillips invokes the 150-year-old sentiment of women and children first in memory of first responders who died on 9-11, claiming that "feminism died in the basement of the World Trade Center." A few of us missed that memo, but I digress: "For the first time in a generation, the American people were exposed to the images and sounds of bold manhood sacrificing for women and children, as more than three hundred firefighters, all of them men [really?], gave their lives in a burning inferno.... May the memory of these men serve to inspire young boys of future generations to raise the standard of Christian chivalry in a world that often forgets that God made men the protectors and defenders of women and children" (Phillips, dedication page). When someone is so transparent, it is easy to see the usefulness and function of protectionist sentiment: to shore up feelings of male inadequacy, especially for those boys who promise to benefit immensely from the subjugation of others.

For a subtler explanation of how life-and-death crises can be canned for vicarious consumption to reinforce hierarchies ideologically through affect, consider the audience member, perhaps even yourself, crying at the end of *Titanic* (any film version—there are too many to choose from). Isn't there some sort of relief in those tears at being a spectator only? Thomas Hobbes wrote, "Those that weep the greatest amount are those, such as women and children, who have the least hope in themselves and the most in friends" (qtd. in Lutz 179). To such thinking, dependency, even inter-dependency, indicates a power differential. Tom Lutz explains, "powerlessness still frames our own cultural understanding of tears" (179). For a concrete example, Lutz describes how "[a]n actor friend told me that whenever he needed tears for a scene, he ... imagined that he was on the *Titanic* as it was sinking (this was before the James Cameron film), and that he was handing his wife and baby son into a lifeboat. This vision could make him break down into sobs almost immediately. When I asked why he thought this worked so well, he said that it was because the image produced the most intense feeling of loss he could imagine." He points out, however, that in this scenario, "his wife and son were not dying" but surviving (264). They then agree that the real reason for the immediate affective power of the imagined scene "was based on the fact that others were watching and approving of what he was doing—the captain of the ship, the first mate, the other men taking charge of the situation. This daydream, this mini-melodrama, makes him weep because in it he consummately fulfills an iconographic social role" (265). Too bad Douglas Phillips didn't realize this deeper and more self-focused incentive in himself before writing his book on the *Birkenhead* drill. He may have spared his reader the alienation and himself the embarrassment of such transparent ego work.

Of course, the popularity of heroic displays of male power also reflects broader adult nostalgia and maudlin denials of the fact that such terrible fates could await any of us. In the public imagination, sentiment placates fears about child vulnerability, but disguising the truth also perpetuates a denial of unpleasant realities which can compromise vigilance. Thus, the most disseminated narratives about shipwreck are romanticized *ad nauseam*, showing a practice of getting women and children in lifeboats first, not because it is representative of reality but because it is very precisely not. Stories about the *Titanic* are popular because its sinking appears as the exception to a rule: it flatters our hopes that children are safe rather than alerting us to problems that beset the small and outnumbered.

In fact, sometimes at sea, the only thing kids were first at was being chucked, stolen, killed, or eaten. In her account of the aftermath of the infamous 1816 wreck of the *Medusa*,[3] on which she and her family had been traveling when she was eighteen years old, Charlotte-Adélaïde Picard Dard notes that "every one pursued the plan he deemed best for his own preservation" (226). This included most of the officers and crew; even the captain, unlawfully, abandoned the ship before others were safely situated. Dard is quite explicit about the particular vulnerability of her younger siblings and of the whole party being burdened with their care. With luck, they reach one of the fleeing boats: "[F]or it is most certain they had no intention of encumbering themselves with our unfortunate family. I say encumber, for it is evident that four children, one of whom was yet at the breast, were very indifferent beings to people who were actuated by a selfishness without all parallel" (227–28). In hindsight, she also is glad to have escaped the ill-fated raft, where "a spirit of sedition began to manifest itself in furious cries. They then began to regard one another with ferocious looks, and to thirst for one another's flesh. Someone had already whispered of having recourse to that monstrous extremity [cannibalism] and of commencing with the fattest and youngest" (234). Even before the wreck, when the *Medusa* was early into the voyage, a "fifteen-year-old sailor lad, leaning too far out of a port to watch the shining display [of porpoises] had fallen overboard" and was simply left behind when "swept astern into the bubbling wake" (McKee 18–19). So perhaps the phrase should be "women *with* children first." The kinless child is in a whole other heap of trouble. When children are defined as property instead of persons, the kinless have little legal recourse to care. Kinship status matters.

Of course, class is a factor in the brutal hierarchies of survival that become explicit in life-or-death group crises, a fact made clear in standard *Titanic* narratives. But race is also, predictably, a discriminating factor. If one reads between the lines of Thomas Nickerson's diary from the 1820 shipwreck of the *Essex* (on which the fourteen-year-old was the youngest of the crew), the black survivors of the wreck died mysteriously in at least one lifeboat, first of supposedly natural causes after food and water ran out, although with enough of a pattern to resemble a bad horror flick (174). It is not clear if all were cannibalized, but records would have us believe that one black sailor refused his food and even willingly offered his body for the others' sustenance (168). Sounds like a conspiratorial lie of troubled conscience to me.

But factoring out race and class, age becomes an obvious but less recognized advantage to survival in a broader context of crises. Catherine Orenstein's *Little Red Riding Hood Uncloaked* is full of examples of real "big, bad wolves" like the inspiration for "Bluebeard" Gilles Garnier, the sixteenth-century serial killer who ate children (96). Using fear to sway kids away from danger is a common didactic practice. Anthropologists in the South Pacific found "[y]oung people were told . . . that if they cried the Americans would eat them" (Lutz 173). But the "eat or be eaten" dilemma of fairy tales is not simply symbolic. Daniel James Brown gives twentieth-century examples of famine followed by the desperation of cannibalism from which "children disappeared the fastest" (178). As a result of floods, drought, and agricultural and economic crises, "famine was so widespread in some rural parts of China that some peasants began to eat the corpses of their fellow villagers, particularly the corpses of children. When they ran out of corpses, some families took to starving their infant daughters and then exchanging the bodies with those of their neighbors' daughters so that nobody would have to eat his or her own children" (178–79). Ok, so I guess you can't factor out gender. But there is particular evidence for age and parental connections as discriminating factors—before and after women and children first became a dominant sentiment or supposed custom of the sea.

A much longer-standing custom particular to sea travel that proved stronger than laws of nations was the drawing of lots to choose who should be killed and eaten when necessary for the survival of others. A surprising number of examples following the custom, from literary and maritime history, involve fictional and real Richard Parkers.[4] In fact, the name has become synonymous with being a young (often orphan) martyr in maritime disasters—a tasty morsel[5] who dies to sustain the survival of others—as in the ballad stanza that appears in this chapter's epigraph (for full ballad see Simpson 1984, verso facing p. 131). The literary legacy links Edgar Allan Poe's *Narrative of Arthur Gordon Pym of Nantucket* (1838) and Yann Martel's *Life of Pi* (2001). In Poe's story, after a mutiny on and shipwreck of the *Grampus*, a character named Richard Parker secures his death rather than sating his hunger when he expresses "cannibal designs" to the remaining shipmates (68). Once others agree to the procedure, he (with poetic justice) draws the losing lot: "He made no resistance whatever, and was stabbed in the back by Peters, when he fell instantly dead. I must not dwell upon the fearful repast which immediately ensued" (70). But, of course, Pym does tell that "having in some measure appeased the raging thirst which consumed us by the blood of the victim, and having by common consent taken off the hands, feet, and head, throwing them together with the entrails, into the sea, we devoured the rest of the body" (71). The telling phrase "common consent" seems to suggest that they are acting on custom, which I will address below. According to this custom and remarkable coincidence, life will, in time, imitate art.

Pym is seen as a source for Yann Martel's *Life of Pi* (see Ketterer), although the only inspiration Martel has acknowledged is hearing of the premise from Moacyr Scliar's *Max and the Cats* (1981).[6] In *Life of Pi*, the name Richard Parker is comically given to a tiger from a paperwork error, and the name sticks. After the ship carrying the animals from his family's zoo sinks, Pi is on the lifeboat with surviving animals: a zebra with a broken leg, an orangutan named Orange Juice, a hyena who eats them both, and Richard Parker the tiger, with whom Pi will travel until he reaches land. So Pi is constantly under threat of being eaten, even when he briefly stays on an island that turns out to be carnivorous.[7] The fantastical island reflects the metaphysical bent of Pi, who had found *Robinson Crusoe* too prosaic for his tastes (73). Depending upon how you interpret the narrative as a whole, Pi offers the ship owners an alternate story—either fabricated but more believable, or a breakdown of the animal tale as an allegory. In it, the survivors on the lifeboat are human: a crew member from the ship, Pi's mother, and the cook, leaving the suggestion that Pi is in fact the tiger. With the second interpretation, one can read a commentary on the animality of humans, which we live daily in denial of but realize in eat-or-be eaten conflicts, just as Pi had learned when he was younger at the zoo: "Life will defend itself no matter how small it is" (38). Michael Titlestad writes (with an on-point nod to William Blake's "tyger") that

> Richard Parker is an avatar of the proximate terror of the wilderness—of the beast facing man in fearful asymmetry. The open boat represents exposure, not only literally but also to a world that is red in tooth and claw. In shipwreck, along with the masts, hull, and decks, a microcosm of sociality is shattered. Castaways are exposed to threats that arise from this disintegration of social, political, ontological, and ethical structures. (207)

So castaways expose the artificiality in such consensually determined realities; in their place a politics of survival emerges. Poe's Pym likewise learned this when the last two lots remained for either him or Richard Parker: "At this moment all the fierceness of the tiger possessed my bosom, and I felt toward my poor fellow-creature, Parker, the most intense, the most diabolical hatred" (70). On one level, both Poe's and Martel's stories focus on how the eat-or-be-eaten dilemma equalizes humans with nonhuman animals.

But, for Martel's readers who prefer the human story, the possibility of the orangutan Orange Juice representing Pi's mother reintroduces the more familiar trope: mother love again. The cook is as indomitable and voracious as a hyena. Pi's mother slaps him, and "it was heroic." She confronts him when he eats the sailor's dried flesh: "You monster! You animal!"—not a word used unreflectively in Martel's novel (308). If Pi is dissociating his own animal self projected through "Richard Parker," he certainly sets up his alibi for turning violent himself: "He killed her. The cook killed my mother" (307). In her struggle with the cook, she protected Pi: "She turned to me and said, 'Go!' pushing me towards the raft," but "My mother was fighting an adult man" (309). Pi is temporarily safe on the raft, but it gets even worse: "He hurled something my way. A line of blood struck me across the face. No whip could have inflicted a more painful lash. I held my mother's head in my hands" (310). I only bring up this particularly gruesome detail to emphasize how much fact can be as strange as fiction. As with the remains of Poe's Parker on the *Grampus*, the cook is following a customary procedure of survival cannibalism: "[S]ailors indeed did just that—they cut off the head as a preliminary to eating the corpse" (Simpson 1984, 142). The true stories surrounding the ritual in maritime history are even more fascinating than Pi's imaginings.

Legal scholar A. W. Brian Simpson has documented such customs at length in his analysis of the *Mignonette* case from 1884. A yacht barely equipped for international travel, the *Mignonette* had a crew of four, including the seventeen-year-old Richard Parker, often referred to as a "boy" or by the nickname "Little Dickie" (Simpson 1984, 37).[8] He was illiterate but receiving tutoring as part of his wage during the journey: "And Richard Parker wrote what was probably the first letter of his life to his foster parents," telling them that "he was happy and comfortable, that all on board were well, and that they had had a fine a pleasant voyage on the way" (43). But the *Mignonette*'s planking could not weather a heavy South Atlantic storm, coming loose and sinking the yacht rapidly. The crew escaped in the lifeboat but without adequate food or fresh water, languishing for nineteen days. Parker was in particularly bad condition due to drinking seawater, so he was killed to be consumed. Upon being rescued, there was little effort to cover up the gruesome details, which Simpson reports with humor: "Brooks [seaman who did not take part in the killing] was given some blood; it was congealed, and there was little of it. He swallowed it as well as he could. It might now be supposed that the three sailors, confronted with the corpse of their shipmate, would be in something of the same state of puzzlement as children confronted for the first time by artichokes—uncertain how to proceed next" (68). The testimonies of the crew became inconsistent, if revealing, with the passage of time, but most accounts indicate that Parker was killed because he was dying anyway. Simpson explains, "The law treated accelerating death as murder; popular culture did not necessarily accept this rigorous line" (65). In fact, even Richard Parker's brother Daniel forgave Richard's killers, and the only public criticism of the crew's action was based on the slim evidence that any proper lot drawing had occurred (Simpson 1981, 4–5). Most accounts fail to mention that protocol, and the few that do indicate that any such drawing was rigged against the youngest crew member: "Accounts of the drawing of lots reflect the idea that this was the proper or appropriate course of action—the right thing to do. This idea has survived in oral tradition; I have had it explained to me by relatives of Richard Parker that the only reason why [captain] Dudley and [mate] Stephens were tried was that they cheated—they did not follow the approved practice, which was to draw lots" (5). So the custom of the sea remained stronger than laws being created against it, guiding, disseminating a rationale for the practice through oral history and ballads: "These old traditional ballads, which survived to this century as a living form of folk art, instructed sailors as to what ought to be done, and their message was reinforced by other ballads dealing with specific cases—such as the ballads of the *Essex* and the *George*. The instruction provided by the ballads could be very specific indeed," revealing procedures with quite contrary priorities to saving the lives of women and children (141).

    Sea lore and historical accounts reveal another pattern with far more sinister repercussions for the young, however. Many cases indicate that the young were directly targeted for survival cannibalism (not just the unfortunate Parkers named Richard). In obeisance to the custom of the sea, stranded sailors who succumbed to cannibalizing may have simply agreed upon a common fabrication for a consistent defense: "It strains credulity to suppose that in all these cases lots were actually drawn, or were fairly drawn, just as it is quite possible that in other cases in which killing was not admitted, death was anticipated by sailors desperate for drink, who feared that they would not obtain blood from one who died naturally" (Simpson 1981, 5). But it also "strains credulity" that the dying lots should be drawn by the youngest, often the kinless, as much as they were. The evidence of picking out the youngest and kinless first (or rigging the lots to choose them) is not particularly well hidden. For example, in 1874, a cargo ship, the *Euxine*, caught fire and had to be abandoned. One of three lifeboats capsized and lost all food and water. Only four days later, "it was proposed that lots be drawn; they were, three times, and on each occasion the fatal lot fell on an Italian boy who spoke little or no English. He was called Francis Shufus—a corruption of an Italian name. This story conforms to a pattern—the lots are repeated, the result is always the same, the odd man out is selected" (8). But the "odd man out" isn't even a man, and this pattern, too, is repeated.

The year 1836 was particularly bad for cabin boys and young orphans at sea. At least one was spared, although not by design: the report of the wreck of *Brig Caledonia* "records only one actual killing but confirms the story that on the thirteenth day they were about to kill the ship's boy" when they were rescued (Simpson 1984, 128). Even more telling is the testimony of the captain of the *Francis Spaight*, which almost capsized in 1836 and had to be dismasted to be righted but lost all food stores. From the captain's report, it is clear that the first drawing of lots specifically targeted only the four young orphans on board: "His opinion was that one should suffer for the rest, and that lots should be drawn between the four boys, as they had no families, and could not be considered so great a loss to their friends, as those who had wives and children depending upon them" (131). Here the overt logic is that the four orphans' youth and kinlessness are a justification for the action. The unlucky one who called his own name for the shortest stick was Patrick O'Brien, whose killing is documented in great detail. Even the ballad "The Sorrowful Fate of O'Brien" shamelessly repeats the rationale of eating kinless boys first: "Our captain cried: 'Cheer up my boys, let those four boys cast lots / They have no wives: to save our lives one of these four must die. / While lots they were preparing, these poor unfortunate boys / Stood gazing at each other with salt tears in their eyes / A bandage o'er O'Brien's eyes they quickly then did tie / For the second lot that was pulled up said O'Brien was to die" (142). The verses repeat details documented in legal record, such as the suspicious method of lot drawing that could easily have been rigged, the cook refusing to kill the boy until threatened with death, and the lots drawn only for those who have no relations on land who could litigate against the killers. Such cases give a sinister spin to the phrase "women and children first."

Clearly, these cases are plotting hierarchical discriminatory killing with a careful rationale. In the drawn-out days of postwreck languishing in lifeboats, sailors are acting under the duress of thirst and hunger, but their protocol can be debated for days before acting—highly rationalized, even hegemonic, based on contradictory values. Although hardly equal in consequence for individuals, for children as a group, whether being prioritized for a space in a lifeboat or being chosen to die first, there is a serious gap between public sentiment and actual practice. Without the operative component of the phrase "*women* and children first" kids were, frankly, screwed.

Even in the doomed Donner party of 1846–47, who had no "custom of the sea" to guide behavior, and where familial ties and proportionality offered greater protections,[9] children, who made up half of the party, did not all simply succumb to the elements: "Three-year-old James Eddy was dead in the Murphy cabin. And a night or two before, Louis Keesberg had taken one-year-old George Foster into his bed with him. In the morning the boy was dead. As Levinah Murphy and the three Donner girls looked in abject horror, Keesberg took the boy's limp body from the bed, carried it to a wall, and hung it on a peg, like a piece of meat" (Daniel James Brown 233). In the account written by Virginia Reed Murphy, who was twelve years old during the crossing,[10] children's deaths are made to seem more comfortably distanced by identifying them through substituting first names with simple possessives: "Mrs. Keesberg here this morning. Son died three days ago" or "McCutchens' child died five days ago" (62, 63). For similar reasons, in an account written for children, *Patty Reed's Doll*, the reader's view is limited to the doll's perspective, and the reader's sympathies are redirected onto parents, as in "Everyone is dying. Mrs. Eddy's baby died yesterday" (129). The historical gap between young readers and these pioneers also gives the safer perspective of distance to such events.

But our denial of children's physical and economic vulnerabilities is two sided (and, I'll contest, not simply evoking them as victims). Children can take part in strategizing survival, which also becomes taboo (as evidenced in Pi's motive for the animal version of his story). According to Daniel James Brown, it was "seven-year-old Mary Donner, the toes of her feet blackened by frostbite" who "could not stand the hunger pangs any longer. She suggested that they eat the dead" (235). Such moments are even less represented, revealing a preference for the child as victim over child as surviving cannibal. In the aftermath of the *Essex* sinking, those (white) men remaining in the lifeboat drew lots: "The awful lot fell upon a young man named Owen Coffin ... who with great fortitude and resignation cheerfully smiled at his fate at this awful moment. The captain wished to exchange lots with him, but to this Coffin would not listen for one moment. He placed himself in a firm position to receive his death and was immediately shot by Charles Ramsdell who became his executioner by fair lot" (Nickerson 174). Although Coffin was eighteen years old, and Ramsdell only sixteen (Rarick 131), when the tale was adapted for the film *In the Heart of the Sea* (2015), both were played by actors in their midtwenties. By way of an ageist double standard, the actual minors who self-determined survival and heroically sacrificed become falsified as unequivocally adult. And the child cannibal has no place in our palatable narratives.

This is in part because the taboo against cannibalism is ideologically created, and taboo by definition utilizes a similar mechanism of denial to that which can make certain children socially invisible (for example, child victims of sexual abuse, especially incest). Within carnivorous societies, eating the flesh of nonhuman animals is selectively sanctioned from what Melanie Joy calls a "carnist" perspective. As Claude Lévi-Strauss has explained: "This view of things makes a carnivorous diet an enrichment of sorts of the vegetarian regime. Some people without writing, however, see it as a barely attenuated form of cannibalism" (113). From such a perspective, eating the flesh of nonhuman animals is just as taboo, indicating through contrast that carnism is ideologically buttressed by selective denials.

One example of this conflated denial can be seen in the case of the Uruguayan air force flight 571 (McKee 286–90), which crashed in the Andes in October 1972. The crash and a following avalanche killed twenty-nine passengers, ultimately leaving sixteen to survive snowbound on negligible food for seventy-two days. Most were male teens and young adults who played on the same rugby team. To survive, they cannibalized those who died before them, although with many consensual controls, eventually even with each other's permission before dying. Yet, after a remarkable rescue, resulting solely from the young survivors' own extraordinary efforts, rejoining their families posed ideological problems. The father of one survivor was angered by the media suggestion that cannibalism may have been involved: "Look, now, you must say that this isn't true." His son confirmed it was true, and "The father looked abruptly at the son with an expression of mild distaste on his face; but later, when he realized that it was something his son had done from necessity, he got used to the idea and was surprised that it had not occurred to him before" (302). But it hadn't occurred to many in the community who still prefer the gloss of a "miracle." After more than two months of not knowing what had happened to their sons, the means of survival could only be seen as unacceptable: "They were aware that many—especially among older people—were appalled by what they had done and considered that they should have chosen to die. Even Madelón's mother, who as much as anyone had believed in the return of her grandson, could not bring herself to contemplate this aspect of his survival"

(308). So this triumph of youth ingenuity and grit is instead remembered as "the Miracle of the Andes" by deniers.

When children rescue themselves and others, the standard tropes break down or at least require a different narrative groove from preferred, self-flattering adult heroism. And a narrative ensuring such a perspective is not as conveniently accessible as the adult-focused compensatory narratives that dominate in history and literature. Even when stolen, captive, and enslaved children are concerned, a literary distancing occurs in redirecting focus on parental hardship: "In written and visual abolitionist rhetoric, tales of land-bound slaves with drowned children or children carelessly buried or sold away from mothers mirror the mourning mothers and abused women on slave ships" (Miskolcze 2007, 83). Child heroism is muted by endless projections of parental perspectives, even in the democratizing microcosm of a ship. Paul Gilroy suggests that "ships were the living means by which the points within the Atlantic world were joined. They were mobile elements that stood for the shifting spaces in between the fixed places that they connected. Accordingly, they need to be thought of as cultural and political units rather than abstract embodiments of the triangular trade. They were something more—a means to conduct political dissent and possibly a distinct mode of cultural production" (16–17). But this potential for participation in dynamic, democratic publics is often denied children, or it is a suppressed possibility in popular narratives. An excellent example of Gilroy's thesis, and an illustration of how it doesn't apply to children, can be seen in mainstream tellings of the *Amistad*'s story.

Like the stories above and the robinsonade tradition to be treated in more detail below and in my next chapter, the 1839 *Amistad* rebellion has been white-washed in retellings: "[T]he history and especially the movie.... have told only part of the story. The drama of the courtroom has eclipsed the original drama that transpired on the deck of the slave schooner. The American actors—abolitionists, attorneys, judges, and politicians—have elbowed aside the African ones whose daring actions set the train of events in motion. Curiously, the American legal system has emerged as the story's hero—the very system which, in 1839, held two and a half million African Americans in bondage" (Rediker 2013, 5).[11] But it has also been "age-washed," for lack of a better term. Little attention has been paid to the children involved in this historical event, who clearly saw themselves as active participants. Nine-year-old Ka'le's letter to John Quincy Adams is pointed about the children's knowing and active participation in the rebellion: "Americans no take us in ship.... If court ask who brought Mendi people to America? We bring ourselves. Ceci hold the rudder. All we want is make us free" (qtd. in Blassingame 34). "We bring ourselves" is a declaration of self-possession and exercised agency, a declaration that enhanced the argument for adult survivors' freedom, but Ka'le and his young cohorts were not so easily interpreted as rightfully belonging to that "we."

Benjamin N. Lawrance does much to redress this oversight by focusing entirely on the six children, aged about nine to sixteen, involved in the successful uprising and trial. Lawrance argues that the *Amistad* orphans' status as minors vastly complicated their treatment and housing arrangements during the two-year period between the rebellion and legal decision, because of "the ambiguity of free status for children." Much in contrast to the "myth of blanket freedom" whereby all were declared free and freedom proceeded immediately,

> [t]he experiences of *Amistad*'s orphans in the wake of the Supreme Court determination were complex, painful, and likely traumatic. In some regards Ka'le fared the best: he was released with the adult males shortly after the ruling.... For the remaining five, however, liberty was often an elusive or ambivalent status ... Covey, ostensibly liberated at the age of nine, but first apprenticed and then detained in the United States under subpoena, was more or less abandoned by the Amistad committee. (180)

Antonio, who was fifteen or sixteen, had worked as a slave for three years before the rebellion and was actually on the *Amistad* as a cabin boy (not "cargo") and not allied with the rebels, so ultimately his only recourse to freedom was to flee to Canada.

More to my point, however, is the aftermath of the trial, necessitating an additional lawsuit to release Kag'ne, Mar'gru, and Te'me (ubiquitously referred to simply as "the girls"), who were "detained as house servants" in the home of Colonel Stanton Pendleton, a supposed benefactor who assured the children they were being protected while actually attempting to have them indentured (Lawrance 180, 201). This complication indicates the extent to which being "free-born" was not sufficient reason for freeing the minors, as it was for the adults. In other words, inalienable birthrights aren't birthrights at all. Rather than being collectively applied, they are selectively distributed according to hierarchies of race, class, gender, history, culture, and geography, conferred when one reaches the age of majority, which is also subject to relative definition.

The Pendletons' ruse speaks to specific dangers of child status in the context of slavery. Manipulation was a common method of control: "children were seen as possessing skills and competencies less accessible to adult slaves, including the powerful dependencies that quickly emerge from emotional vulnerabilities during childhood. Slave traders realized that child slaves craved security and protection" (Lawrance 29). To be sure there is evidence of childlike fears, although in light of my examples above, perhaps they are not irrational ones at all. Part of the children's self-defense points to their fear of being eaten by the *Amistad* cook. Ka'le wrote, "Cook say he kill, he eat Mendi people—we afraid—we will cook" (Blassingame 34). This element appears in a children's book on the rebellion, *Africa Is My Home* (2013), in which Mar'gru reports that the cook "pointed to some barrels nearby, mimed throats being slit, then chopping.... They were going to eat us! There was now no doubt about it—they were planning to kill us for food!" (Edinger 12). Perhaps they knew that it is easier to eat something than someone. Considering a person, property has its way of soothing cognitive dissonance. One case in point is "the loss of the brig *George* in 1822, when one Joyce Rae was eaten by her husband, a detail which added a certain piquancy to a routine procedure. He claimed prior rights in the corpse arising out of the marriage, a principle of family law now obsolete" (Simpson 1981, 5). Redefined as property, a person cannot own oneself but can be claimed as someone else's. So most certainly the *Amistad* orphans learned, if they did not know already, that it is also easier to exploit something than someone. It is the greater ease with which children could be defined as property that is particularly revealing about their separate and subtle entrapment.

Obscuring the sometimes artificial distinction between familial and property relations, Mar'gru and Kag'ne had been pawned for debt in Sierra Leone by their fathers, and the family they resided with after the rebellion and during the trial was attempting to have them bound into more permanent servitude. In the words of the fictionalized Mar'gru (later to be named Sarah), the Pendletons' scheme sounds like a textbook protection racket: "We had been living with the New Haven jailer's family, the Pendletons, since shortly after our arrival, and they vehemently did not want us to leave. I now know that is because they used us as household servants, but at the time I thought it was because they genuinely cared for us. They were the only American family I had lived with and knew well, and so when they told us that they were the only ones who could protect us from being sold into slavery again, I believed them" (Edinger 43). The emotional power of familial obligation, even affection, was particularly useful in controlling children: "Slave traders preyed on the emotional insecurities of children to strengthen the master-slave relationship and reshape it with the paternal dimensions of a pseudo-family" (Lawrance 29). Whereas adults can often forge their own families, a child's familial place is defined biologically at birth or legally determined by others.

As Paul Gilroy has suggested, the ship can foster new "cultural and political units." The adult mutineers aboard the *Amistad* were able to forge "a means to conduct political dissent" that successfully protected their "free-born" rights. But kinlessness is a whole different legal beast for minors—there is plenty of precedent for viewing them as someone's property to be claimed, freeborn or not.¹² For example, in Melville's *Moby-Dick* (1851), the mere threat of another's claim to him as property renders Pip powerless. When he jumps out of a whale boat interrupting pursuit, second mate Stubb berates him and warns, "Stick to the boat, Pip, or by the Lord, I wont pick you up if you jump, mind that. We can't afford to lose whales by the likes of you; a whale would sell for thirty times what you would, Pip, in Alabama" (597). The unfortunate cabin boy jumps again, is abandoned, and loses his mind before being rescued almost by accident. Even geographically remote from a slave-holding state, his potential exchange value will only protect him if it exceeds the object of their hunt in the economy of the ship. For those caught up in such sinister calculations, their lack of property rights and potential ownership by another can doom them.

Minors who lack agency within commerce can easily be trapped within domestic economies. The experiences of the *Amistad* children highlight the relative fluidity yet rigid consequences of family definitions. While the "unit" forged by adults is deemed valid and authentic, the "pseudo-family" granted the children is certainly not. The unique, extreme disempowerment of enslaved children also points to how all children and the enslaved share a common problem in regard to the recognition (or granting) of civil liberties—their subjectivity to property laws. Early family law reflects this shared complication. In *The Origin of the Family, Private Property and the State* (1884), Frederick Engels wrote, "The original meaning of the word 'family' (*familia*) is not that compound of sentimentality and domestic strife which forms the ideal of the present-day philistine; among the Romans it did not at first even refer to the married pair and their children but only to the slaves. *Famulus* means domestic slave, and *familia* is the total number of slaves belonging to one man" (121).

These common roots of patriarchy and privatization of property explain the broader meanings of "family" in Daniel Defoe's *Robinson Crusoe* (1719), in which the title character swings easily from slave owner/trader to being a slave and back again without so much as a pang of consciousness (56–57, 63, 70, 73–74, 148) yet continually calls his servants, slaves, and even animals his family (128, 206, 250, 299). Although on an uninhabited island, he nonetheless sets about a somewhat absurd task of creating "enclosures" (129, 140), which, far from being simply defensive borders, become (the reader is to believe) his "plantations" from his effort alone, without recognition from any local populace or law but solely a "first-come" colonizing claim (170, 246). Two of the primary themes of the book, beset with assumptions of beneficent slavery and paternalism, are family and private property—neither of which, at first thought, would be expected or deemed relevant on an uninhabited isle.

The primary inner conflict of Robinson's personal development is set up as stemming from his desire for (and possible error of) escaping a cautious middle-class existence advised from within his nuclear family: "I broke loose, though in the meantime I continued obstinately deaf to all proposals of settling into business" (47). Helena Wall positions *Robinson Crusoe* as a response to "parental tyranny" (133), which makes sense in the context of primary accumulation: privatizing property through enclosures, family intensifying through nuclearization, and class identity replacing community roles. If one considers the slowly shifting family dynamic in such a context, it is easier to understand how Robinson's experience in the home of his nuclear family might be interpreted as oppressive parenting:

> As well as isolation, a further price is exacted by the nuclear family: the overintensity of the parent-child relationship. When there is no ease of the village, no margin of the street, no relief of the extended family, when a child "belongs" only to its parents, when an entire childhood depends on just one or two relationships, the psychological stresses are bound to be appalling—more than kin and less than kind. . . . Everything depends on that one thread. There are no other ropes and no safety net. (Griffiths 166)

By breaking off these ties, Robinson and his creator, Defoe, suggest the necessity of escaping the private sphere of domestic determination. Teresa Michals points out, "In Defoe's time, the economic world was not an adults-only place. Economic relations crossed our familiar divisions between public and private, adult and child," but this paradigm was being replaced by structures that would come to be dominant in the nineteenth century, wherein "children and childlike people belonged in the home, and adults belonged in the economic world outside" (27, 26). For much of the narrative, Robinson protests, although his actions repeatedly suggest a different message, that he should have listened to his father's warnings:

> He told me it [going to sea] was for men of desperate fortunes on one hand, or of aspiring, superior fortune on the other, who went abroad upon adventures, to rise by enterprise, and make themselves famous in undertakings of a nature out of the common road: that these things were all either too far above me, or too far below me; that mine was the middle state, or what might be called the upper station of low life, which he had found by long experience was the best state in the world. (44)

In contrast to familial expectations, Crusoe amasses his own capital, rather than rising within the self-stabilizing methods of his class. After all, the middle "station" requires preserving class relations and property distribution, as Stephanie

Coontz explains: "[T]he intermediary layers or classes of capitalist society, however, distinctive their outlook from labor's or capital's, can produce no alternative ways of organizing society. Their special place, indeed, *depends* upon the polarization of labor and capital; their privileges flow from their role as a buffer between the two." This constant deferral to a centerless but normatizing function can only remain reactive, not proactive: "Ultimately, the middle layers have no independent program or basis for structural change. However discontented they may be with big business, their dependence on existing property relations has led them to sanctify the same market forces that favor expansion of large blocs of capital" (1988, 187). It is clear that Robinson's father believes in operating within this safer mode, advising "that kings have frequently lamented the miserable consequences of being born to great things, and wished they had been placed in the middle of the two extremes, between the mean and the great; that the wise man gave his testimony to this as the just standard of true felicity, when he prayed to have neither poverty or riches" (44). But his son embraces a darker demand of capitalistic processes, the need for expansion through conquering land and the bodies/labor of others. Robinson continually repeats his father's advice of the middle (class) way and that he should have listened, but his individual trajectory relies entirely upon building capital through plunder (slaves and land providing the means for producing sugar), depending on perspective, retrogressing or class climbing, through the recourse he gains by being at sea.

The island Crusoe claims as his own serves as a microcosm not only of colonial capitalism (by which expansion and the subjugation of others is rationalized as necessary for profit) but also for the changing position of children and families under expanding and privatizing property. Ownership expanded for wealthy capitalists while access to land dramatically shrunk for everyone else, including children. Jay Griffiths explains,

> The experience of children was mirrored in the treatment of the land. Although some early Enclosures had taken place in the thirteenth century, it was the fifteenth and sixteenth centuries that saw a wave of Enclosures, with an extreme peak in the eighteenth century, falling off by 1830. Map this with the history of childhood and something fascinating emerges: children were subjected to increasing discipline from the very end of the fourteenth century to the fifteenth and sixteenth centuries, reaching its height in the eighteenth century, until the tide began to turn by about, yes, 1830. (32–33)

So, *Robinson Crusoe* (1719) represents a milestone in a new trajectory mapping and historicizing childhood as well. Robinson's journey and cultivation of the island reflect an optimism about breaking away from the nuclearizing family and a naïve but sinister faith in privatizing property. Griffiths concludes, "The nature of the land and the nature of the child were both to be controlled, fenced in. Enclosure, both literal and metaphoric, was enacted against land and childhood" (33). No surprise, then, that the most famous island tale emerged in the midst of such changes, and robinsonades have flourished in the past two centuries, in particular (these will be the subject of my next chapter). In the collective imaginations of vicariously sailing readers, the sea came to represent freedom and the island an enclosure providing safety through restraints.

Consider as points in contrast two sea stories for young readers that focus on young sailors who work their way into full participation and even positions of (symbolic) power on ships. Jules Verne's *Dick Sand; or, A Captain at Fifteen* (1878) and Avi's *The True Confessions of Charlotte Doyle* (1990) were composed a century apart, spanning a period of intensified nuclearization of families and the privatizing of childhood. Both Dick Sand and thirteen-year-old Charlotte Doyle become captains, if initially only by accident and symbolic title. The microcosms of the ships on which they sail constitute self-contained publics, unaffected by on-shore familial politics while at sea. Verne's protagonist is an orphan named Richard (fortunately not Parker) "because it was the name of the charitable passer-by who had picked him up two or three hours after his birth. As to the name of Sand, it was attributed to him in remembrance of the place where he had been found; that is to say, on that point of land called Sandy Hook, which forms the entrance of the port of New York, at the mouth of the Hudson." His belonging to nothing but a beach uniquely qualifies Dick to develop without the restraints of family protections or projections. He is a full participant, beginning as a crew novice: "At fifteen he already knew how to take a part, and to carry out to the end whatever his resolute spirit had decided upon" (10). This self-determination and ability to "take a part" is thus unhindered by the care or concern of others. Nor are his successes credited to others: "[H]e had made himself—being already almost a man at an age when others are still only children" (11).

Much of the difference between this boy's possibilities and those of Avi's Charlotte Doyle is of course due to gender and class. Charlotte is from an upper-middle-class family with rigid gender expectations and classist pretensions. But it is clear that having an intact family expecting her return creates the largest obstacle to her budding interest and skill as a sailor (at least within the fictive reality Avi creates in the novel). What's of interest to my own argument is the way both novels separate family from sea life. In *The True Confessions of Charlotte Doyle*, as the title might imply, conflict hinges on a journal she has kept at sea. In it she recounts at first being manipulated by a cruel captain, then a mutiny in which she plays a role, her education in sailing, and happily shedding the old life for sailor's threads and action. Accustomed to her freedom at sea, however, she forgets that she had been instructed to keep the diary for her father's approval (even at sea her privacy is violable). Upon her return, he reads it, disbelieving her account as "rubbish of the worst taste. Stuff for penny dreadfuls" (218). Her experiences are so far from the control he expected the journal to represent (as his power of oversight while she is out of his sphere)[13] that he forbids her to ever speak of the trip again to him or to her siblings. What happens at sea stays at sea. But Charlotte's reaction, captive in her solitary room for punishment, suggests the importance of not only her taste for "confessional" honesty but also her need to write her own narrative: "I did not read. Instead I used the books, the blank pages, the margins, even the mostly empty title pages to set down secretly what had happened during the voyage. It was my way of fixing all the details in my mind forever" (219). It doesn't take her long to rescript her life and go to sea again, the reader presumes, this time for good. Her only choice can be the protection of family and home on shore or giving it all up for a life at sea, as Zachariah has told her, "[a] sailor chooses the wind that takes the ship from safe port ... but winds have a mind of their own" (221). Families (biologically or socially created) cannot guarantee solutions to both protecting children and allowing for their gradual participation. For the protected middle-class child, choosing risk can mean subjecting oneself to the otherwise invisible constraints of family expectations. Perhaps enumerating the dangers is how we keep children safe in port, reading about rather than living great adventures.

Modernizing childhood has been a project of containment. With the enclosure of property and children (often themselves as property), the nature of parenting changed and, of course, is still changing. Tom Lutz characterizes later stages of this continuum in which "[t]he most significant change in the American culture of parent-child relations over the last several decades is a change from thinking of that relationship as one of child rearing to one of parenting. 'Child rearing' (or management or care) is a set of responsibilities, techniques, and tasks, while 'parenting' creates an identity, a way of being that includes a cluster of attributes, like sensitivity, intuition, nurturance" (170). Emotionalism dominates modern concepts of family, parenting, and children. Depending upon how it is exercised, parental love can be limiting.

To recognize a child's capacity for participation, we need to honestly assess the restraints, whether necessary or unfairly imposed, that come as conditions for protection. Methods of containment, within and against which growing children should be free to practice emerging agency, outline boundaries we should visualize and make permeable. Child captains like Dick Sand and Charlotte Doyle are fictions, but children's literature can imagine possibilities for participation, expose where reality is lacking, and, where safe enough, close the gap. Intensified norms, even essentialized roles in our imaginations, are often disconnected to quite diverse realities already in play. But privatized childhoods in isolated nuclearized families don't teach us how to love, protect, or honor the independence and privacy of other people's children—in fact, we are prone to blaming other people's children and other parents whenever our unitary sense of security or integrity is in question—and on an increasingly petty scale. One contemporary example of this can be seen in the experience of Janis Couvreaux, who spent a decade living on a boat, raising two young boys there, and got complaints from concerned parents when she blogged about a thirty-day transatlantic trip with her infant and toddler shown in photos without lifejackets. Defending their everyday practice, she explains that their boat was their home (her children no strangers to boats or water): "Our daily reality was that it was not feasible to have two young children bound up like sausages from dawn-to-dusk." Knowing that car accidents and drownings (in pools) are two of the top causes of child death in the United States (shootings a close third), parents likely see boating accidents and drowning as likelihoods at sea, but personal fears are not the best motive for making collective, protective decisions.

Transportation is a risk, but context matters. Couvreaux, who is committed to "raising kids out of the box," took reasonable precautions and knew that her kids had better sea legs than their landlubber counterparts—living on water was their norm. Lenore Skenazy points out, "Children are built to survive. And until very, very recently, adult survival depended on them too. That's because throughout most of human history, kids and adults worked side by side" (70). But a recent "survey by polling expert Tom Smith at University of Chicago asked fourteen hundred people ... At what age do you think adulthood begins in the United States? The answer: twenty-six" (71). By that age, most of us have gained independence, full participation, and many are already parents themselves. But this poll reveals that childhood is now defined not by physical maturity but by protectionism, the only contours of childhood we prolong this late. These closing contours, and the legacy of Crusoe's island, will be the subject of my next chapter.

2
No Child Is an Island
Robinsonades, Islanding, and the Right to Roam

> Sail, little ships in your glass bottles,
> safe from every contact,
> safe from experience,
> safe, above all, from life!
> —D. H. Lawrence

In a 1939 single-panel cartoon by Margé (Marjorie Henderson Buell), we see Little Lulu floating a ship in a bottle tied to a string (Buell 25). Looking on in envy, curiosity, or perhaps confusion are two boys with their own, far less elaborate toy boats (see figure 2.1). The gag was repeated in other comics, like a 1939 Kings Comics book with Popeye and Wimpy on the cover holding a can of spinach in a bottle. In Buell's context, it is clear that Lulu is the cleverest of the children, but her bottled boat seems to me indicative of an entrapment this rebel character usually not only escapes but mocks, thus heightening the nuance of the image. None of these children's vessels are quite satisfactory to them. Not only is Lulu's ship tied to a string, incapable of its own navigation, but by being encased in glass, it is suggestive of both the containment and the fragility increasingly surrounding and isolating children in the twentieth and twenty-first centuries. Of course, Buell couldn't have predicted that these limitations would become as problematic as they are today, in a bourgeois culture

LITTLE LULU

Figure 2.1. Little Lulu on Parade, by Margé (Marjorie Henderson Buell). David McCay Company 1941. Appears with permission of the Buell family.

where some college administrators refer to coddled young adults as "teacups" because they break so easily when suddenly on campuses with unfamiliar independence (Skenazy xxi). But to me the ship in a bottle (tied to a string no less) is symbolic of a process that has curbed the young from participation, freedom, and exploration in an overprotective and anxious parental culture. As D. H. Lawrence's poem "Ships in Bottles" reminds, a life without risks may be inauthentic and robbed of fulfilling experiences. Sometimes being adrift is just that much better than being led by a string.

In sharp contrast to sailing narratives of the century before, child adventure became a contained event by the Progressive Era. Allen Guttman discusses the popularity of "broad paths, a pond, toy boats," as stock items taken from impressionist imagery and exemplified in American "scenes with neatly dressed middle-class children decorously at play in Central Park, sailing boats on Lilliputian Boat Lake." Such appropriations resulted in a mood decidedly "culturally distant from [Winslow] Homer's unfenced field" (149). And, indeed, this iconography idealized childhood as more containable than that which we see possible in Homer's *Yachting Girl* (see cover, 1880). The popularity of sea stories, and their afterlife in robinsonades of the twentieth- and twenty-first centuries, would result not from continued celebration of expansion and domination, but as an investment in imagining the island destination as an enclosable safe haven for impressionable youth. This motif is concretely reconceived for a contemporary audience in Laurel Snyder's *Orphan Island* (2017), in which a rotating society of nine "orphans" live alone on an isolated but "safe" island with built-in protections. *Orphan Island* is a robinsonade in the tradition of Rousseau, where each child learns through trial, error, and risk. It fits Marx's ideal of unalienated labor[1] for sustenance in a use-value microeconomy. But it also investigates a childhood imagined without parents, or even knowledge of parents. A contained educational experiment it may be, but it is also a contained child public. However, the boat that connects this island to the outside world, and the rules that establish who rides and when, is clearly out of the children's control: "Nobody had any idea how the boat worked. It arrived at this same spot, through the thick mist. As if pulled by an invisible string" (5).

Understanding this shift in emphasis—from disconnected expansion to attached containment, from risky adventure to controlled safety—will help us to trace the ascent of familialism and protectionist motives in child-rearing culture. In *Adult Supervision Required*, Markella Rutherford argues that "there has been a historical trade-off between the private and public forms of autonomy experienced by parents and children in American culture. Both parenthood and childhood have increasingly been constructed around private freedoms at the same time that they entailed growing public constraints" (10). As a result of "a decline of community level solidarity," and "heightened sense of children's vulnerability," parents are "keeping a tighter leash on their children—restricting their freedom of movement" (11). All the while, the public seems aware of a need to protect children from harm but unaware of the need to protect their freedoms: "The overwhelming focus on privatized and individualized freedom of emotional expression has tended to obscure cultural recognition of the public dimensions of both parenthood and childhood" (10). By historically expanding our view of such changes, the loss of particular liberties will come into better focus.

The connection of contemporary protectionist childscapes with those emerging in the wake of an earlier era of primary accumulation (enclosing and privatizing property) might be made clear by a text that hints back to early phases of the transition: Roald Dahl's *Danny the Champion of the World* (1975). Like most of Dahl's work, this one is in keeping with trickster traditions, whereby skillful lying and stealing appear as clever and sometimes necessary attributes. Whereas adults in Dahl's books are usually the bad guys, and smaller children are the sympathetic protagonists, in *Danny the Champion of the World*, the villain is the wealthy landowner, and the heroes are the poor who defy his enclosure of presumably once-communal land and wildlife for his own sport, reminiscent of deer parks[2] in the nineteenth century. As in the proverbial "old days," Danny walks "two miles" to school, and "the walk took only half an hour and I didn't mind that in the least" (16). He discovers the family secret of poaching pheasants from Hazell's wood (a six-mile walk away), demonstrating resistance to privatizing property, which is not only justified in the book, but it is also treated as an art form (29). Danny's father explains the necessity behind the tradition that he learned from his own father at age ten: "[I]n those days, just about every man in our village was out in the woods at night poaching pheasants. And they did it not only because they loved the sport but because they needed food for their families. . . . [S]ome families were literally starving. Yet a few miles away in the rich man's wood, thousands of pheasants were being fed like kings twice a day" (30). There is no question in the text that Hazell's wood, aside from the possessive name, truly belongs to the people. Hazell's deed is a violation against community and, so, is delegitimized within the fictive text. There is also awareness throughout the book of the isolation such enclosure effects. Mr. Hazell "was rich beyond words, and his property stretched for miles along either side of the valley. All the land around us belonged to him, everything on either side of the road, everything except the small patch of ground on which our filling station stood. That patch belonged to my father. It was a *little island in the middle of the vast ocean* of Mr. Hazell's estate" (my emphasis, 42).

With enclosures of "private" property, childhood itself is seen as becoming privatized within nuclearizing families and dwindling terrain on which to roam freely. Helena Wall describes the early social impact of this emerging order, saying that "as the relationship between parents and children tightened, the relationship between family and community loosened" (131). Richard Sennett saw the "isolated family group" as "the encompassing medium of face-to-face relations in the community" in the industrial US, describing urban and suburban middle-class homes as "little islands in the midst of an enormous city" by the beginning of the twentieth-century (53). Spatially oriented scholars refer to this combined isolation of children from public spaces and segregation from community as the "islanding" of children, a process that continued throughout the twentieth century to an especially damaging degree in the twenty-first, in which, according to an often-cited but anecdotal piece, "children have lost the right to roam in four generations" (Derbyshire). John Gillis paraphrases "islanding" from Helga and Hartmut Zeiher, who coined the usage: "By this they mean not only the insulation of children's spaces from those of adults but also the separation of one child's space from another's" (116). Helga Zeiher has argued that contemporary "[p]laces geared toward children's needs, often toward the needs of children of a particular age, are scattered like islands on the map of a city at greater or lesser distances from one another" (66). Slavoj Žižek includes daycare in such a process: "[C]hildren are increasingly cared for not by parents but by paid nurseries or child-minders, and so on. We are thus in the midst of a new process of the privatization of the social, of establishing new enclosures" (144). No wonder that robinsonades became a staple of child reading while family intensification increasingly isolated minors, especially in the United States where sentimentality was at a premium: "The American publishing history of *Robinson Crusoe* clearly demonstrates that in crossing the Atlantic Defoe's novel also crossed age categories, becoming much sooner and more completely than it ever would in Britain, a book for child readers" (Sánchez-Eppler 2013b, 127). It is as if adults had come to realize that in order to provide "a childhood" like that which they had experienced as minors, imagining complete isolation from current geographies was necessary.

In the 1930s, when more than 250,000 American minors were economically forced to leave their nuclear families, riding the rails in desperate pursuit of employment, comic-strip tales perpetually stranded kids (or characters they loved) on islands.[3] Perhaps the most relevant of these are the robinsonades of Harold Gray's *Little Orphan Annie*, Elzie Segar's *Popeye*, and Milton Caniff's *Terry and the Pirates*. Each of these strips had a robinsonade arc that was eventually published separately due to popularity (for Gray and Caniff, the desert isle story is considered by many to be their best work). King Features released a "Popeye Shipwreck" board game in 1933, and Caniff produced a Big Little Book called *Terry and the Pirates Shipwrecked on a Desert Island* (1938).

In the "Shipwrecked" sequence from June 15 through November 12, 1930, Little Orphan Annie becomes stranded on an uninhabited island with Spike Marlin, an experienced but somewhat lazy sailor, who is in charge at sea but plays her Friday on the island (2009, 3:90–154). In a transparently derivative and crudely plot-driven story characteristic of Gray's melodramatic bent, Annie experiences the same conflicts and resolutions that Robinson does on his island: building a raft for unloading the wrecked vessel, losing the timber from it in a second storm, finding turtles on the other side of the island, creating enclosures, taming goats, and falling ill with fever and rationing limited "medicine" (3:97, 109, 101, 120–21, 127–35). Neither helpless victim nor superhero,

Annie depends upon a message in a bottle for her rescue. Sure, her survival on the island is to her credit, and Daddy Warbucks pursues her earnestly, but Gray draws out the journey of that bottle as the main impetus of suspense. It is this fragile missive with her coordinates that ultimately saves her, but only after being tossed around at sea, discovered by an illiterate fisherman, stored carefully on a shelf by his wife who thinks it important but also can't read, accidently broken while in storage waiting for a visit to town to find someone who can read, paper preserved but lost in a drawer, until Daddy Warbucks reaches the couple, who find the paper with the message (August 18–October 8, 1930, 3:118–39). There is also a Sunday strip highlighting the bottle of dwindling medicine for Annie's fever, perhaps intended to parallel the drama of the message in a bottle (September 28, 1930, 3:135).

Ultraconservative Gray harkened back explicitly to a supposedly bygone era, admitting in his own promotional material that Annie is a mouthpiece for "rustic drivel" that John Huston would later call "American folklore" (Smith 76, 110). The politics and sentiments of the strip made it immensely popular, but primarily to long-time, loyal readers who were boys or young men when it started running. When papers began dropping the strip in the 1960s, "kids didn't care" (79). One key to its continued success with an older generation was its appeal to self-reliance, individualism, and optimism in spite of Gray's resolve to never provide a happy ending. These qualities were oddly countergendered in Gray's mind: "I could never bring myself to draw Annie as an innocent, sheltered, prissy little angel" (13). But the vast literary and folkloric tradition of orphan figures was the primary influence. Gray depicts Annie's independence in relation to her kinlessness and freedom from nuclear family: "At the time, some 40 strips were using boys as the main characters, only three were using girls. I chose Annie for mine, and made her an orphan, so she'd have no family, no tangling alliances, but freedom to go where she pleased" (9).[4] Any reader of fairy tales and children's literature will note the common lack of familiar support therein for primary characters as a means for allowing conflict. Likewise, the isolati of comics—orphans like Bruce Wayne, Clark Kent, or Annie—necessarily lack the full structural supports of community but in some cases serve the community all the better without such structure. This is not just coincidence or American individualism but a reaction to the changing social dynamics of family and emerging anxieties about childhood in the face of growing invisible constraints and shrinking communal supports. After all, no matter how isolated, no child is an island.

Thimble Theatre's Popeye regularly visited islands (especially in short sequences during his first year in the strip), often with treasures he carelessly waylaid (his lack of interest in money served to contrast the greedy Castor

Oyl but also as comic relief). But most of these islands are reached safely and inhabited—by stereotyped natives or even, in some storylines, capitalists trying to hide their fortunes (think off-shore accounts). Eventually, elements of shipwreck entered in the board game in 1933 and extended storyline from April 17, 1935, to March 19, 1936 (4:153–67, 5:7–41). Whereas Gray simply restages plot elements from *Robinson Crusoe*, Segar subverts the earnest Defoe novel in a parody of colonial expansion by making Popeye "dictipator" of "Spinachova" (July 1935, 4:165). More importantly to my argument, Elzie Segar harkens back to another robinsonade theme in this sequence, titled "Popeye's Ark": the emerging centrality of reproductive nuclear family and questioning its constraints.

The possibilities of this theme in the robinsonade tradition were made especially explicit in another prototype, the Johann Wyss novel, *Swiss Family Robinson* (1812). First, there is the central concern of sustainability. Often this is achieved through references to Noah's ark and detailed accounts of animal husbandry. In a humorous episode in which the eldest boy, Fritz, finds an innovative method of saving animals from the wrecked ship (for their dietary use), he explains: "[L]et us tie a swimming-jacket round the body of each animal, and conceive to throw them into the water; you will see that they will swim like fish, and we can draw them after us in the same manner" (84). Problem solved: "By and by the two dogs, the fowls, the pigeons, the sheep, and the goats, had all assembled around us, which gave us something like the air of sovereigns of the country" (93). In this sense *Swiss Family Robinson* concentrates on the sustainability through animal husbandry (and agriculture) that we see in *Robinson Crusoe*. But, as Sheng-Mei Ma points out, Wyss "reworked the tradition in a significant way: he introduced a family rather than a single individual stranded on an island," reinterpreting "colonization not only as acts of personal heroism but as a family enterprise. Women and children (women are often viewed as children) played a key role in imperialism; moreover, they came to rationalize its existence" (39). By stranding a nuclear family on the island, Wyss ensures at least a symbolic legacy of sustainable expansion. But women's presence in the robinsonade has a problematic history. Andrew O'Malley explains,

> As the domestic sphere was invested with ideas of purity and morality, its security required, paradoxically, a disavowal of the very sexuality necessary for generating nuclear families. In the robinsonade, the anxieties over obscuring the connection between homemaking and sexuality lead to some quite complex narrative contortions.... In children's editions of *Robinson Crusoe*, the tension between female domesticity and sexuality, at least reproductive sexuality, is defused by keeping women off the island entirely. (57)[5]

Figure 2.2. Popeye, July 27 and 28, 1935. Copyright © E. C. Segar, Courtesy of Fantagraphics Books (www.fantagraphics.com).

Elzie Segar both circumvented such contortions and reveled in the paradox by having both Popeye and Olive Oyl stake their claims and establish their own nations whose shores are in sight of one another.

Even before soon-to-be-dictipator Popeye lands on the shores of his new nation, he evokes the story of Noah's ark with his own scheme: "I yam go'ner take male an' female of all kinds of people an' animals in me ark, sail away an' discover a new country an' build a new umpire. I'll take two doctors, two lawyers, two cows, two horses, two newspaper editors, one comic artist . . . on account of I don't want them to multiply" (April 24, 1935, 4:154). Not to be bested, Olive Oyl establishes, at least in name, her own realm: "I name myself Queen Olive—and I do hereby name this country 'Olivia'" (July 24, 1935, 4:167). The competition that develops between their shores wryly exploits the historic erasure of "femininity" in the robinsonade tradition, as Olive explains, "There are no women in Popeye's new country" so she will "dance upon the beach and draw his people to my island with my womanly grace and charm" (August 8, 1935, 5:9). This is all done with great comic effect (see figure 2.3).

By making anxieties about female sexuality and reproductive survival a humorous impetus for his robinsonade, Elzie Segar breaks from the capitalist colonialism of *Robinson Crusoe* or privatizing familialism of *Swiss Family Robinson*. *Thimble Theatre*, which in its first decade focused on characters

Figure 2.3. Popeye, August 7 and 11, 1935. Copyright © E. C. Segar. Courtesy of Fantagraphics Books (www.fantagraphics.com).

from Olive Oyl's nuclear family, eventually focused almost entirely on Popeye's patched-together but decentralized network of supporting characters. Although his father comes into the plot intermittently, he does so very much as an adrift isalato himself, and Popeye's "littl'un" Swee' Pea is a foundling (to be discussed at greater length in my next chapter). Popeye and Olive's relationship usually resists any static definition in some nuclearizing familial sense. Likewise, Little Orphan Annie finds a father figure in Daddy Warbucks, but his protections are often yearned-for denouements that simply punctuate beginnings and endings of conflict. These strips are already about kinlessness, imagining adventures from outside hegemonic views of family.

Milton Caniff's *Terry and the Pirates* perhaps follows a more traditional mold, creating adventure through geographic remoteness rather than kinlessness in one's own community. Piracy becomes the escape from the domestic drudgery and safety of a protected childhood. The thrill is there but without the risk of any real consequences. The precursor to Terry was Caniff's Dickie Dare, who was inspired by "books about Robin Hood, Robinson Crusoe, and Aladdin" (Harvey 2002, viii). The Chinese setting and organized crime in *Terry and the Pirates* are romantically remote but inspired by the real Lai Choi San, upon whom the Dragon Lady is based, once described as a "female Chinese version of Robin Hood" (Lilius 29). In the memoir that inspired many elements of the strip, *I Sailed with Chinese Pirates* (1930), by Aleko E. Lilius, the actual pirate leader, Lai Choi San, is described quite differently from Caniff's, and the contrast between her land-lubbing attire and boat business garb is stunning in the original source, not details intended to please the young paper-doll-cutting fashionista or sex-starved teen reading the comic strip.

In a chance meeting with the "Number One Master" on land, Lilius writes, "She was exquisitely dressed in a white satin robe fastened with green jade buttons, and green silk slippers. She wore a few plain gold rings on her left hand; her right hand was unadorned. Her face and dark eyes were intelligent.... Every move she made and every word she spoke told plainly that she expected to be obeyed, and as I had occasion to learn later, she was obeyed (25–26). Later, when on her ship, he reports that "she was entirely transformed. Now she wore a jacket-like blouse and black trousers made of the strong, glossy material commonly used by coolies for garments.... As soon as she stepped on board she kicked off her slippers, and for the rest of the voyage padded about barefooted" (31–32). Those bare feet are my favorite detail in the book. This woman is no-nonsense about her business. Aleko's Lai Choi San, the real one, is a far cry from Cinderella (or a foot-bound courtesan), whereas Caniff's Lai Choi San became the general Asian stereotype of a "Dragon Lady" (Ma 5), who appears in various elaborate costumes exposing as much of her legs, chest, and especially

Figure 2.4. Photo of Lai Choi San, by Aleko E Lilius, 1930. Courtesy Earnshaw Books.

midriff as sartorially possible.[6] In a somewhat hagiographic introduction, Robert C. Harvey describes the resulting effect: "To the stock femme fatale of melodrama, Caniff had added two final and masterfully delicate touches: a note of doubt about her ruthlessness and the poignant suggestion that perhaps the Dragon Lady would rather be loved of men than lead them" (2002, xi). By making her subservient to heterosexist desire, Caniff assured male readers that her power (both to tantalize and reproduce) was fully in male hands, thus keeping property in patriarchal line.

Much in contrast, however, the real Lai Choi San appears as a fully capable commander and mother of a twenty-year-old son who has finished schooling and is about to marry and a five-year-old son who is already sailing: "He was going to be a sailor, all right. He was already in training on another of her junks. One day he was going to inherit all her ships and the 'trade.' He was a

Figure 2.5. Dragon Lady from Terry and the Pirates, by Milton Caniff. © Tribune Content Agency, LLC. All Rights Reserved. Reprinted with permission.

real little man, she explained, and a brave chap. He smoked like a man too" (51). This child is the subject of two photos in the book (49–50). Lilius explains, however, "She did not want him to sail with *her* on her ship; it was better that he should stay away from his mother. But whenever the junks were in harbour at any of the islands she always had him brought over" (51). If the hierarchy of Lai Choi San's "trade" is built like "family," in the mafia's sense of the word, it is certainly matriarchal. Caniff erases any sign of this more complicated yet integrated vision of female power in his strip, but he does allow a (however limited) view of boy power. The sentiment of women and children first still echoes in *Terry and the Pirates*, just in altered form.

Figure 2.6. Lai Choi San, by Susan Synarski from *Booty: Girl Pirates on the High Seas* by Sara Lorimer, 2002. Courtesy of Chronicle Books.

If the Dragon Lady has some power in the strip, the conveniently placed female love interests of Pat (Terry's protector) seem to appear only as testaments to his virility. In the robinsonade sequence from March to May, 1935, Normandie Drake is a necessary burden, protected by the males and put in a life belt not unlike the livestock in *Swiss Family Robinson*. Terry calls her a "dead weight" and Pat calls her a "little girl" as they carry her after, of course, she faints (March 13, 1935, 156; May 15, 1935, 174). While drama plays out on the island, she eventually proves herself not completely clueless, but still her role is just to be there and wait things out in her evening gown with plunging neckline. In a direct revelation of the chivalric purpose of the rescue-ready female, she must ultimately be passively saved, and Terry, a minor but a male, seems to demonstrate his agency in contrast to the female character he attempts to carry. But even Terry's freedom and agency are safely limited by Pat Ryan, to whom he is sidekick. By falling back on nineteenth-century sentimentality, Caniff's strip could entice boy readers with the heroic ideal of protecting women and children first—defining themselves as men in training through contrast. The policy it evoked would be more accurately translated here as "protect girls first, then women (especially if they are wearing dresses or heels), then boys, and finally, every man for himself," which always carries its contrasting truth, "freedom for men first, boys next, women, and then girls last." Like the romantic adventures that inspired Milton Caniff's *Dickie Dare* and *Terry and the Pirates*, there is a built-in genre expectation of safety. The thrill is like plunging into dangerous waters with a life jacket. Without any true sense of risk, travel becomes presented as canned adventure—contained like ships in bottles with someone else pulling the string.

Over time, the focus of the robinsonade seems to have drifted away from adventure through risk and toward the safety of the island. John Gillis writes, "The mythical geography of childhood emerged simultaneously with the physical islanding of children" (318). This seemingly contradictory interrelationship between the shrinking territory of childhood and inner colonization of imaginary spaces was already clear in nineteenth-century juvenilia of writers like young brothers Thomas and William DeQuincey, as well as the Brontë children: "Mimicking in their literary play the acts of discovery, exploration, and colonisation that generate a shared history and create a national culture, as they constructed their imaginary kingdoms to populate the blank spaces on the map, these little Britons were also engaged in projecting 'home' upon an imagined 'away'; they were imagining empires" (Harty 96–97). Such young authors reveal their indoctrination as imperial subjects, but according to Joetta Harty, they also revel in potential subversion: "While their elders were forging a nation and a sense of nationalism that would have far-reaching implications overseas, in their juvenilia, little Britons were writing, mapping, colonizing, and ruling over imaginary kingdoms that were, on one level, so many little Britains, and on the other, subversive acts that reiterate and reframe cultural ideology in a new context. Autonomously scripting youth freedoms, "[t]hese youthful creators of paracosms challenge not only historical but contemporary cultural and literary conventions by creating spaces where child authors have the ultimate authority. As authors, child writers are kings and queens not only of the imagination, but also of the pen" (117). But reign over fantasy spaces and "the pen" comes at a cost. And contemporary child readers and writers are less likely to have access to moors on which to ramble like the Brontës, or

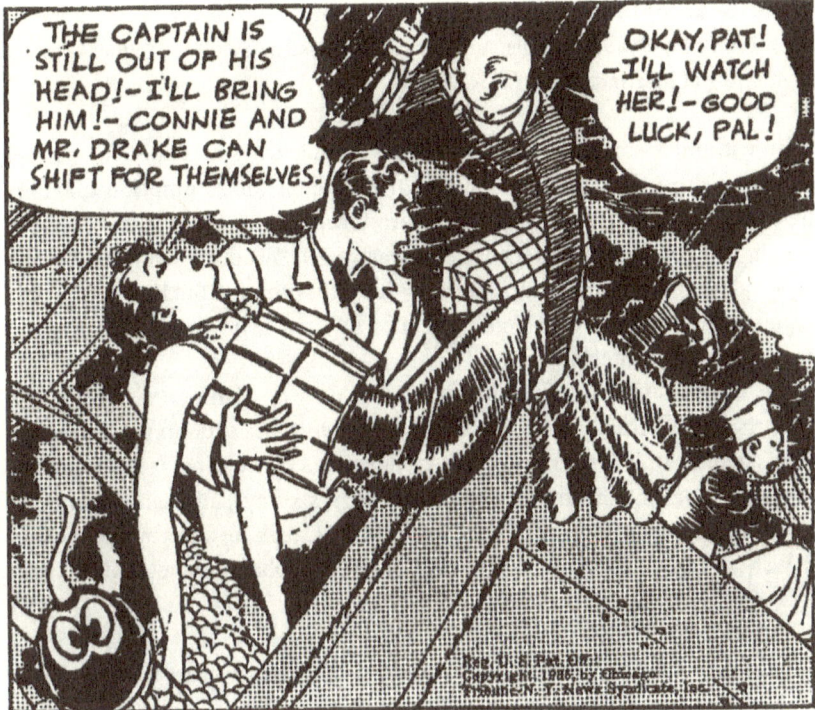

Figure 2.7. Terry and the Pirates, March 12–13, 1935, by Milton Caniff. © Tribune Content Agency, LLC. All Rights Reserved. Reprinted with permission.

even permission to roam. Such imaginings cover up the trade-off of access to limitless space for make-believe voyages. The double edge of the protectionist agenda is clear in adventure tales and especially fantasy spaces of childhood.

Even where dangers seem real, the possibilities of projection are invoked, often in terms of surveillance (even Charlotte Doyle's journal speaks to the adult gaze and control). There is a very telling yet subtle instance of this in one of the most influential and antithetical robinsonades (in stereotyping of minors, at least), William Golding's *Lord of the Flies* (1954). An early foreshadowing and framing contrast of conflict to come results when Roger (one of the biggest boys) watches one of the smaller boys, Henry, rapt in play on the beach:

> Roger stooped, picked up a stone, aimed, and threw it at Henry—threw it to miss. The stone, that token of preposterous time, bounced five yards to Henry's right and fell in the water. Roger gathered a handful of stones and began to throw them. Yet there was a space round Henry, perhaps six yards in diameter, into which he dare not throw. Here, invisible yet strong, was the taboo of the

old life. Round the squatting child was the protection of parents and school and policemen and the law. Roger's arm was conditioned by a civilization that knew nothing of him and was in ruins. (81)

Even without a watchful adult eye, Roger's conscience is described in terms of someone else pulling the strings. The insult here is the assumption that fairness and nonviolence are solely adult-produced values. The fact that the boys are on the island in part because of a war waged by adults seems irrelevant, especially as they unravel into clannish violence without adult leadership, only regaining their consciences (as evidenced by their tears) when rescued by a requisite adult protector.

Jay Griffiths tells quite a different tale in *Kith: The Riddle of the Childscape*: "For there has actually been a real-life *Lord of the Flies* situation and the children's behaviour was the opposite of that depicted by Golding" (189). Her story takes place in Tonga, where "One day in 1977, six boys, all friends, from the Friendly Islands, set out on a fishing trip" (190).[7] Caught in a storm that lasts for days, their boat is wrecked on the beach of an uninhabited island. Griffiths asks,

> What do they do, this little tribe of children? How does the story continue? Authored by Golding, the story would involve cruelty and humiliation. Authored by the children, the story involves sense and grace. They made a pact never to quarrel, because they could see that arguing could lead to mutually assured destruction. They promised each other that wherever they went on the island they would go in twos, in case they got lost or had an accident. They agreed to have a rota of being on guard, night and day, to watch out for anything that might harm them or anything that might help. (190)

After fifteen months of survival, order, and peace, "two boys, on watch as they had agreed, saw the dot of a new future approaching, tiny at first, a speck of a boat on the horizon. The boys were found and rescued, all of them, grace intact and promises held" (190). I prefer the true story.

Libba Bray celebrates a similarly peaceful yet subversive possibility in the islanding of teen girls (trans, gay, bi, and cis) with her postfeminist adaptation and parody, *Beauty Queens* (2011). In this version, an airplane full of teen beauty contestants is in transit to a pageant and crashes onto a desert island. Reflecting on *Lord of the Flies*, one girl remarks that "it wasn't a true measure of humanity because there were no girls" and asks "how it would be different if there had been girls." Another replies, "Maybe girls need an island to find themselves. Maybe they need a place where no one's watching them so they can be who they really are." Like Roger, they are shedding their socialization, but in contrast to Golding's little savages, unlearning the lookism they've been raised with serves them well in resisting parental and societal oppression: "There was something about the island that made the girls forget who they had been. All those rules and shalt nots. They were no longer waiting for some arbitrary grade" (177). The former control of their consciences through media, advertising, and commodification is made far more explicit and critiqued in interchapter portraits of each contestant. The loss of authenticity in their heavily mediated identities and the omnipresent unreality of reality shows and pageants is emphasized throughout the novel. Learning through trial and error, they are led to gender-transcending awareness by Adina, the one contestant who was there to take the pageant down: "[A]ll those romances they feed us are wrong. They make us think it's supposed to be hearts and wind machines and boys who slay dragons for you" (29, 124). Mary Lou, Miss Teen Dream Nebraska, realizes that "when it came to love, the message for girls seemed to be this: Don't. Don't go after what you want. Wait. Wait to be chosen, as if only in the eye of another could one truly find value" (125). Bray demonstrates how deeply damaging these girls' socialization has been, showing the cracks in their indoctrination as it falters. Soon they are no longer divided into two bands, the Lost Girls and the Sparkle Ponies(!), but united as fledgling feminists, never too earnest for humor. Tiara asks, "Do you think my new feminism makes me look fat?" (251). Milton Caniff would have been very challenged to draw these characters *and* remain faithful to the text.

Even the resolution of the primary conflict (discovering an arms-dealing, genocidal corporation that has been on the island all along exploiting the survivors' struggles for a reality show) is resolved through a televised pageant which the contestants subvert, now in solidarity:

> It was the most highly rated Miss Teen Dream Pageant ever. Though there were only thirteen contestants, the curiosity about seeing these survivors—fanned by an Internet ad campaign that hinted at unsavory sexual secrets and possible cannibalism—drew a record number of viewers. Sadly, without continued sponsorship from The Corporation, the program was canceled and replaced with new episodes of the reality show about Amish girls rooming with strippers, *Girls Gone Rumspringa*. (380)

Corporate misdeeds behind the not-so-uninhabited island are exposed, but consumer capitalism remains for the reader to realistically grapple with. Accordingly, the girl who had the most difficulty in shedding her socialization, Taylor Rene Krystal Hawkins, Miss Teen Dream Texas, decides to stay on the island, because "[s]he had a busy day scheduled. There was an island to tame.

Creatures to name. A world to build ... Whatever would she wear?" (380). In the end, the satire upends most of the conventions of the genre, especially the infantilization of young females waiting to be rescued.

If adults have trouble giving youth agency credit, young readers clearly do not. Karen Sánchez-Eppler offers an early example from a child reader, Nelly Hale, who wrote her own revealing robinsonade in *Mary Lowell or the Desert Island* (1865): "Escaping a shipwreck Mary packed *The Swiss Family Robinson*, her sewing kit and 'plainest dresses.' Gender distinctions clearly affect the flotsam boys and girls collect." (2013b, 141). Like Bernardin's Virginia, Nelly Hale reveals her awareness that dilemmas of what to wear don't cease for a female, even during shipwreck and the privacy of being a castaway. But Sánchez-Eppler also detects subversion in Hale's reimagined version:

> As an instructor in gender norms *The Swiss Family Robinson* offers only a slightly more limited role for women than Defoe's all-male island story. The Swiss father narrates, knows and does, while the 'exemplary' mother mostly cooks and worries. In contrast, although the shipwreck stories penned by Nelly and her friends contain rather heroic cooking, and even some worrying, they are characterized by a sense of female possibilities lacking in Wyss or Defoe. When Mary first finds herself alone on the abandoned ship she bursts into tears, but "soon remembered that crying makes no difference, so I stopped and began to think how to save myself." Ultimately the provisions Mary salvages from the ship do include "a gun (for my father had taught me how to use one)." Thus while Mary's resilience and prowess require explanations that the boys never bother to provide, the similarities of these castaway tales suggest that one of the pleasures of island life may lie in the opportunities these literary fantasies offer to flout gender conventions. (2013b, 141)

Clearly, readers can vicariously imagine their own survival and contemplate their tools for survival. They have probably always done so.

Young readers clearly respond to depictions of young self-reliance, self-discovery, innovation, and resilience against the elements and dangers far from human help. The risks and rewards in contemporary survival stories embrace child power not parental protection. As Lenore Skenazy puts it, "Control is a figment of our imagination"—no amount of helicopter parenting can prevent the miniscule odds of danger to our kids (92). Toward such (unlikely) events, "the best way to keep your kids safe is to worldproof your baby. Or at least worldproof your growing children" (xii). This is a bit more practical than the impossible babyproofing and kidproofing of the world.

Gary Paulsen has built a career on writing survival narratives like *Hatchet* (1987) and its sequels for a loyal, young fanbase. In *Hatchet*, thirteen-year-old Brian Robeson survives a plane crash alone in the wintery Canadian wild and learns to procure food, heat, and shelter through trial and error. Like the gun that alludes to Mary's father and his practical protection extended into practice, a hatchet Brian's mother gave him before the flight is helpful in his survival, as are memories of his mother's cooking evoked throughout his ordeal, suggesting her protective influence through preparation. But it is clear that his survival depends entirely upon his use of that preparation. So, Brian's mother in *Hatchet* may have saved his life with the gift of the hatchet; Mary's father may have made the difference by arming and instructing his daughter how to shoot. Ultimately both better protect their children by preparing them for conflict rather than shielding them from unpleasantness, but neither of these fictional children would survive without independently using these tools sensibly. Would we know what resources of resilience we truly have without being tried and applied? Certainly, Rousseau, who thought *Robinson Crusoe* to be the only book worth a child's reading, would approve of Brian and Mary's method of learning through trial and error how to survive (Rousseau 184–85).[8] We all have to learn at some point that risk, no matter how small, is a necessary part of life.

As with Uruguayan air force flight 571 discussed in my first chapter, plane-crash survival stories like Bray's and Paulsen's are pretty much the shipwreck stories of our own time. Air travel is considered necessary for participating in more than adventures. Like ship travel before it, there are vocational opportunities even in the fuzziest sense of training for independent living. But all travel, no matter how mundane the purpose for it, entails some risk. Child psychologist Adam Phillips points out that adolescent risk not only is a necessary part of life at times but also is necessary to pleasure and inherently linked to our capacity for engagement and solitude, so it is also integral to robinsonades:

> From adolescence onward the link between risk and solitude becomes a vivid and traumatic issue. But pressing the question of risk is clearly bound up with something that certain psychoanalysts after Freud have seen as central to early development: a capacity for concern. We create risk when we endanger something we value, whenever we test the relationship between thrills and virtues. So to understand, or make conscious, what constitutes a risk for us—our own personal repertoire of risks—is an important clue about what it is that we do value; and it also enjoins us to consider the pleasures of carelessness. (33)

More on the slippery concepts of care and carelessness in my last chapter, but here let us just focus on the role of risk in solidifying independence and concern for that which is outside of the self (environment, others). Conservative camps are in agreement with such a priority, spinning pedagogy and epistemology likewise toward a resilience movement: "Two centuries ago, Goethe declared that the job of the educator was to find the germ of virtue concealed in the kernel of every fault. The resilience revolution has brought us full circle, back to the wisdom of early pioneers who saw positive qualities in even the most challenging youth" (Brendtro and Larson 199). Proponents of youth resilience see in it a necessary revision of how we think about protection: "courage only comes from experiencing adversity. Thus, adults should not shelter children from all difficulties, nor allow them to become discouraged.... [E]ven serious disruptions in a child's life can offer unexpected opportunities for growth" (194). That ship in a bottle can ride waves but needs a little crack every now and then.

A concrete and almost visceral appreciation for both the necessity and pleasure of risk can be found in a true story that resembles the fictional survival of Paulsen's Brian Robeson, Norman Ollestad's *Crazy for the Storm: A Memoir of Survival* (2009). Written more for an adult audience but capturing his childhood experience of the 1979 airplane crash that killed his father, his father's girlfriend, and the pilot when he was eleven years old, Ollestad provides clear-eyed details of his risk-filled childhood and the challenges of being stranded on an ice-encased mountain (conditions unpassable to rescuers, not unlike Uruguayan air force flight 571, which also had to be traversed by minors saving themselves). This struggle, like Brian Robeson's, is only part of the story. Much of the narrative focus is on family dysfunction and how much Ollestad's father pushed him in extreme sports (or extreme for his young age—the cover shows a photo of Ollestad, barely a toddler, papoosed to his father's back as he surfs). Surfing and skiing always off the beaten track, he is pushed in dangerous conditions to take risks that would concern a social worker today. His incredible postwreck journey down the mountain is directly tied to such earlier moments of his father's questionable judgment in putting him at risk so repeatedly. When he has reached safety and is being carried for the last steps to safety, he stares back at the formidable mountain he has successfully descended:

> Although it was smothered in boils of cloud, I knew vividly what was inside that storm, and for an instant the whole arc of my life was clear to me: Dad coaxing me past boundaries of comfort, day after day, molding me into his little masterpiece.... Every misadventure, every struggle, everything that had pissed me

off and made me curse Dad sometimes, rippled together, one scene tripping the next, the pieces speeding forward like falling dominoes into a streak. I glared at the storm as it feasted on the mountain, hammering on my dad still trapped in there. It did not get me. And I knew—I knew that what he had put me through saved my life. (210)

As the title, *Crazy for the Storm*, indicates, Ollestad is not advocating quite so much "crazy," but he has definitely learned the importance of risk taking and perseverance. As a father himself, he tries not to overprotect. His epilogue ends with him admitting to his son, "My dad made me do lots of things that I'd get arrested for making you do" (259). But he does push him. The book concludes with a ski run when his son Noah was seven years old (he learned to ski at four). After completing a difficult black diamond, Ollestad wants Noah to ski an icy, rocky pass. Noah is frightened, and once under way, he begins to cry and protest: "You shouldn't have taken me here" (269). Ollestad admits, "I sensed that I had crossed the line." But there is no turning back with skis up a mountain. Noah "began writhing and bawling uncontrollably" (270). Ollestad continues to advise, waiting. When his son recommences down on his skis, something wonderful happens (I might be projecting here, but stay with me)—the child overcomes his fear and gains momentum. And I'll let Ollestad take over: "I yelled for him to stop at the tree line. But he ignored me and disappeared in the woods below. I found him at the chair lift and skied up beside him, expecting a blast of anger," but instead, "What took you so long? he said, full of gusto" (271). Norman Ollestad took a risk that might have hurt his son, but he was valuing some risk as worth taking to train for life, and in this scene we see his son coming around to understanding why.

Maybe your own moments of childhood risk and bliss were a bit less extreme—the pleasure of a tire swing over a quarry, skipping fast on train tracks, perhaps a trampoline, skateboard, or go-cart? But I want you to try remembering such a moment—of overcoming fear, riding the edge of control as long as possible, getting as close to human flight as your neighborhood could allow. Such thrills don't just give us pleasure, they build us up, familiarize us with our bodies, teach about our limitations, integrate the bodymind, helping us to discover strengths we might not have recognized or developed otherwise.

Islanding children and serving them canned adventures will not control them. You can only control the bubble they are in for so long. Like a ship in a bottle, childhood's containment is fragile—our efforts to steer it ultimately just a tug here and there in the right direction.

As in the fictional cases of Golding's Roger and Bray's beauty contestants, the primary Western method of socially controlling children is through parenting and guardianship. A reminder of the centrality of privatization and the nuclearizing of families can also be found in Paulsen's *Hatchet*. Although the main focus of the whole narrative is a life-or-death solitary struggle in dangerous conditions, the impending divorce of his parents is treated, nonetheless, as a primary conflict of the novel, even framing the triumph of survival with the emotional conflict of keeping "the Secret" (Brian knows about his mother's extramarital affair), which forms the final words of the novel: "Brian tried several times to tell his father, came really close once to doing it, but in the end never said a word about the (other) man or what he knew, the Secret" (195). That emotional struggle is threaded through his much more consequential one of survival—an author's choice that leaves this middle-aged "child" of amicably divorced parents a little queasy. Is divorce really that big of a deal in comparison to surviving in the snowy wild for fifty-four days alone as a thirteen-year-old? My guess is that adult assumptions about the sacredness of nuclear family in maintaining a perfectly isolated, contained, and idealized childhood is the deeper adult priority being projected in the narrative. As with *Robinson Crusoe*, solitary survival in the wilderness is merely a backdrop for testing the ties of nuclear family around an individuating member.

We need to take a look at the larger picture in which childhood is defined within property relations of family, and how family itself is defined in the broader community and state. Even if we see them as fixed in our daily lives, they are neither fixed nor consistently or ubiquitously experienced in reality. Stephanie Coontz has written: "The family is both a place and an idea. It is above all an *idea*, a 'socially necessary illusion' about why the social division of obligations and rights is natural or just. . . . And the idea has some material base, for the family is also a *place*, distinct from household, from which people derive particular connections to rights, resources, and duties" (1988 14). Children need community and access to their own sense of place within this larger geographic and historical picture. Jay Griffiths argues that children need more than kin; they need kith *and* kin: "I was interested in how children belong, needing their kith, their local acre, as they need their kin. An entire history of childhood is in that one word 'kith,' which is now used as if it means only extended family, whereas in the phrase 'kith and kin,' 'kith' originally meant country, home, one's land" (ix). When we isolate each other in nuclear units that may or may not be adequate (that just depends on the luck of birth), we overlook too easily our responsibilities to each other's children, and we limit their discovery and choice of spaces that can nurture and negotiate identity.

Is there any space in which children can forge their own kith and kin relationships? Terry Pratchett's *Nation* (2008) is about children forging both. In this corrective to the traditional colonialism, racism, and sexism of the robinsonade, the main characters are orphaned (one temporarily, the other permanently), but they discover the importance of forging kith, not just kin. Like the boys in the Tonga case, Mau is caught in a holding pattern by a great storm. Going away is how one becomes redefined as his own man in a rite of passage wherein boys were left on another island and had to carve a canoe and return: "He'd lived for a month on the island of the boys, hadn't he? Just surviving on that place was enough to make you a man" (12). Note that the liminal transition requires solitude. Once afloat, "You left your boy soul there and were given a man soul when you get back to the Nation." Like Brian Robeson and his hatchet, Mau is "allowed to take only [his] knife to the island" (13). But his fate is determined by a Tsunami. Mau is swept out to sea in his canoe, without community bestowal or recognition of his man soul, for a far more perilous quest than he had planned for. When he manages to return to his island, he finds his Nation decimated. Now he is an orphan on his own island, where he must rebuild kith and kinship.

Daphne, the only survivor from the wreck of the *Sweet Judy* on the island in the same storm, has an even less socially prepaved transition to make, as Mau comically muses, "Boys had to live on the island and build a canoe before they were officially men, but with girls it just happened somehow. Then they magically knew things, like how to hold babies the right way up" (123). Like the sleeping, fake-dead, and comatose girls of fairy tales awaiting their prince, his kiss, and true love, girls have few and pretty negating models for the transition from childhood to womanhood. Together, however, Mau and Daphne learn the power of community that transcends units of biological family or tribe, even that which transcends an individual's lifespan: "One person is nothing. Two people are a nation" (252). This is not to say we need a social unit to be actualized, but that we can forge community ties that are as strong, or stronger, than biological kin. By creating and participating within a public sphere, taking responsibility for each other and the physical environment we depend upon to sustain life and group identity, we forge kith.

One right that many of us take for granted is the right to those ties that are integral to identity. It is something that many simply think of as organically happening in a child's development. According to the Convention on the Rights of the Child, "Children have the right to an identity—an official record of who they are. Governments should respect children's right to a name, a nationality and family ties" (article 8). At first glance it might be hard to see how this is any different from one's right to having family, but it is—especially for those (like Mau) who must actually build their own support network or be granted new legal identities (as in cases of international adoption or foster care, to be discussed more at length in the next chapter). Having community ties to counterbalance potential family isolation is crucial for all people, and children are people. That simple syllogism often breaks down in everyday rhetoric—especially in the case of minors asserting self-determination rights to forming their own social ties, claiming independence, and anything else that may conflict with their protection as it is defined by an adult responsible for their care. As the territory that children can freely roam dwindles, so do diverse extrafamilial links to the community—at least their abilities to create their own social net, which is instead, if present, prescribed by parents or state-determined guardians.

One fascinating example of the conflict between child participation and state/parental protection—the very issue that first got me interested in the larger focus of this chapter—is the unusual but surprisingly repeated incidence of teens trying to set new records as the youngest to sail around the world unassisted, for speed, or taking the trek nonstop. Recognizing that this could only continue encouraging younger and younger sailors to attempt solo circumnavigation, the World Sailing Speed Record Council stopped keeping such records in 1999, no doubt in part to avoid litigation for incentivizing hazardous attempts on the part of minors (Jessica Watson 57, 316–17). A nonsailor might find this example arcane, but, in fact, there is a large genre of books about such journeys, most likely inspired to varying degrees by the early classic (in a larger genre of circumnavigation narratives) by Joshua Slocum, *Sailing Alone around the World* (1900). The subgenre of such memoirs by teens (three of which are coauthored with older and more experienced writers) include Robin Lee Graham's *Dove* (1972), Tania Aebi's *Maiden Voyage* (1989), Jesse Martin's *Lionheart* (2000), Jessica Watson's *True Spirit* (2010), Mike Perham's *Sailing the Dream* (2011), Abby Sunderland's *Unsinkable* (2011), and Laura Dekker's *One Girl, One Dream* (2013). These sailors would go through many changes in their journeys—one leaving as a virginal teenager but returning with a wife expecting their first baby, and another even changing her nationality, by the end of their global treks. Their educations are, like Ishmael's, anything but conventional.

Robin Lee Graham's first experience with global sailing was at age thirteen with his parents, who took him out of school for the year in order to experience the classroom of the seas. Then there is the botched attempt at sailing with school friends from Long Beach to Hawaii that resulted in a $25,000 rescue (12). By the time Graham was sixteen, in 1965, with the old-school sextant, cats, and personal travel library in tow, he headed out for his own global adventure.[9] And it didn't take long for the media to catch on and spew protectionist rhetoric that sounds more like the 1860s, questioning his parents' judgment for "allowing a schoolboy to face 'not only the dangers of the deep,' as one newspaper correspondent put it, 'but the perils of savages'" (23).

Others romanticized his quest but were likewise infantilizing—as Graham says, "so many newspapers wrote about me as if I were Little Lord Fauntleroy" (25). Strangely, one reporter refers to Graham as the "kid who had sailed the Pacific in a teacup," perhaps referring back to the patched-up boat in which he first tried to sail to Hawaii (48). But just for the record, Graham's *Dove* was a twenty-four-foot sloop, not china dinnerware.

If, in fact, Graham had perished at sea, protectionist rhetoric would have stuck with his story in public memory. Sixteen-year-old Abby Sunderland, whose 2010 circumnavigation attempt failed due to her boat *Wild Eyes* being dismasted in in the Indian Ocean, experienced harsh criticism of her own mission and her parents, whose son, Zac, had succeeded as solo circumnavigator in 2008 at age sixteen. International rescues can cost millions of dollars, especially in the Southern Hemisphere, which is very aqueous and has fewer resources much further apart. Some grumbled about the expense (even though the French and Australian agencies that paid for it did not). Geraldo Rivera claimed that the trip was just for sponsorship and a potential reality show about the family's adventures (Sunderland 191–99). And, of course, the protectionist rhetoric got nasty: "[I]t is the height of irresponsibility to allow a child, indeed almost any sailor in a vessel of that size to sail in those waters" (197). Abby points out in her book, *Unsinkable*, that her age was a matter of positive interest before the trip, and that people only "freaked out about my age" after the rescue (197). If a teen sailor is successful, however, the media plays it up and is ready to be there all along just in case good copy is on the horizon.

Sometimes sponsorship helps to pay for part of the voyage, giving it the feel of a canned media event. Mike Perham's and Jessica Watson's boats were even named by their sponsors. Book deals seem to be agreed upon before departure, even when the sailor is not a particularly riveting writer (and that's ok. They are accomplishing something much bigger than writing a book. I'm just saying I wouldn't recommend most of these, and my students made very clear why I should not each time I did). Even in Robin Lee Graham's day, before computer boards and satellite communication in real time, he had a deal with *National Geographic* to write a three-part series on his trip (Graham 91, 97, 139, 154).[10] His memoir, *Dove*, would be marketed to both adults and younger readers (one juvenile edition was even titled *The Boy Who Sailed around the World*).

Like Pratchett's Mau, Robin Lee Graham's transition into adulthood felt more amorphous while away from a community that would define and recognize him in that role: "At sea I was a man, but when I thought of the business of making a living in a civilized society I knew I was still a child" (169). Whereas decades later teen sailors, like Jesse Martin, Mike Perham, and Jessica Watson, would get competitive about solo sailing for speed, nonstop and unassisted,

Graham's journey took five years, with many long stops where he would work long enough for repair money, gaining immersive international experiences. This must have seemed like an agonizingly slow yet suddenly eclipsed adolescence to his parents, who rarely got to see him but would hear of his exploits, sometimes through gossip they'd rather not hear. Tensions developed between father and son over Graham's freedom and what that meant: "[W]hen he still wanted to control me from afar, I had to remind him that he had given me my freedom. I learned that our ideas of freedom were different" (24). As with landlubber adolescence, the conflict sharpens with a love interest, Patti. Graham wishes to marry but legally needs parental consent, as he is still a minor: "This was a shock. I couldn't understand why anyone should still be able to control me when I was half a world away from home" (106). He does have a point. His parents, not surprisingly, refuse permission: "They talked about my completing the voyage and that there'd be time enough—that sort of thing. They believed they knew best what was right for me. I wrote back and told them Patti and I considered ourselves married anyway" (107). He finishes his trip solo, but he is able to see Patti while at port. By the time he returns, his wife will be about to have their first child, Quimby. He also returns to find a nation in which the young are revolting against their parents' generation: "I understood some of the reasons for their revolt. Wasn't my voyage prompted by the same longings for freedom, the same desire to get out of the rut and routine, to prove something to myself—to prove perhaps that a kid doesn't have to be *boxed in* until he is a mental and spiritual dummy in a business suit?" (my emphasis, 169). The lid kept on the box of childhood would become more snugly affixed in following decades.

Graham's island hopping provides a useful contrast to islanding.[11] With such travel, one can get the rare sort of experiential learning that seems a revolutionary change to identity. In contrast, nonstop sailors like Jesse Martin and Jessica Watson experienced fewer revolutions in their worldviews but some tension over independence. Sixteen-year-old Jessica Watson would report the mental shift during her return: "I hope I don't upset Mum and Dad by mentioning it. I was really looking forward to seeing everyone, but sometimes, when I thought about it, I felt claustrophobic. I wasn't sure how I'd go settling back into living at home after having so much independence out on the water" (284). But she also describes being boatbound the whole time as constraining: the competitive choice of sailing nonstop seems to contain and conform to social definitions of adolescence from home a bit more without cultural contradictions from experiences abroad. Nonstop narratives tend to focus on the athletic accomplishment, self-sufficiency, and gained confidence—more on psychological, even metaphysical changes brought on by the intensive solitude, mechanical trouble-shooting, and physical rigor rather than structural changes that can result from stopping to get to know other cultures, terrains, and people. Perhaps it is also in part from the longer travel time, but those who stop to island hop, although episodically relieved of the solitude, can experience a different sort of revolution. Graham truly returned a changed person, but he demanded the rights of a person (no matter how young) from the beginning of his trip. Thinking further outside of the box and taking even greater liberties than those offered her decades after Lee's trek, Laura Dekker completed her ambitious voyage but actually refused (at first) to return to her country of birth.

Teen circumnavigator Laura Dekker's greatest challenge was not even her voyage, which she wisely extended, like Robin Lee Graham, with visits in different locales, taking full advantage of learning opportunities such travel can allow.[12] Her biggest challenge was the child protection mechanisms in her own country of birth, the Netherlands, giving her an extreme sense of the containment Graham had come to understand as being "boxed in." First of all, as with the women-and-children-first policy, girls are not particularly credited for having great survival skills. When Jessica Watson planned her circumnavigation, "criticism of Mum and Dad got really bad.... There was even a report that the Queensland government was going to investigate ways to stop me" (76–77), which leads her to rightly wonder "if the outrage about me attempting to sail around the world would have been as intense if I was a teenage boy" (29). In Laura Dekker's case, Dutch authorities launched a far more consequential and long-lasting effort to stop the then fourteen-year-old (she had also attempted at age thirteen). In *One Girl, One Dream*, she recounts, in the selective, gradual, and strained manner of someone traumatized and still healing (75–76), the "bureaucracy nightmare" of being "treated like a criminal" and "interrogated for three hours by police and lawyers working for Child Protection" without even being "allowed access to my own lawyer or my parents" (273, 19). To control against the dangers of global solo sailing and out of concern about Dekker's education, Dutch child protection agencies subjected Laura and her family to six court cases in eleven months, and the Dutch state intelligence and security service (AIVD) continued to hack her computers and tap her phones as routine surveillance (18), all in an effort to prevent her exposure to risk. According to Laura, "The Child Protection official asked the judges to have me put into a closed institution immediately and to terminate my dad's parental rights. Fortunately, the court had no good grounds to do so" (17). When she tried to circumvent the rules, her boat was seized in St. Martin (18). The media circus and real threat of sabotage required her family to have a security detail during the legal ordeals and even throughout her midjourney stop in South Africa (272, 276–77).

Child protectionists had a difficult case to weigh but went astoundingly too far. Using rules already on the books, they attempted to thwart the planned voyage in smaller ways, too. Especially indicative of my larger argument is the following result: "Back in the Netherlands I'd wanted to install an SSB radio with an email facility on *Guppy*, but this wasn't possible as you need a special license to own a radio with such a high transmission power. They thwarted every attempt I made to get one and I ended up leaving without one. So the only means of communication at sea is via satellite telephone" (66). In other words, child protection made her less safe at sea. A fairer concern for repercussions on even younger sailors brought about yet another somewhat absurd compromise: "[I]n 2009, the Dutch authorities had also made the *Guinness Book of Records* liable for any possible consequences of record attempts by minors, which resulted in the *Guinness* scrapping these records. All in the hope that I would give up" (273). Ironically, as often happens in such cases, "I recently read that since the news of my plans to sail around the world went worldwide, more kids have been joining sailing clubs. Good to know" (43). Dekker was likewise inspired by Tania Aebi when she was younger (120). No doubt the authorities were just as aware of this possibility if Dekker succeeded as they were concerned for her own safety if she failed. And, as always, the public loves a winner: opinion began to turn in favor of the teen as hopes got higher for her safe and successful completion (121).

How to estimate individual cases of competency continues to baffle. As far as making snap decisions in the face of life-threatening conditions is concerned, teens are well equipped. Their motor control is at its peak, and although more formal reasoning peaks later (descending by about age thirty), someone who has been sailing throughout childhood already has as much specialized training in their teens as most of us get before starting careers (Epstein 173–77). Laura Dekker's first solo voyage, with her dog Spot, was her "first holiday on my own for six weeks when I was 10" (71). Although Dekker's parents initially disagreed about permitting Laura to take her global attempts, both eventually supported her. But such carefully debated decisions nonetheless get a lot of scrutiny from the broader public. The questioning of her parents' judgment is an understandable necessity in child protection, as one clinician argued: "[P]arent objectivity is clouded by pride, and perhaps their own needs and desires. A parent vicariously receives kudos, pleasure, and enormous satisfaction from their child's successes. One only needs to visit a sports oval at the weekend to realise that some parents' investment in a child's sports performance is more about their own gains than the child's" (Roseby 286). But Dekker had all the requisite training. For example, "I had passed my Yachtmaster's Offshore Certificate exam at the age of 13, but then received a letter saying that, although I had passed,

I wouldn't be issued a license because I was a minor" (29). Protection is just a step toward justice for minors, who should also be assured a reasonable amount of participatory discretion and procedural leeway for variant competencies to be measured and declared.

Born while her parents were living at sea, off of New Zealand, Laura Dekker had the option of dual citizenship, and her experience with a punitive level of Dutch "protection" led her to change her national affiliation: "In Australia I replaced the Dutch flag with the New Zealand, and I haven't regretted it for a moment" (248). Although she eventually revisited the Netherlands in a professional capacity, she now considers New Zealand her home country, truly exemplifying her chosen "kith." Most of us don't get to choose our nationality, but we can define our community. While many teen sailors find that voyages grant independent perspective, self-sufficiency, perhaps even credibility, Graham was also able to redefine his kinship and Dekker her kith. Like the islanding in children's robinsonades, the experiences of minors can be somewhat contained and media representations canned, but their actual experiences are far from mythical fantasy. They might even be deadly, and people of all ages do disappear at sea.[13] But following arbitrary absolutes about age-appropriate behaviors can be unjust if unbalanced by respect for a reasonable level of participation in that determination. Backlashes that punish ambitious minors and blame parents when support is just as feasible make no sense. There need to be alternatives to being "boxed in" and some way to enable an outlet for roaming more safely *and* freely.

As children lost the right to roam throughout the late nineteenth and twentieth centuries, they were offered the inadequate compensation of symbolic freedoms, or as Mathew Thomson has said of the postwar norm: "On the one hand, it encouraged and justified a closing in of the landscape of the child: the most important thing for the child was the protection and love of home and family. On the other hand, it also emphasized the importance of play, freedom, and social relations within that setting." Such are the benefits and compromises of islanding. Thomson summarizes the effects of tethering children to the private sphere: "As such, freedom was lost but also gained: lost in the sense that children were increasingly tied to the protection of home and had less access to the outside world; gained in that there was a new emphasis on freedom within the home and institution" (79). Protections are available within family models and even from abuses within family, but opportunities for participation, even mobility, have decreased. By focusing solely on children within or toward this model, larger sociostructural problems get obscured. Kirsten Isgro, channeling Lauren Berlant, argues that "privatization of citizenship, as part of a conservative cultural agenda, diverts people's attentions from the more substantive causes of economic, racial, and sexual inequality. To maintain a nation's core image, it is easier to divert public debate to people's private lives." She offers as a salient example the solipsism of simultaneously abandoning and blaming privatized, nuclear families for larger social problems: "[W]hile this discourse sees the large number of children currently living in poverty as a serious concern, the only solution it offers is familialism" (49). Resorting to familialism only reaffirms insular family attitudes and community shirking responsibility through blaming parents when problems arise. It also can leave children temporarily without familial supports and permanently with fewer public supports.

We may island children, but no child is an island.

3

Babies in Boxes

Finding and Loving Other People's Children

> And what did the boy who belonged to himself do?
> The boy who belonged to himself curled in a warm little heap and went to sleep. And he dreamed his own dreams.
> That was what the boy who belonged to himself did.
> —Margaret Wise Brown, *Mister Dog: The Dog Who Belonged to Himself*

Orphans, foundlings, changelings, and kids in contested custody or foster care all have something in common—they change places, change hands, or change guardianship, often moving from what is traditionally called "family" today (biological relatives) to community care. Within progressive child protection agencies, transfers of responsibility are full of seemingly necessary bureaucratic compromises. Win-win solutions are rare. But occasionally minors will trade their "protection" for freedom—and sometimes it's a worthy swap. Like the "boy who belonged to himself" in *Mister Dog*, they may discover they can choose where they live and with whom, even choose their own dinner: "[T]he boy's little boy bought a big lamb chop and a bright green vegetable and trotted home" (Brown). But how does he pay for it? Who pays the bills?

If marriage is about establishing paternity and property lines, both of which narrowed conceptions of family, and being unclaimed or emancipated casts a child outside of family, neither property holder nor property of family, can a child, at least, own herself? When you follow the money, a strangely hidden-in-plain-sight history of childhood emerges in which the privatization and nuclearization of families take on deterministic roles. Within a nuclear family, as with the marriage that legally seals it, structure, rules, custom, codes of behavior, and roles have historically been connected with money/property rights, but the middle-class norm is not to talk explicitly about economic factors, other than to vaguely refer to "poverty" as if it is a temporary, contained social problem that isn't maintained by this very denial among elites contributing to the disproportionate distribution of wealth. Or, in contrast, we may admit to a "comfortable" income, which could be anything from a family wage to billions, although the euphemism identifies its speaker as somewhere at neither extreme but safely, suppliantly, in the middle. This denial is consequential for kids: "In our desire to re-create for our children the feelings of safety, comfort, and opportunity of that mythic middle class of the American dream, we are continually reaching for a life that's increasingly unaffordable and unsustainable," but "[w]hen fulfilling an emotional need creates a financial reality, our feelings about money can get pretty contradictory and twisted" (Perle 64, 66). Middle-class denial of economic realities behind child dependence confuses our awareness of what it takes to be independent. Money and property determine major life decisions but are considered unseemly to mention, which only keeps larger interests of vulnerable parties more difficult to evaluate as economic power is mystified. Joline Godfrey gives this simple but excellent example of how absurdly this mystification plays a role in the protectionist paradigm: "A man once told me that he had just given his daughter a substantial amount of money because he wanted her to be financially independent. I looked at him and said, 'No, you don't understand; you just made her financially dependent!' It's a strange and cruel conundrum: The families who—in the most loving, well-intentioned ways—give their children the most are in fact undermining them" (qtd. in Perle 66). The middle-class avoidance of openly addressing the very real monetary issues affecting children not only excludes them from decision making and understanding how things work, but it can actually make them more vulnerable.

We cover up economic realities with sentimental narratives, but in the United States before 1813 (and 1836 for the British), the "best interests" of children were still determined by who was financially most fit to own them. As women could not own property, "the children's 'owner,' the father had a legal right to the economic benefits of his children" (Walker 80). With the rise of sentimental value of children this gave way over time to favoring the mother, without child input, as the most appropriate caregiver for young children: "The tender years doctrine served to protect children, not to include them in decision making" (Walker 81). In these contexts, children operate as transferrable property with unmentionable exchange value, whose protection was initially seen as a financial imperative but over time gave way to the tender-years doctrine with an emotional cast. In custody, "best interests" became redefined not as financial but as emotional. This shift in thinking about children also meant that anyone profiting from the transfer of children, which had formerly seemed a commercial enterprise, became morally suspect: "If child labor was no longer legitimate, a working home was an anachronism. If children were priceless, it was obnoxious to profit from their misfortune. Thus, baby farming was singled out as uniquely mercenary 'traffic in children'" (Zelizer 2011, 62).[2] Protectionism conveniently masks the pecuniary aspects of treasuring kids.

And yet, the financial dependence of children and necessity of economic support for those unclaimed has always been a central factor for child welfare. Lack of funds is a contributing factor in child harm, so a reversal in fortune becomes necessary to assess in the business of child protection. Incentivizing the safe placement of unsupported children, or simply donations to fund it, exposes the ugly inequities of reigning ideologies. Untoward trade of children for indentured labor was part of the operating procedure for Maria Rye and the emigration of tens of thousands of British Home Children from England to Canada during the second half of the nineteenth century. For some, it was an escape from abusive homes or basic survival—but it was always controversial. John Thomas Barnardo utilized the same method for abused and neglected children, riding a fine line between protectionism and kidnapping by removing them from their biological kin and native kith. He was depicted as everything from angelic, self-sacrificing saint and Christ figure to accused kidnapper and even Jack the Ripper suspect. In 1869, George Cruikshank critiqued such advocates' "Sweeping measures" in his cartoon *Our Gutter Children*, showing three adults sweeping up tiny ragged children and shoveling them into a cart, while Maria Rye is shown overseeing them with a long whip in hand, saying: "I am greatly obliged to you Christian ladies and gentlemen for your help and as soon as you have filled the cart I'll drive off to pitch the little dears aboard of a ship and take them thousands of miles away from their native land so that they may never see any of their relations again" (transcribed in Diamond 236). Cruikshank also places emphasis on Maria Rye's emigration of *girls*, not boys. Anxieties about the sexual exploitation of girls motivated Rye's efforts, but also Cruikshank's critique, demonstrating the difficulty of finding common ground for agreed-upon solutions and communal care.

Some of the perennial controversy surrounding child protection stems from the fact that people are always more absolute in judgments concerning "other people's children" than they are with their own family. In much the same way today, this problem has been repeatedly made clear to me in both training and working as a CASA for children caught up in the protective mechanisms of foster care in the United States. Ambivalence abounds even in the happiest of resolutions, mostly because the circumstances that bring parents and children into the process are never happy ones. Many would rather be in denial about such circumstances existing in the first place, offering unhelpful critiques as a defense mechanism because they don't want to help and wish to be spared the tug toward emotional expenditure that empathy threatens to require, so they convince themselves that the system is broken, but nothing can be done about it. Popular narratives for an atomized reading public perform a similar function. Kristine Moruzi writes of evangelical waif novels that set the prototype: "While there is little doubt that these texts produced emotional and affective responses in previous generations of readers, emotion and affect were used in conservative ways that suggested individual responsibility but failed to consider more radical social change" (49). Consciousness raising is often coupled with compensatory narratives, sentiment sugar-coats the alienation of privatization, and learned helplessness relieves guilt.

Another cause of discomfort for armchair critics is the factor of child work. Those in the middle-class comfort of safe homes and well-provided-for children could easily see child work as an affront to childhood innocence and an intrusion upon education. But from the perspective of poverty, some families and children would look at child work as a necessary corrective for the lack of opportunities promising a family wage. Both views may have been implied cynically by one of Maria Rye's most successful critics, inspector Andrew Doyle. In a damning 1875 report, he cites a perceptive sixteen-year-old girl who told him, "'Doption, sir, is when folks get a girl to work without wages" (qtd. in Diamond 244).[3] Although Victorian child savers hoped that emigrating children would increase the likelihood of their being adopted into new families, like the *Amistad*'s Mar'gru, most became unpaid servants in the exchange. When grafted onto the structure of a nuclear family without clear conditions of inclusivity (participating member or paid employee?), children lose even more potential for financial independence, indeed, becoming more exploitable to "work without wages."

Public opinions about children were often slower to shift along with the sea change of policies surrounding their options for care. Within private spheres, individuals could recognize the limitations of defining best interests and linking child welfare to money and the dangers of not acknowledging psychological parentage of nonbiologically related caregivers. But when it comes to "other people's children," facts get fuzzy. One *Titanic* story demonstrates many of the extremes possible for temporarily kinless kids: that of Michel and Edmond

Navratil, who became famous as the "Orphans of the Deep, Titanic Tots" (Geller 91). Traveling with their father, who had kidnapped them during a custody dispute and so bought tickets under falsified names, they were separated by the women-and-children-first policy, which doomed their father but found his children safely in seats on a lifeboat. Their mother, who was still searching for them in France, where they had been living until taken by their father, had no idea they were at sea.[4] Once the unclaimed "waifs" were safely on the *Carpathia* after rescue, the story was reported as if it were a Cinderella tale: "Speaking barely understandable toddler French and with no identification, they were taken into the willing arms of different passengers—one to First Class and one to Third. Traumatised, they sobbed for each other until reunited. . . . Enter the story's fairy godmother, New Yorker Margaret Hays" (92). Hays, a wealthy urbanite, was able to care for the children and sleuth out their parentage, eventually reuniting them with their mother. Although not fairy-tale magic, this endeavor was sensationalized as a heroic mystery. But when Dorothy Dix reported on the reunification in the *New York Evening Journal*, she "lamented the boys' return to their 'poor' mother when they could have been adopted into a better life by a 'rich' American. She suggested strongly that Madame Navratil was being selfish by forcing her sons to grow up with little education and few advantages" (93). To print such offensive nonsense, it is clear that buying children or indenturing them to servitude might be out, but lucrative charitable adoptions had become acceptable enough in popular sentiment to disregard "tender-years" sentiment selectively based on classist and nationalist bias.[5] Nonetheless, the distinction between buying children and charitable adoption was still blurred, especially if a tidy profit stood to be gained.

The exchange value of children in the liminal but semipermanent position of kinlessness (or in temporary transition between different kin and kith arrangements) often reveals much about discriminatory hierarchies. The tender-years doctrine may appear to favor mothers but could also be seen as an excuse for actually keeping the financial burden on men while relegating the tough unpaid work of actual parenting to women. And as a result of the sentimental impetus behind it, there was preference for supposedly emotional and malleable girls in adoption. Viviana Zelizer explains that racial bias was explicit as well: blue-eyed, curly-haired blondes were the ideal (2011, 63). Not only were gender, race, and class factors in determining *who* might be adopted (poverty the largest underlying factor), but also in the patronizing ideal of "lifting" the poor orphan child out of poverty. Zelizer dates "a very special adoption market that began in the 1920s," and "[b]y 1937, infant adoption was being touted as the latest American fad" (62–63). Comic strips and comic books played an important role in building up Americanized orphan mythologies from the *The Yellow Kid* to *Batman*.

Nowhere in popular culture has this fad been more explicit than Harold Gray's *Little Orphan Annie*, which from its beginnings in 1924 correspondingly records the rage for rags-to-riches adoption and complicated sentiments surrounding it. The strip's premise reaffirms patriarchal best interests but also tracks changing paradigms of child welfare in the Progressive Era.

In the beginning of *Little Orphan Annie*, the title character is little more than a curio to Mrs. Warbucks, who takes her on a trial basis. Gray intentionally kept her in a kinless state, "meeting the sentimental criteria for faddish, wealthy adoption and matching the plot-driven, melodramatic mode of the silent film era. Like evangelical waif novels of the nineteenth century, the comic strip operates almost entirely on an emotive and affective level." (qtd. in Bruce Smith 9).[6] The standard orphan fare takes on a fascinating social dynamic, which may be the only original element of the strip. Annie's closest father figure, Daddy Warbucks, is, despite his nickname, not particularly fatherly. His relationship is protective but also fickle: he leaves her often, and when she leaves, she manages to stay away for long periods of time, sometimes under the care of others but often not. Daddy Warbucks doesn't always search for Annie, and even when he does, her return to the safe fold of his providing can be a year-long adventure arc. It's a bit difficult in today's culture to find the right words to describe their relationship, but at the time the strip was conceived, the term "sugar daddy" was gaining recognition (Willard), and in the twenties there was a sensational case of which many would later recognize echoes when *Little Orphan Annie* hit the papers in 1924: the adoption campaigns of Edward West Browning, New York elite and real estate developer who was needy for publicity (think Trump, but smarter and with better hair). In 1918 Browning and his first wife sought a daughter with the following ad in the paper: "PROMINENT WEALTHY OLD NEW YORK family of highest standing with palatial home and no children, would like sweet little girl of about 4 years, who would have every advantage and care, with privilege of adoption. Write full particulars, Knickerbocker, 122 Times" (qtd. in Greenburg 49). Michael M. Greenburg writes, "Such adoption advertisements were fairly common at the time and laws preventing the farming of children were only in the initial stages of development. Orphanages and other childcare institutions were falling out of favor, and the placement of children with families had become the growing trend" (49). After a successful search, adoption, and few years had passed, the publicity-loving Browning made another public search to find a new sibling for his first adopted daughter. By now, Browning, often called the "Cinderella man" for his rags-to-riches adoptions, had another nickname that would permanently stick, "Daddy" Browning. One syndicated news article from 1920 would announce, "Browning Tots Rival 'Alice in Wonderland'; Are Idolized by All Little Kiddies in Land," with a picture of the pampered daughters superimposed on an image of Browning's rooftop garden, complete with an angular pool and rowboat (Jacobs 12).[7] Michael Greenburg writes, "The *Annie*-esque irony of it all became a sensation, as word of these two charmed adopted children began to spread" (51). Daddy Browning appeared to be collecting little girls.

Harold Gray admitted to using daily headlines as inspiration for his comic strip but despised and denied claims that Daddy Warbucks was based on Daddy Browning. I bring it up, not to make any salacious claims about either, but to point out that a strange blend of romantic paternalism pervades both stories, fictional and nonfictional. And Browning's third adoption campaign reveals the gray areas between them. After a divorce in which his previously adopted daughters were separated in custody, one with her legal adoptive mother and the other with her legal adoptive father, Browning yet again put an ad in the paper: "ADOPTION—PRETTY, REFINED GIRL, about 14 years old, wanted by aristocratic family of large wealth and highest standing: will be brought up as own child among beautiful surroundings, with every desirable luxury" (Greenburg 68). In this search he claimed he would interview all 12,000 applicants personally. Two finalists who competed as if auditioning for a part were photographed on Browning's lap as if they were much younger. Mary Louise Spas dressed and played up the Cinderella role best, but it turned out, in a scandalous reveal, that she was actually twenty-one (see figure 3.2). The facts that she could (supposedly) convince Browning, and that the public was willing to play along to some degree, indicate the extent to which the ideal of the innocent waif of poor means fooled them: "Mary's claim of Cinderella innocence and deprivation was crumbling beneath her feet" (84). Perhaps Browning got what he was really paying for.

But in the long run, the scandal (at least the only actionable misstep) was not the finery lavished upon his adopted daughters (and later on his girl-bride Peaches in a short but sensational, publicity-hit marriage) that caused any legal troubles. If the similarities of these relationships went further than explicitly recognized, that is unclear in the obscure sexual coding of the time. It was a gift of money for Mary's biological sister's care that sullied his last adoption: "As a token of goodwill, Edward Browning then provided to Mary's parents what was described as a surprise present for the purpose of defraying the mounting expenses of Mildred's illness. He wrote a check to each for $500, and he would soon regret ever doing so" (Greenburg 80). This offense was too threateningly explicit about the material motives that were nonetheless at the core of Browning's relationships with girls. It broke the pretense.

Viviana Zelizer provides this more representative sentiment about adoption from Browning's contemporary counterparts: "As one grateful adoptive father

Figure 3.1. Little Orphan Annie, August 11, 1924, by Harold Gray. © Tribune Content Agency, LLC. All Rights Reserved. Reprinted with permission.

told a *Good Housekeeping* reporter in 1927, 'Talk about children owing their parents anything! We'll never be able to pay what we owe that baby'" (2011, 63). By mystifying financial arrangements, such testimonies keep them unacknowledged but out in the open for historical record. The incompatibility of material and emotional realities further mystified the shift from best interests to tender-years doctrine, adoption for hire (as in orphan trains), and sentimental adoption, causing avoidance about the former, keeping the economic entwined but denied. Zelizer explains that with the charity-adoption fad that swept "comfortable" society, "the value of a priceless child became increasingly monetized and commercialized. Ironically, the new market price for babies was set exclusively by their noneconomic, sentimental appeal.... Commercial child placement emerged as a significant social problem in the 1920s in large part because it violated new professional standards" (64). Demand for sweet,

Figure 3.2. Mary Louise Spas, Daddy Browning, and Sylvia Mullen, August 8, 1925. Courtesy New York Daily News Archive/Getty Images.

white babygirls was higher than supply, but such economizing became taboo in child placement. Perhaps this ideological conflict surrounding the exchange of money for parenting is one of the deeper discomforts some still have with foster care and expensive international adoptions. It might also explain how "May-December marriages," like that of Peaches and Daddy Browning, have become remythologized with "gold-digger" stereotypes that allow audiences to imagine girl-brides as having street-smart business motives precocious for their years. Profit corrupts.

"*Annie*-esque" combinations of romance and paternalism have lasted beyond the life of the strip and long after public memory of Daddy Browning. In fact, Martin Charnin, the primary force behind its musical adaptation, *Annie*, would describe the orphan-millionaire relationship in this way: "[W]e didn't want to make it an adventure story. We wanted to make it a love story between two orphans. Warbucks is as much an orphan in this musical as Annie is. He doesn't find his parents, he finds his child" (Smith 91). But even if Warbucks had no family, he is a wealthy, white, privileged, adult male—almost as far from Annie's powerless orphaned status as you can get (without getting into race and ability politics). Making a musical out of the strip required radical alterations[8]—making Warbucks more relatable, altering the political spin 180 degrees. Whereas Gray despised FDR, even having Warbucks dance on his grave in the strip, the musical has FDR singing along and even shows Warbucks excited about the New Deal. It also required making the "love story" more strictly filial-paternal. In contrast, reading the original comic strip through the lens of historical hindsight feels a bit like when latch-key kids of my generation heard rumors that *The Brady Bunch* actors who played Mrs. Brady and her son, Greg, were sleeping with each other—not a legal problem but a little creepy to those of us who came home from school to watch this surrogate family on television. Interestingly, Charnin's reconfiguration of the characters opposes adventure to romance, seemingly aware that for Daddy Warbucks to be seen as fatherly, Annie's adventures will have to remain contained within his sphere. Charnin too readily glosses the extreme differences in power afforded the characters as a result of class, gender, and age. Annie, as a fictional character, and one without traditional family ties, is able to experience and overcome conflicts that middle-class readers want to believe real children are protected from. And by thinking of their own children, people completely miss that children in greatest need of protection are either in quite different homes or in none at all, explained away as other people's children or other people's problems.

A defining characteristic of Western childhood is dependence, yet the bourgeois baggage of denial about money sometimes makes it too easy to also ignore need. Differences in power are too easily unacknowledged within the emotionally-hidden financial structures of nuclear family or simply the domicile. These microeconomics can operate invisibly but potently to trap children emotionally and so seemingly not in any "real," structural, material way: "Exchanging obedience for love comes naturally—we were all once children after all, whose survival depended on the caprices of love. And thus you have the template for future intimacies: if you love me, you'll do what I want or need or demand to make me feel secure and complete and I'll love you back. Thus we grow to demand obedience in our turn, we household dictators and petty tyrants of the private sphere, who are in our turn, dictated to" (Kipnis 93–94). Such are the hidden exchanges within power that control children. Or to spin it more theoretically, Slavoj Žižek compares government, market, and family politics: "[R]epresentative democracy in its very notion involves a passivization of the popular Will.... [T]he ruling order is itself already doing all the undermining necessary. In the same way that (market) freedom is unfreedom for those who sell their labor-power, in the same way that the family is undermined by the bourgeois family as legalized prostitution, democracy is undermined" (135). The Daddy Browning case and even the comic-strip sugar daddy's name,

Daddy Warbucks, encapsulate these often unremarked, uncomfortable realities. You don't have to read much Gray to know he in no way associated these two figures called "Daddy," but one can see why an ambiguous link may have been occasioned in the public mind, as both reassert patriarchal best interests in the tenet, "If I pay the bills, I make the rules." [9]

Good intentions and sweetness don't pay the bills. With pluck and ingenuity, Annie does get to work for her own wages at a grocery store during a role reversal in which she supports the temporarily down-and-out Warbucks, which threatens his sense of mannish superiority: "Great scott! Has it come to this? Warbucks practically supported by a girl?" (qtd. in Smith 25). So of course, he goes off to make some money and be worthy again, abandoning Annie out of privileged pride. In spite of this making him redouble his capitalist efforts, he never fiscally secures her future. One reader, an attorney from New York, wrote to Gray: "I'm a little tired of seeing Daddy Warbucks disappear and periodically leave Annie broke as a result . . . I therefore am willing to set up, free of charge to the parties concerned for my services, a trust fund by Daddy Warbucks for the benefit of Annie. . . . I just cannot stand the thought of Annie being left on the rocks next time Daddy leaves town, nor can my little seven-year-old niece at whose insistence I write" (qtd. in Smith 77). Indeed, when Warbucks dies, leaving Annie without an official caretaker, a social worker named Mrs. Bleating-Hart interferes in a possible adoption opportunity (with Mrs. Hold), telling the judge overseeing the case that "the child shows decided traits of juvenile delinquency" (September 10, 1944, 11:18). So instead of adoption Annie is taken away to live with Bleating-Hart on a "trial" basis for six months of the strip. To make sure his audience hated this villain enough, Gray had her call the dog catcher to take Sandy, locking Annie in the closet when she protests: "I'll just lock you in this closet, where you can considah how silly you're being ovah a nawsty old mongrel!" (October 15, 1944, 11:205). Letters poured in to respond, including one eight-year-old reader, Thelma Anderson Delmont of Nebraska, who said, "Dear Sir, My brother will take a billy club after you if you don't save Orphan Annie's dog. Why don't you have Mrs. Bleating-Hart put in jail? Please have Orphan Annie's dog save [sic] for she is a friend of mine" (Heer 13). Others wrote in general of Gray's ability to create tensions between good and evil. John Updike, then fifteen, wrote to Gray, "Your villains are completely black and Annie and crew are practically perfect, which is as it should be. To me there is nothing more annoying in a strip than to be in the dark as to your evil-doers" (Heer 5).[10] Mrs. Bleating-Hart touched diverse political chords— among conservatives like Gray, she confirmed vicious stereotypes about child protection bureaucrats; among lefties, she no doubt served as a reminder of some very real problems surrounding the still fledgling business of child saving.

As with some of the British Home Children's hopefully adoptive but eventually indenturing sponsors, Mrs. Bleating-Hart basically gets Annie to work in her own home without pay: "Mrs. Bleating-Hart is, oh, so-o-o sweet and understanding . . . At least, she understands how to get a perfect maid—for free!" (September 24, 1944, 11:196). In characteristic form, Gray lays it on thick, having Annie do *all* the house work—cleaning, cooking, laundering, and struggling for any time to do homework for school, playing up the concurrent sentiment against child labor and for compulsory education. Bleating-Hart, a hypocrite whose own children attend private school, even restricts Annie's access to others through public school because she is a "delinquent" with a "black record," ironically telling Mrs. Keyhole, "I nevah allow her to associate with othahs outside of school hours—awftah all, we do owe something to ouah deah community" (October 8, 1944, 11:202). Child savers in the 1920s advocated orphan care in private institutions and eventually private homes, whereas progressives called for more widespread and regulated institutional changes. The British Home child who called adoption "work without wages" understood the oppressing power of keeping such workers tethered to the domicile, without as many opportunities for public solidarity. Far from being character-building chores, work without wages within a private sphere is more disempowering because it severs possible links to the community or opportunity for sufficient self-reliance that working publically with pay would. Yet, most sentiments against child work, and for labor reforms, focused on paid but exploitative work in the public sphere. (Even today the term evokes industrial factories rather than domestic servitude, in which children are still enslaved.)

Like the *Amistad* orphans, Annie's freedom does not protect her from being exploited for unpaid labor. But as in Cinderella tales, it is Annie's willingness to do all the work without complaint that makes her sympathetic, even admirable, strangely avoiding appearances of bucking against adult authority while demonizing a specific "type" of adult and the system she vaguely represents. In fact, scapegoating allows refocusing that reduces action against the appropriate, larger systemic target. And, of course, as in many fairy tales, children can be reduced to working without wages by the restructuring that follows the death of one parent, only in this case the parent is wealthy and simply fails to protect the child by providing inheritance or even the legal claim of parentage that is called "permanence" in the business of child protection. Of course, Gray's is a reactionary stereotype of social work, but one that resonated with readers who knew how possible maltreatment could be. One reader, signing as "Orphan Dorothy," wrote to Gray, "Please get Orphan Annie out of Mrs. Bleating-Hart's clutches real soon. . . . Having been placed in one of those so-called opportunity homes after losing one of my parents, I had about the same experiences, yes, some worse than Orphan Annie's. Sad to say there are plenty of Mrs. Bleating-Hart's sort, who being too lazy to do their own work offer out of the kindness of their big hearts an opportunity home to some orphan, an opportunity for whom, and what?" (qtd. in Gray 61). Dorothy is asking an important question—what is the goal of community care? Should it offer opportunities for financial support (private donation or state funding?); should it provide emotional support (impossible to measure or provide through public works); or, more realistically, should it provide opportunities in learning how to independently care for oneself?

Tension between private child-saving efforts and publically institutionalized models has always been part of the conundrum of balancing protective and participatory recognition of child rights, especially in the placement of children who have been removed from homes because of alleged neglect and abuse. Private efforts are more likely to lead to adoption but harder to standardize and oversee as adequately protective, training of foster parents is costly (in time and money); public options, of course, like our underfunded public schools, focus so much on the letter of the law in terms of standards that care is less likely to meet the spirit of the law, in which regulations are meant as protective, therefore providing less wiggle room for adequately individualized attention. Of foster care in the United States today, the chaotic conglomeration of triage operations in place have an impossible task of providing support, reuniting with biological parents where possible, and ensuring emotional support until that happens. Kids will love their biological parents, and want to be with them, in all but the most extreme cases of abuse and neglect because of the basic need for lasting attachment. Cris Beam argues that "the basic tenet of foster care, and its core complication, is that foster care is meant to be a temporary solution" and so foster parents are "generally trained not to attach" (14). Beam cites Eliana Gil, who "interviewed one hundred kids in foster care, asking them why they thought they were there. Ninety percent said it was because of something they did" (101). State wards easily blame themselves for their removal even though it was allegedly caused by their parents' actions, especially if they are secretly grateful for the change and they fear their filial loyalty is in conflict. That emotional burden can only add to the greater challenges of growing into independence without a permanent, caring adult anchor. Imagine how such guilt intensifies when in fact the child unintentionally provided the evidence interpreted as neglect or abuse that prompted separation. Deja Joefield, a five-year-old who was told to go to her grandmother's across the street in case of emergency, did just that when she woke up after bedtime and didn't see her mother anywhere (mother Maisha was in the tub wearing headphones, so she couldn't hear her daughter). According to the "new Jane Crow" that disproportionately punishes single, black mothers in low-income, densely populated areas, this mix-up warranted state interference.[11] Scott Hechinger, a defense attorney in such cases, explains, "There's this judgment that these mothers don't have the ability to make decisions about their kids, and in that, society both infantilizes them and holds them to superhuman standards. In another community your kid's found outside looking for you because you're in the bathtub, it's 'Oh, my God'—a story to tell later" but "in a poor community, it's called endangering the welfare of your child" (qtd. in Clifford). Maisha Joefield also recognizes her young age (twenty-five) as a discriminating factor in this case: "This is my opinion: they factored in my age . . . , and they put me in a box" (qtd. in Clifford). From an individual perspective such injustices can be traumatizing for life. From an ideological and institutional perspective, such failures of the system are a distressing sign that we have barely progressed since the earliest efforts in child protection. Elizabeth Young-Bruehl, speaking of the ageist prejudice that unfairly punishes children (which she calls "childism"), writes that Progressives "saw the great, prejudice-based weakness of the philanthropic child-saving organizations: the child-savers approached children's issues singly and on what came to be known among social workers as the 'deficit' or 'residual' model" (287). In contrast, philanthropists like Warbucks (and Bleating-Hart, who sees herself as one) privately "dealt with children whom a childist system had already classified as destitute, delinquent, or neglected, and then dealt with them in a punitive, childist fashion. Their childist outlook legitimated their childist actions" (287). This is the "box" that Maisha Joefield found herself and her well-cared-for child in, one that has predefined theirs as a dysfunctional domicile and looked for proof rather than presuming innocence and recognizing diverse parenting styles in relative contexts. Not to mention, the punitive prejudice overlooked an older and far better strategy for child protection: crossing the street to get help from an extended family member or neighbor is taking advantage of the child-care role we can all play in well-functioning communities. In my opinion the Joefields were modeling a far more effective method of community care.

For minors who remain "in the box" until they age out, our foster care system may provide the structure of family without attachment, bonding, permanency, or interdependence; taking in the orphan as servant, charity case, burden, job—anything but from a sense that embracing others as part of community is part of being in a community.[12] Those who foster parent often go far beyond these institutionally reinforced values—impossibly offering support, even love, without a view to permanency, but are inadequately compensated either way. So part of the problem in meeting the urgent and complex needs of children in crisis stems from our methods of imposing an ill-fitting sentimental model based on a dated and classist definition of nuclear, biological family rather than larger cooperation in the community in situations where the biological family simply needs support or isn't functioning "appropriately" (up to a disturbingly inconsistent, class-bound range of interpretations). Victoria Rowell, in *The Women Who Raised Me* (2007), demonstrates that as a foster child, funding was a constant struggle, but emotional support came from a vast patchwork family of community members—a happy circumstance not guaranteed by the "system" but by individuals—and most importantly, through them she learned to care for herself, mothering and fathering herself.[13] She also lucked out by getting a caseworker and a few fosters (official and unofficial) who were motivated, diligent, and innovative enough to bend the rules to meet the kinds of idiosyncratic needs we have as individuals growing up. A few points from Rowell's memoir serve as counterpoints to Harold Gray's twist on the "pluck and luck" orphan ideal he kept alive so long for his audience in daily papers. Offering one of the rarer positive depictions of foster care in memoir form, Rowell describes that it was the "pluck" of many committed women and the "luck" of finding a community "anchor" through ballet that worked in her favor growing up as a ward of the state. She writes, "I was never meant to be raised by one mother, but by many." Instead of allowing bureaucratic hiccups all along the way to discourage and exhaust them, these determined women worked, because they had no other choice, within the system by bending and breaking the rules so it would work, recognizing the various idiosyncratic needs that individual development demands. In Rowell's case, this meant scraping as many dollars as the state could provide for ballet training at top schools and being geographically flexible with many "respite" providers to be able to attend them.[14] Although this means being treated with affection in a piecemeal but impermanent fashion, Rowell makes clear that even though she had never been in her biological mother's care, she nevertheless experienced the filial guilt Beam discusses above: "I didn't know if I should embrace Dorothy [relative stranger but biological mother] in front of Agatha [primary foster mom]. Would I be betraying the mother/daughter loyalty between Agatha and me? I desperately wanted to hug them both but couldn't" (161). Of course, children of divorce with stepparents also know this feeling well, but it is especially magnified for state wards, who often don't get unsupervised visits with biological parents while "in care," and hand-offs always involve an audience of both biological parents and fosters, or at least a caseworker.

Victoria Rowell also indicates the central importance and her awareness of money in her foster upbringing. She is keenly aware of the exchanges involved in her care, and her own exchange value in that arrangement, overhearing one foster couple discussing the inadequate compensation they get from the supposed welfare state: "'She's only bringing in $87.00 a month and drinks too much milk.' I heard that with my own ears." Can you imagine a kidnapper asking for a ransom of $87.00? The sense of having a price on your well-being is difficult enough, but such a low one tells a foster kid some very demoralizing truths about the culture, society, agencies, and government in which they live. Rowell writes, "Something happens to a child when they hear themselves scornfully valued by a dollar amount. They either let it affect their esteem or they don't. I had to keep telling myself not to own those words, not to be dependent on dollar amounts, which were just paper, remembering that I had emancipation three years around the corner" (172). Such moments help to explain why Rowell's biggest life goal becomes to own her own home. Her economically savvy primary caregiver, Agatha, was well invested as a multiproperty owner who taught her the importance of property, independence, and self-sufficiency. Most importantly for my question above is that the looming deadline of "aging out" necessitates, above all, that fosters model the means to independence, emotionally and fiscally: "[U]ltimately I alone needed to be responsible for my things and my welfare" (167). She knows that it takes more than pluck, luck, and a millionaire sugar daddy to age out and still have the safety net so many with intact, middle- and upper-class family members take for granted.

By condemning the system of public care for orphans and "throwaway" children, but not providing Annie "permanency," Harold Gray took responsibility away from community, instead indulging us in a fantasy of her impermanent safety net of a millionaire (those are pretty hard to come by in the roster of willing foster parents!).[15] In doing so, he carried some of the changing notions of his times into his strip, but for the most part stuck to his dated brand of conservatism. Gray would explain in a letter to Congresswoman Claire Booth Luce that "since Annie is supposed to be a part of her community" and "what community is without politics?" he reasons that a "strip that is properly handled has tremendous power. As a political weapon it must be handled much as Swift handled the British problem of his day in *Gulliver's Travels*" (Smith 96–97). Yes, he compares himself to Swift. No comment needed. But it is no surprise why one reader would respond to the death of Daddy Warbucks in this manner: "Congratulations to Harold Gray for bumping off that loathsome character Daddy Warbucks. Please instruct him to get rid of Orphan Annie sometime in the near future in the most violent manner possible, and bring an end to years of wasted newsprint. She is the most awful character ever, with her eternal prying, snooping, preaching and stale philosophy" (qtd. in Smith 60). The stale philosophy of pluck and intermittent, random luck, struggle without lasting support, and best interests in patriarchal power, would resist change if only in the panels of a daily strip.

In refreshing contrast, Elzie Segar pressed all the right buttons when he introduced his famous foundling to *Thimble Theater* in 1933: Swee'pea (or Scooner Seawell Georgia Washenting Christiffer Columbia Daniel Boom). Like Annie, Swee'pea packs a punch and never seems to grow, instead remaining a perpetual foundling. Unlike Daddy Warbucks, Popeye couldn't care less about money or patriarchy: the former fits the demands of "best interests" in the monetary sense, and the latter is all "tender years." All the treasure he's fallen into in previous years has already been given to the "Chil'rens Hospital" and "Orphinks' Home," and he models his nervous new nurturing entirely upon the wisdom of women (August 21, 1933, 3:75). The strip for August 7 finds him holding Swee'pea on a park bench and learning how to burp babies from another first-time mother (in this sequence he includes himself in that category). A week later, when he finds a "mother's only" sign on the lecture about childcare he wishes to attend, he attends wearing a dress (of course, riding that sometimes fine line between derision and drag, but come on, it's Popeye—campy, but sincere). Like most continuity strips of the time, as the backstory develops, it becomes the stuff of melodrama: Swee'pea's parents had been shipwrecked off the coast of Demonia; his mother sends her baby to Popeye for protection from Demonians, a superstitious lot who worship little Scooner as crown prince because of lucky seven moles on his back.

But most often, the repeated reason for Swee'pea needing the protection of Popeye is to keep him from being "spoiled," which is uttered as if that is the worst fate possible for a child. In contrast to the royal treatment, Popeye christens Scooner in spinach, baptizes him in the ocean ("I yam pabcizing him in ocean water on account of I wants him to be 'salts of the eart'"), and protects him from the goons sent to kidnap and return Demonia's crown prince. The repetition of "protecting" from "spoiling" in the Segar strip suggests a somewhat unexpected flexibility in concepts of protecting kids. Overprotection reads in many contexts as spoiling, but we have to consciously override such impulses to protect kids from the "rotten" effects of pampering.[16]

Early uses of the term "spoiling" (cockering, over-indulging) reveal the economic roots of the concept. According to the *Oxford English Dictionary*, sample usages from the fifteenth century to the eighteenth are synonymous with divesting, pillaging, or financially ruining someone. From the seventeenth to nineteenth centuries, a "spoil-trade" indicated inequitable trade, a raw deal, bargaining without gain. When child rearing is all give and no take, a defining characteristic of "the new standards of selflessness" dominating middle-class parenting from the nineteenth century to the present, the fine line between support and ruination is unclear (Habermas 47). Sentiments demanding that parents "put their children first," ensured a "spoil-trade" in economic terms but promised a huge emotional "payoff." Often concerns over spoiling were part of the mother-blaming bias common in abandonment accounts. In fact, when Jean-Jacques Rousseau felt remorse in later life for abandoning his five offspring at a foundling hospital, one of his excuses was that it was to protect them from their mother's overindulgence, or "the certainty of Thérèse's spoiling ways" (Kessen 156).[17] In contrast, Swee'pea's biological mother; his adoptive father, Popeye; Popeye's girlfriend, Olive Oyl; and Popeye's clan of community supporters are committed to avoiding overprotective or carelessly indulgent tendencies, promoting independence and self-sufficiency as goals instead.

Popeye certainly dotes on and pampers the baby when it comes to providing, even buying a year's supply of diapers right away: "I wants some baby's underwear—the square kind—I wants good stuff, too—I suppose I better get silk" (August 2, 1933, 3:72). But it is "spoiling" on a damaging scale he fears. His boss tells him, in no uncertain financial terms, "This youngster is worth very, very much to a certain country," and warns, "If they get your baby they will treat him like a god—such treatment would spoil him" (August 22–23, 1933, 3:75). In Popeye's circle, there is a consensus that saving Swee'pea from spoiling is important enough to keep him in Popeye's custody rather than the biological mother's, yet Popeye acknowledges that such valuations are culturally relative: "Bein' worshipped by them ignorant people would spoil him—I suppose that's why the mother brang him away.... They means him no harm—in fack, they'd treat him like he was the god of luck hisself." But Olive Oyl reminds him that is too great a risk: "If they treated him like a god it would spoil him entirely" (August 26–27, 1933, 3:76). This emphatic repetition explaining motives puts the decision in direct contrast to opinions, like that of Dorothy Dix on the Navratil case above, that "best interests" are purely monetary, while at the same time protesting Swee'pea's "value." A cynic might point out here that Popeye and his community of nurturers might also be motivated by Swee'pea's exchange value (would this have changed with a female foundling of color?). Perhaps it is merely an inversion of class contexts, but I think it also suggests an emerging acceptance of the importance and potential of psychological parenting, to be later codified by Joseph Goldstein, Anna Freud, and Albert J. Solnit: "[F]or the child, the physical realities of his conception and birth are not the direct cause of his emotional attachment. This attachment results from day-to-day attention to his needs for physical care, nourishment, comfort, affection, and stimulation. Only a parent who provides for these needs will build a psychological relationship to the child on the basis of the biological one and will become his 'psychological parent' in whose care the child can feel valued and 'wanted.' An absent biological parent will remain, or tend to become, a stranger" (17). Popeye claims Swee'pea as his own, becoming his psychological parent, even aggressively defending his claim as a paternal right.

But the character alterations in Max Fleischer's cartoons seem self-consciously realigned according to gender norms. No longer is Swee'Pea Popeye's foundling son, but he lives in Olive's care (and, of course, they are rewritten as biological kin). In "Little Swee'Pea" (1936), Popeye takes him to the zoo, and the typical physical humor devolves into repetitive mindless displays of masculine might. Popeye even ends the sequence by singing, "There's no ifs or maybes / I'll never have babies / I'm Popeye the Sailor Man!" This comes as a pretty strange denunciation within the context of the original story, and a telling one. In contrast, Segar's Popeye not only had considered Swee'pea "me child," but he is prepared to defend that position and his son by any means required. Even though Popeye's main shtick is brainless braun, Segar's story resists gender norms, marriage, and conforming to conventional family structures. Popeye and Olive don't marry, live apart, and instead Popeye surrounds himself with an even bigger chosen family, or as Donald Phelps puts it, "a preserve, the lightest of domestications for the wild things that Popeye had gathered around him, not subservient to any confining norms, but free as ever in their new, adopted styles" (no pagination). There is even a suggestion that the notion of nuclear families is completely foreign to Popeye: he is himself an "orphink" until he finds his father in a 1936 strip. When in a *Kings Comics* book from November, 1939, his father, Poopdeck Pappy, decides he wants a wife, Popeye protests, "But Poppa, I don't want any momma!" (no. 43). His pop argues, "Ya needs a momma an' yer adoptit orfspring needs a granmomma," but Popeye firmly says "no!" One could probably find evidence in *Popeye* for a reading of the strip as having a viewpoint marginalizing women (or an exclusively homosocial viewpoint); after all, he does comment, "I don't think much of a woman which'll ditch her child" (3:72). But this is immediately followed by a flattered and affectionate change in tone that reveals his recognition of female authority: "She knows I'll be good to 'im, eh?" (72). Nine days later, we see the foundling's mother peeking through the window at her son in his cradle by Popeye's bed with his hand gripping Popeye's finger as they sleep, approvingly saying, "Thank heaven he really loves him" (74). Segar's use of her approval suggests that the dominant viewpoint in no way alienates a maternal perspective, authority, or power.

One might even argue that Swee'pea's pseudo second birth to Popeye from a package suggests a bit of womb envy.[18] After all, he spends some time confused about gender: "I been tryin' so hard to be a mama to him I forgets I yama male sex" (August 7, 1933, 3:73). For one thing, Segar gives Swee'pea's debut onto the *Thimble Theater* stage a stunning five days (29 panels) in which to occur. The narrative pacing alone suggests the importance of the event (see figure 3.3). Donald Phelps writes, "His crated arrival was Segar's funny, loving tribute to the puppet aspects of his stage.... More, it represented the opening step, as might the delivery of tools and timber, in Popeye's doughty, makeshift carpentering of his own Peaceable Kingdom" (vol. 3, introduction). This "crated arrival" explicitly evokes an old trope–the miraculous disembodied delivery, like stork stories, but containment is more pronounced.

Throughout this book, I note frequent images and rhetorical tendencies toward containment (lifeboats, enclosure, islands, ships in bottles, boxes, baskets, playpens, and cages). In accounts of child abandonment, transition, discovery, and even childcare, containment plays a surprisingly consistent role as the reliable prop conveying protection and safety through restriction and security. Amy L. Richman and colleagues write that the trope is particularly resonant in American culture, where, in contrast to other cultures, children undergo greater "containerization," spending "a considerable amount of time [about quadruple] in various sorts of 'containers,' such as high chairs and playpens." They say that comparing a sample from Boston, for example, with one tribe in Kenya, "U.S. infants have their activities restricted by either holding or containerization about the same amount of time that Gusii infants are held.... Yet the practice of putting children in containers is quite distinct from being carried, for it precludes physical contact with others" (70). With the "high chair, infant seat, or playpen" a parent's "first strategy is childproofing, or rearranging the environment so that potential hazards are removed. A second strategy is to restrict the child's movement" (69). Of course, such methods are not simply confining: "Allowing the infant freedom of movement within a small, safe environment (that is, a childproofed area) was the preferred means for integrating two competing goals: that of hazard prevention with that of intellectual development" (70). But with the trope of the boxed birth (or gifting), the precious package also implicitly sets, as part of the scenery, a fading suggestion of the exchange and commerce inherent in protection: freedom for family security, an amassing debt while nonetheless becoming another's property, and the burden of parental power and responsibility.

These tensions between protection and freedom, confinement and contact, exchange and embrace create controversy in child care. And boxed-in babies trigger our awareness of those elements a protectionist view typically erases: that protection is necessary but also necessarily limits freedom. Containment is represented throughout history in transfers of children from biological family to communal care in foundling wheels of churches used for anonymous abandonment and oblation, baby hatches and drop boxes used in foundling hospitals or community health centers, and baskets of swaddled infants being left at orphanage gates. Nonetheless, such realities are met with controversy when aired in public. All it took was calling B. F. Skinner's original Air-Crib a "baby box" to make his otherwise successful solution to child rearing demands unpalatable for many readers of the *Ladies Home Journal* and beyond (October

Figure 3.3. Popeye, July 22–28, 1933. Copyright © E. C. Segar. Courtesy of Fantagraphics Books (www.fantagraphics.com).

1945). In Skinner's article introducing the contraption to a general audience of presumed nurturers, the title, "Baby in a Box," no doubt drew in interested readers, but the wording connotes commerce, neglect, even abuse—implications that damaged his influence in any lasting, practical way with the average consumer. In spite of Skinner's protestations that his "baby tender" was built to reduce the overburdens of childcare and give mothers more time for bonding, the public associated his invention with his earlier studies on boxed animals. His defense, however, is worthy of consideration, as it points to the heart of the rhetorical problem—our knee-jerk rejection of something so close to what we already practiced in childcare: "The baby cannot get out, of course, but that is true of a crib as well. There is less actual restraint in the compartment because the baby is freer to move about." Other elements of his reasoning have not aged as well in an era of attachment parenting: "Easier care is sure to be better care. The mother will resist the temptation to put the baby back into a damp bed if she can conjure up a dry one in five seconds. She may very well spend less time with her baby, but babies do not suffer from being left alone but only from the discomforts which arise from being left alone in the ordinary crib." His control of restraints and freedom supposedly allows some interactive participation: "How long do we intend to keep the baby in the compartment? The baby will answer that in time" (425). Even so, most of us flinch when we first hear of Skinner's baby box—a sure example of the disconnect between our sentiments and practical investigations of child care; after all, Skinner's methods were in keeping with the priorities of his time—remaking motherhood an attractive, trouble-free, and "proper" role for women.

The initial reaction against such innovations is primarily semantic, but it also taps into adult guilt over restricting children for the sake of convenience (whether or not this is actually what we do, parental care is laden with guilt triggers). We already seem to know the motif and have our defenses ready-made. Daniel W. Bjork writes that "Skinner's study with its sleeping cubicle was the last boxlike world he had invented," yet the "box motif became identified with him" and his "life as a scientist, social inventor, and intellectual was inexorably tied to a world of boxes" (3). Even though the intent was to provide less restraint with greater control of temperature and humidity, he is remembered for mostly false stories from the unrestrained imaginations of critics. His daughter, the test subject and first temporary inhabitant of the "baby tender," writes of these in her article, "I Was Not a Lab Rat." She was said to have been raised in a "laboratory box," in a "cramped square cage that was equipped with bells and food trays" (Buzan). But she didn't lose her sense of humor: "Then there's the story that after my father 'let me out,' I became psychotic. Well, I didn't. That I sued him in a court of law is also untrue. And, contrary to hearsay, I didn't shoot myself in a bowling alley in Billings, Montana. I have never even been to Billings, Montana" (Buzan). Like her father, Deborah Skinner Buzan explains that the actual contraption "was a wonderful alternative to the cage-like cot." The fact that this view has been popularly clouded by urban legends that "made the rounds of psychology classes across America" speaks much more to our imaginations than to Skinner's reductive behaviorism.

In spite (or because) of the fact that we "containerize" childhood, Americans still bristle at baby boxes. When the Finnbin, a box of supplies for newborns distributed in Finnish hospitals that can also be used as a safe starter crib, captured global attention, the response from Americans was jumping immediately to the same irrational fears, in spite of the fact that Finland has had great success in lowering crib death, no doubt contributing to its significantly low infant mortality rates.[19] Rachel Rabkin Peachman explains that the "boxes, which come filled with items such as clothes, diapers, nursing pads and a snug-fitting mattress, are given to new parents as part of an educational campaign about safe sleeping practices for infants." As with Skinner's Air Crib, the emotional public response blew realities out of proportion, missing the learning points we could build on. In fact, "Most parents in Finland don't even use the boxes as a baby bed. A recent survey found that just 37 percent of families there used the baby boxes as a sleeping place," which brings into focus to the more valuable structural insight that Finland's success with infant survival is more profoundly and consequentially linked to the country's universal health care for mothers, children, preventative medicine, and counseling systems.

Sentimentality (as with women and children first) is one of the most pervasive and lasting protections we've offered our young as a safety net, but it isn't always matched by structural support (law, aid) and sometimes can even comfort adults too much by casting real dangers in an obscuring rose-tinted view. Some of the emotional response to the box motif springs from discomfort with darker realities in child care. Take, for example, South Korean pastor Jong-rak Lee's "baby box" for anonymous abandonment of infants. The "small box in a wall is stirring controversy about child abandonment and human rights" (McDonald). From 2009 to 2014, 383 children were left at the church, although 120 parents did return to reclaim children. In a 2015 documentary, *The Drop Box*, Lee's privately funded effort in providing temporary protection to anonymously surrendered infants (before most are handed over to orphanages) is shown in a somewhat unproblematic, even at times heroic, light.[20] But such facilities cause legal troubles for the state and possibly interfere with more organized procedures for homing abandoned children: "Caregivers leave their child without official records of when they were born, who the parents are or why they are being abandoned" instead of "formal relinquishment where parents officially renounce their parenting rights and consent to the adoption of their child. . . . The children will most likely live at orphanages until they turn 18 or 19. They cannot be adopted internationally because they haven't been formally relinquished" (McDonald). Being left undocumented violates the

U.N. Convention on the Rights of Children: "Therefore, the U.N. Committee on the Rights of the Child opposes so-called baby boxes, the heated incubators located at the exterior wall of a hospital where a baby can be left anonymously and an alarm sounded" (Oaks 23). The CRC clearly emphasizes the primacy of biological parents to children, as in the objection of Szilvia Gyurkó (child rights delegate for Hungary) that an anonymously relinquished child "will never have a chance to know her/his birth mother, her/his health history, or siblings" (qtd. in Oaks 23). But there is a class bias to this logic that overlooks risks in not having anonymous options. Supporters of the practice claim that such operations reduce incidences of infanticide.

If we rethink giving top priority to bioparentage, are we guilty of individualist hubris? No doubt Rousseau told himself something of the sort each time he and his partner, Thérèse, abandoned their children, but I'm not simply talking about some bureaucratic passing of the buck. In Rousseau's time, a growing sense of the need for state-guaranteed care would eventually result in policies after his death: "During the French Revolution, the state assumed care for abandoned and foundling children, and the decree of 1811 mandated that all hospices for abandoned children have *tours*, baby boxes located in an exterior wall with a way to swivel the cradle into the hospice, allowing anonymous child surrender" (Oaks 32). The care of our young needs to be a priority in the way we govern, and communities need to accountably ensure reciprocity and interdependence for children to thrive.

As might be expected, literary depictions of such issues reveal less about actuality and more about our uses of sentimentality. In *The Kindness of Strangers: The Abandonment of Children in Western Europe from Late Antiquity to the Renaissance* (1988), John Boswell documents in great detail multiple practices of child abandonment, transfers of care, and child offerings (as in oblation) from ancient to early modern societies (primarily European), demonstrating that swaps and simple abandonment have always existed, leaving parents and children vulnerable to scams or worse. Literary representations of abandonment, however, grapple with sentiments surrounding and obscuring these dangers. Bowsell reports,

> The frequency with which fictional shepherds find abandoned children and rear them in Arcadian simplicity before restoring them to their natal parents may strain credulity: the inspiration for this seems so obviously the mythical archetype of Oedipus, or Romulus and Remus. Aside from the fact that the archetypes themselves may arise from some social reality, it is worth noting that there was actually legislation in the later [Roman] empire prohibiting the upper classes from "handing their children over to shepherds," and many

indications both that infants were regularly sent to the countryside for rearing—because this was thought to be healthier for them—and that this could give rise to separation from, or at least possible confusion about, the identity of young children. (97)

Poverty is generally recognized as a primary cause for abandoning, selling, or indenturing children, but usually it is the exchange of money that is depicted as most problematic, not the child's welfare. Boswell notes, "The sale of children receives literary attention, although less frequently than other forms of abandonment because it is relatively difficult to portray sympathetically" (381). Gilles de Rais, more than likely the original inspiration for Bluebeard, was memorably depicted (as foil to Joan of Arc) in Michel Tournier's *Gilles and Jeanne* (1983). But the horrific and mostly historically accurate portrayal of events from the fifteenth century also echoes Tom Thumb tales in the sense that economic hardship can lead to child abandonment, dramatized with the worst-case scenarios of consequences to children. The exchange of money in buying children for his sadistic and psychopathic sexual assaults, torture, and murder attests this power differential. When one victim is purchased, he "is helped up on to the horse. They gallop off. The weeping mother makes the sign of the cross. The father counts over the money again" (46–47). The mother's behavior allows us to pity, but the father's almost suggests that the child wasn't properly valued, thus redirecting our sympathies. Many look at such anomalous extremes as examples of how brutal human experience was before the supposedly wonderful growth of agriculture, industry, and wealthy nations, but what we are really doing when we indulge in this logic is a delusional historical distancing of brutal realities, which is, in fact, completely inaccurate, like the denial of "that wouldn't happen to us—it happens to other people's children" but on a grander scale. By doing this we also imagine such tragedies are completely out of one's control, but we can control how we deal with them as communities.

In actual experience, like that of *Amistad* orphan Mar'gru, it is usually not villainy that prompts sale, indenturing, or enslavement, but a wide range of complicating factors:

> Parents abandoned their offspring in desperation when they were unable to support them, due to poverty or disaster; in shame, when they were unwilling to keep them because of their physical condition or ancestry (e.g. illegitimate or incestuous); in self-interest or the interest of another child, when the inheritance or domestic resources would be compromised by another mouth; in hope when they believed that someone of greater means or higher standing might find them and bring them up in better circumstances; in resignation, when a

child was of unwelcome gender or ominous auspices; or in callousness, if they simply could not be bothered with parenthood. (428–29)

Selling or "exposing" (abandoning in plain sight) children could be a result of any combination of these factors. John Boswell also finds some heartening trends usually clouded by harsher realities like the targeted infanticide of disabled or female babies treated elsewhere in scholarship. In spite of these ugly truths, Boswell demonstrates a kinder precedent intermittently observed throughout history that he usually calls "fostering." Of course, most fostering situations involve that now-familiar cash flow, but in some cases it was at least an honored practice. After a laboriously sweeping trove of evidence, Boswell concludes, "Most abandoned children were rescued and brought up either as adopted members of another household or as laborers of some sort. Whether they were exposed anonymously (in which case the aim was usually to attract attention), sold, donated, substituted, or 'fostered,' abandoned infants probably died at a rate only slightly higher than the normal infant mortality rate at the time." Of particular relevance to my argument is that such rescues by an engaged, interdependent community were negatively impacted by the growth of industry: "Humans were the major source of power in ancient and medieval Europe, and it would require extraordinary circumstances—for example, a great oversupply of workers and a very high cost of food—to render children valueless to anyone in such a society. And even where economics might have created such a situation, the 'kindness of strangers' in every age seems to have been sufficient to rescue most abandoned children" (429). He notes the modern downturn in fostering, in part with Christianity "insisting more rigidly than any other moral system on the absolute necessity of procreative purpose in all human sexual acts, and by providing, through churches and monasteries, regular and relatively humane modes of abandoning infants nearly everywhere on the continent" enabling child abandonment on a mass, organized scale (430). Of more widespread and lasting consequence was that "the increasing social significance of lineage and birth in the Middle Ages gradually rendered adoption an inherently troubling and risky concept." As families became standardized along with private patriarchal property and nuclearized through heterosexual and biological kinship, such developments "ultimately undermined the status of foundlings as a group by implicitly denying the ancient idea that adoptive parent-child relations were not only as good as, but in some ways better than their biological counterparts" (431). In contrast, chosen, nonmarital, alternatively nurturing, interdependent units became delegitimized, deeming some children "illegitimate" in the same way many nationalists essentialize undocumented immigrants as "illegals."

Being born is not a crime. But even "legitimate" biological parentage is no guarantee of safety, especially due to the biological reality of unavoidable parental deaths and shifts in family lineage through multiple marriages. In *The Truth about Cinderella: A Darwinian View of Parental Love*, Marin Daly and Margo Wilson argue that abuse occurs more when children live under the care of a "nongenetic" parent. As the subtitle indicates, they are a bit biodeterministically biased, completely missing adoptive parents who psychologically experience their relationship to their children as "genetic" parents do. But in contrast to fairy-tale blaming of evil step-monsters, "[f]ilicides by genetic parents certainly occur. In absolute numbers, they actually exceed the cases perpetuated by step-parents, although the latter occur at much higher per capita rates" (34). Theodore Dalrymple spins such studies in a more practical light: "The sociobiologists argue that the reason for the increased violence of step-parents is that step-children represent competition for the resources that might otherwise be available to their genetic offspring. This seems to me to be ludicrously reductive. If step-parents are many times more likely to be violent to children than biological parents, the fact remains that most of them are not violent" (236). Even if in blended families a step-parent (and I assume, step-sibling) is more likely to be abusive relatively and proportionately speaking, the greater number of children living with biological, abusive family members is certainly underrepresented in popular culture—a consequentially misleading bias. Cinderella stories rarely hold the passive father who fails to protect her responsible.

Adeline Yen Mah's *Chinese Cinderella: The True Story of an Unwanted Daughter* (1999) allows teen readers to comprehend this connection to fairy-tale versions, while keeping to Mah's personal experience as a daughter who is considered to be bad luck because her mother died in giving birth to her. She experiences targeted physical and emotional abuse while her step-siblings are treated as "special," but it is the lack of love, not lack of protection, that is most damaging. Her identity is threatened, as when her father is dropping her off at a boarding school and it becomes clear that he has forgotten her name: "A pang went through me. I meant so little to him, I was such a nobody, that he didn't even remember my name!" (125). Mah demonstrates how psychologically complicated her roles become, especially as she tries to gain recognition as an individual, in school and the community, especially as she has to remain as invisible as possible at home. Particularly fascinating is the exhausting pretense she has to keep in a steadfast effort to maintain her personal dignity: "I never spoke of my family, neither issued nor accepted any invitations outside of school, and always refused to eat the candies and snacks brought by my friends.... No one from home ever came to be with me on prize-giving day, regardless of how many awards I had won. They didn't know that in front of them I was desperate to keep up the pretense that I came from a normal, loving family" (54). She avoids being the object of pity and develops a strong sense of property and reciprocity: "Though my classmates often brought snacks, I never dared accept because I knew I could never reciprocate in kind" (70). When she gets lost on her way home from school in the first grade, no one notices she is gone. Relying on herself, she comes to the profound resolution that allows for her surviving less scarred: "*[T]here's obviously nobody looking out for me. I'll just have to find my own way*" (31). So she learns to read a map.

Adeline Yen Mah is also keenly aware, from her earliest days, of herself as an economic burden and the larger forces that threaten to keep her in place: "Times were hard, and on my way to school in the early mornings, I had seen infants wrapped in newspapers left to die in doorways. Beggar children in rags routinely rummaged through the garbage cans searching for food. Some were reduced to eating bark peeled off the trees lining the street on which we lived" (117). She wonders whether she might be sold, like the child she sees at the entrance to a hotel with wealthy patrons: "As we approached the entrance, I spied a little girl standing forlornly beside a man kneeling on the ground with his head bowed. Both were in rags. On the pavement was a sheet of paper describing their miseries and a plea for help. The child had a large placard hanging around her neck on which was written, MY NAME IS FENG SAN-AN. I AM FOR SALE" (160). The realities of poverty have motivated such market offerings throughout the world and history: "The sale of children by parents . . . seems at first startlingly callous, but close attention to the desperate circumstances that often inspired it renders the parents' actions more understandable. If sale was the best hope for the child's survival, it was little different from drastic measures any parent would take to save a child" (Boswell 430). But in wealthy modern states, we convince ourselves that for every child in rags there is a possible future in riches.

American uses of the Cinderella trope and tale type reveal our naïve fixation on the riches, not rags, of the formula, making the elements of servitude, abuse, and discrimination within the family somehow just part of setting the mood. But Malinda Lo's retelling *Ash* (2009) emphasizes the servitude within a changed family dynamic as well as Ash's agency with and against the fairy realm rather than passively benefiting from another's well-timed magic spell. There is always an exchange; you don't get something good for nothing. And she learns something too about emotional economics: "Do not fall in love with those who cannot love you" (202). Reciprocity is not simply a survival tactic; it is part of demanding equity and recognition as a full agent for one's own protection and welfare. These Cinderellas learn what it takes to turn their positions as family castaways into self-determination and strength, but they also demonstrate the dangers of being defined within familial relations according to the whims of emotional economics that can have very real structural consequences.

Malinda Lo delves deeper into these dynamics in her treatment of changeling lore in *Huntress* (2011). On a quest, her heroine passes through a hamlet in which there is talk of jinlike beings called "Xi" stealing children. One informant explains, "The mother says it's still her babe, but the father came through here just yesterday. Looked as though he'd lost everything. He said the child is a monster, and his wife has gone mad" (76). Although within the fictional context of the story the babe has indeed become inhabited by a demon of "dark magic," several details remind the reader of the unmagical reality behind the compensatory tales of changelings—justifying the killing of unwanted babies, especially those deemed "illegitimate" or marked by misunderstood differences. When the mother reports that the father has left her, she explains, "He—he believes I have betrayed him. . . . He says the baby is not his" (85). After calling the babe's monstrous form to show itself, Kaede "plunged the iron into the monster's chest," but as in many changeling tales, the baby retains its original form, only dead: "[T]he monster shriveled up until there, in the woman's bloody arms, was a baby with an iron knife protruding from its still belly" (89). In contrast to Cinderella tales, there is rarely a happy ending to changeling tales, especially when you recognize their function, but they do emphasize a consistent, subtle curiosity: while suggesting that babies are not equal, interchangeable, and thus replaceable, they nonetheless leave unquestioned the exchangeability of infants.[21] In this sense, changeling tales may be reflecting men's fears about ensuring their own patrilineage and guaranteeing male control over reproduction.

Eloise McGraw's *The Moorchild* (1996) and Francesca Lia Block's *The Waters and the Wild* (2011) both conceive of changelings as alienated from and within families. Expected parental bonds are absent in their experiences. Perhaps this is in part necessary for plot—creating distance that will allow the reader to tolerate abuses, as requirements to reinstate proper kinship through a re-exchanging of babies is a brutal business. In *The Moorchild*, Bess, the local good witch, tells the changeling's parents: "I have heard—but I cannot swear it—that the Folk will come and take their creature back if—if it be thrown into a well—or onto the fire—or sorely beaten" (10). But it is clear that in such rescues and returns, it is not so much kinship that prompts the rescue, especially in Saaski's case, because she is the "misbegotten" offspring of a fairy and a human fisherman. And among her original kin, there is no real parental bond recognizing and possessing the young as individuals after they are weaned. When the fairy folk discover her half-human parentage, they call the mother to identify her, which she does after hesitation: "Oh, is it you, little duckling? What a dear baby you were! Sweet as honeycomb!" (30). This is all the recognition she gets before being exchanged.

Emotionally untethered from family, changelings can operate outside of and/or redefine kinship, signaling a departure from conventional notions of biological belonging. In *The Waters and the Wild*, Francesca Lia Block somewhat contemporaneously intreprets changelings as social outsiders who have "abandonment issues without necessarily any cause" (2). Bee, the changeling, is also threatened, in this case by the human she replaced: "They frightened you with steel. You don't like steel, do you? Put an effigy of wood where you lay to curse you. Or you'd be whipped to make you confess. Then you would turn into your true self—a hideous elf that just lay there, not moving, drooling down your chin. If you didn't pass the test they'd make you drink water poisoned by witches' gloves. Or they'd drown you in the river. They'd shove you in the oven. Burn you to death alive" (82–83). What doesn't work in this novel is that the audience is expected to understand Bee's lack of emotional ties, but without being fully developed, it is hard to understand how easily she gives up the human family she has been living with to right kinship wrongs and return the unsympathetic human daughter, whose desire for reunification is described in an almost visceral way: "The girl missed her mother in a monstrous way. She missed her with a fanged longing, a zombie ache. Not having her mother was like not having a soul" (75–76). In contrast, of course, Bee is described in terms of not being possessed, owned, or missed: "The girl was nobody's" (76). What is clear upon rereading, however, is that Bee was only temporarily there, and the reunification of the nuclear family is only a back plot to the unification she establishes between two other social outcasts—peers Stephanie/Sarah and Haze, a reincarnated slave and an alien spawn, whose unusual beliefs alienate them in school. When they meet, Sarah says, "It looks as if we have found our kindred" (46). Bee is not interested in a nuclear family, but she does crave her kith, and with her school friends, she redefines kinship as a matter of choice.

The theme of the exchangeable child not only enables possibilities of constructing one's own family, but also represses anxieties about loyal, monogamous, biological property lines. Fairy mothers in *The Moorchild* are not just maternally but also sexually unrestricted: "No youngling knew its mother—only that it must have one. Each mother cosseted and adored her baby until the Nursery took over, then she forgot it and returned to the Gathering and a different mate and the careless life of the Folk" (16). John Boswell gives a related example of such anxieties from the Qur'an in the "women's pledge" to "not kill children and, interestingly, not to substitute babies—a problem one would expect in a society with a good supply of abandoned children." In another example from the Qur'an, "a mysterious stranger kills a youth because he is troublesome to his parents, 'so that their Lord might replace him with a better one'" (187). Boswell finds examples in tales from many regions, all supporting his interpretation that changeling lore "encouraged the belief that the devil might replace a good child with a bad one, for whom parents need feel no moral responsibility. Such notions might easily excuse or even inspire the abandonment of a troublesome child" (380). Although this may seem a stretch, I've actually heard similar attestations by women threatened with losing their parental rights to the state or adopting fosters in my experience as a CASA. One, who was losing five children, claimed she could always have more and "get it right this time around"; another was ready to give up parental rights to one son to prevent him from "ruining the chances" of reunification with her younger two children. I bring up these examples not out of disrespect (in fact, I have deep respect for the second speaker) but to suggest how close to home, socially conditional, and absolutely possible such thinking about children can be. It simply goes unrepresented unless through vilifying, mother-blaming sensationalism.

In one Scandinavian example, racism plays a clear role, with a plot that will sound familiar to anyone who has read Mark Twain's *Pudd'nhead Wilson* (1894): "A queen abandons twins who are so dark and ugly that she is ashamed of them, by forcing a servant to exchange for them her own beautiful son.... Ironically, the handsome child turns out to be cowardly, and the ugly twins to be brave and noble, a twist of fate which subtly draws attention to the optimistic prospects of foundlings, and—somewhat paradoxically—to the importance of lineage and blood" (389). And, of course, it could be read specifically as a cautionary tale to women to protect bloodlines, which really means protecting patriarchally defined property through dutiful sexual fidelity. But, again, the focus seems to be on the raw deal of interchangeability, the fact that the exchange is not equal or profitable rather than a damning of exchangeability itself.

In fact, the gifting and swapping of children are probably as old as human history, and certainly societies developed laws and methods for handling them in ways that were deemed appropriate within their familial and communal structures. In most, children had to be given freely by parental consent or meet with punishment. For example, in seventeenth-century Germanic tribes, "kidnappers were handed over to the relatives of the child, who could kill them or sell them into slavery. But, as in the case of Roman law, these measures were actually designed to protect status more than children: parents could farm their children out at a very low fee and forget them, so long as they were not made slaves; slave children became the property of those who found them (as opposed, for example, to the rule in the East by this time that all abandoned children were free): only natural children could inherit" (Boswell 207). Oblation was one such highly organized invention borrowed from an earlier precedent in Ming and early Ch'ing China, allowing parents to commit their child to lifelong service within a monastery. John Boswell suggests, "Oblation was in many ways the most humane form of abandonment ever devised in the West," because it guaranteed survival (238–39). But, of course, children who became oblates had no say in the matter.

In *The Golden Compass* (1995), Philip Pullman spins oblation as a violation in which adults clearly do not know what is best for a child. One way he does this is by making his villains complicit with a corrupt but powerful church abducting children supposedly for the betterment of humanity. Abduction fronts as protection. Although oblation in the novel occurs without the parental consent given to the church in the actual centuries-old tradition, Pullman highlights the lack of child consent in either type of exchange by making it outright kidnapping. The looming threat of being taken by Gobblers (General Oblation Board) is the object of children's scariest tales and taunts. When Lyra tries to rescue her friend, Roger, who has been taken, she discovers that oblation involves a surgical procedure called "intercision," in which children are severed from their daemons (animal alter egos and companions) to immunize them from Dust, a metaphysical occurrence yet unexplained. Mrs. Coulter heads the nefarious organization of the GOB, explaining, "It's not something for children to worry about. But the doctors do it for the children's own good, my love. Dust is something bad, something wrong, something evil and wicked. Grownups and their daemons are infected with Dust so deeply that it's too late for them. They can't be helped.... But a quick operation means they're safe from it." But Lyra can see through this eerily familiar logic, pointing to the hypocrisy of the adults in charge: "If he's got Dust and you've got Dust, and the Master of Jordan and every other grownup's got Dust, it must be all right" (283). Insisting upon her disingenuous romantic view of childhood and scientific basis in development, Coulter explains that "at the age we call puberty, the age you're coming to very soon, darling, daemons bring all sort of troublesome thoughts and feelings, and that's what lets the Dust in. A quick little operation before that, and you're never troubled again" (284). In the name of protection, the Gobblers rationalize that they are fixing their victims in a permanent state of childhood innocence, but it is clear they are keeping them controllable, revealed by the fact that only their adult employees have had the intercision. The fact that most oblates come from poorer families also suggests that the procedure is selectively useful for maintaining social control, not the welfare of children.

Although Lyra is saved from intercision by Mrs. Coulter, she eventually discovers her true biological parentage (she had been living as an orphan in the care of her school administrators). She also discovers that, like the intercised and malleable adults, she has been used by both of her parents as a pawn in their experiments to lure other children—any protection or affection they have granted her was designed to harm other people's children. All for the sake of their quest against Dust—they would not sacrifice their own child, but they would sacrifice anyone else's. The fact that the ending—with child sacrifice, parental betrayal, and Lyra's recognition that she and her daemon, Pan, are completely alone in any effort toward justice—was bizarrely absent from the film adaptation speaks to how threatening it was to family sentimentality. But in the novel, the conflict yields the insight that forces Lyra to realize her solidarity with other people's children and give up on the strange hidden family romance that would provide her with parents.

Even the Gyptians who aid her in her quest to find Roger have their own motives, and they fail to take all of her strategies seriously in spite of their belief that she is a prophesied protector of the people (205). Iorek Byrnison, who becomes a heroic sort of psychological parent to Lyra, not only puts the child first in terms of protecting and following her leadership, he also is able to model a liberating autonomy for her. Whereas her biological parents had been, each in their own way, sacrificing children to sever their soulmate-daemons, the ice bears create their own.[22] Iorek tells Lyra, "My armor is made of sky iron, made for me. A bear's armor is his soul, just as your daemon is your soul" (197). Later when he explains that "I made it myself from sky metal. Until that I was incomplete," she comprehends that "bears can make their own souls" (224). This is, I think, a rather powerful declaration of agency, encouraging us to further consider the ways in which we make ourselves and make our own families—even those aspects of our lives that we are born with, the identities biologically essentialized through family conventions, can be cultivated according to choice and free will.

Mr. Scoresby says of Lyra, "[T]his child seems to me to have more free will than anyone I have ever met" (310), which is funny from a traditionally religious standpoint; after all, within a metaphysical framing, free will is something we either have or we don't—it is what we do with it that matters. But the comment draws attention to another matter close to my argument: perhaps she *exercises* free will more because she is technically not tethered to family. Sara Ahmed argues that "willfulness is deposited in the figure of the child" because the "child also signifies the not-yet-subject, as well as the subject-to-become" (123). She also expounds, "I think this might be why some of the most positive representations we have of willful children are also of children who happen to be orphans, and thus have a certain freedom from the family" (232).

A child's "soul" is not just for bartering away to the church or for subjugating to reflect an adult "owner's" power, just as a child is not for selling into servitude or slavery, kidnapping for ransom, adopting as a prop in conspicuous consumption, isolating on a safe but inaccessible island, or the means of getting that foster care check every month.

Exchanges involving children also shouldn't be for the sake of nonconsensual experimentation and unwilling harvesting of body parts, cases against which most of us would agree that willful, kinless children should be able to band together as collective participants, especially where family, institutions, or states fail to offer necessary protections. There are many obstacles to children creating solidarity amongst themselves as a political group.[23] A major one is the privatized isolation of nuclear family, in which their earliest peer bonds may be limited by how many siblings they have. Orphans, throwaways, and the cast out have been conveniently (whether or not painfully) freed of such emotional and structural tethers. A penetrating dramatization of child isolation within family, and family isolation within community (without interdependence or reciprocity), can be seen in Neal Shusterman's *Unwind* (2007), about a dystopian future in which children can be "unwound" (disassembled for harvesting parts) at the request of parents who are dissatisfied with their development and want a do-over. This, of course, allows for the customizing of kids over time, eliminating undesirables, and viewing them all as property to be manipulated as biomatter when they reach the "age of reason" (223). Once they are assigned to be unwound, kids go from being their parents' property to the state's, which means that AWOL teens, by running away, are committing a "federal crime" of "stealing ourselves" (56). In a context in which having children is a little bit like buying a car, parents' consumer choices feel like freedom, and that delusion co-opts future consumers into gratitude toward the system, as one child who got a lung from an Unwind expresses: "The only reason I'm alive is because that kid got unwound" (169). Which I guess means we are supposed to believe with all this harvesting and transferring of organs, they can't just sign their driver's licenses as donors[24] for when they actually die of hopefully more humane causes. Or, they are so deceived by the ideologies of their culture that they can't think "outside of the box" that a technological capacity for unwinding has built around them. Shusterman takes this scene far enough into the absurd for his entire audience to get his satiric jibe: "unwinding does help people. If it wasn't for unwinding, there'd be bald guys again—and wouldn't that be horrible?" (168). And perhaps he is pointed about the unethical role played by allopathic medicine, like the disposable consumer culture surrounding it, neglecting preventative health measures in favor of expensive, exclusive, shorter-term triage: "If there wasn't unwinding, they'd go back to trying to cure diseases instead of just replacing stuff with someone else's" (169). Shusterman's futuristic fictive reality dramatizes something we can see in the limited choices made in the twenty-first century as well: unregulated markets are rarely a good thing for the disempowered young.

Where there is "free" trade, there will also be discriminatory practices. To use an example relevant to my larger argument, consider international adoptions. As an unevenly regulated market, consumers with enough wealth can customize their children to order, controlling for various traits rarer in supply rather than caring for those in need. Of course, racism plays a role in demand: "U.S. racism, not a shortage of babies of a certain skin color, facilitated the turn to transnational adoption" (Oaks 173). Why do some celebrities adopt children whose only biological relatives will remain in their native country, when there are legally adoptable children of color in their home country who have neither a mother nor father able (or allowed) to care for them? Whether you call it a "consumer trend" or idiosyncratic personal choice, it is an ideological valuation, inflected by globalizing paternalism, rather than a priority to meet the needs of community. And a similarly discriminating valuation leaves local children in group homes or homelessness stateside. Michele Goodwin wrote in 2010 there were "more than five hundred thousand children live in foster care arrangements," indicating "the strain on the current child welfare system to serve the needs of all kids. But as interesting is what such statistics reveal about potential parents. Each year, thousands of children are adopted from abroad, often through cumbersome, complicated processes that can take years" (10). It is also prohibitively expensive: "Adoption is a multi-million-dollar transnational service, in which aesthetics and genetic traits are significantly scrutinized. However, there are pitfalls in the free market model, in which wealth and the ability to navigate complicated systems with the aid of sophisticated lawyers may prevail over child welfare. In such cases, the best interests of children are subordinate to adult preferences" (Goodwin 10–11). Consumer choice for would-be parents trumps child needs.

Exchange value of children needing homes can also be affected by circumstances of their relinquishment that fit into well-worn sentimental narrative grooves. For example, children surrendered at safe havens have the cachet associated with rags-to-riches stories of the nineteenth and early twentieth centuries. In such cases, adoptive parents become heroic benefactors. One adoptive parent of a legally abandoned baby admits, "We wanted to adopt, but adopting a Safe Surrender baby was even better" (Oaks 174). His choice of words here is curious—suggesting that the act of adopting a surrendered baby is more ethical (thus self-righteously motivated), or that somehow these babies are simply *better* babies (afforded greater exchange valuation). Laury Oaks comes to the latter conclusion in her response: "The superlative value of safe haven infants is demonstrated not only in their rarity, but also in reports about the outpouring of interest in adopting specific babies when their cases are covered in the news" (174). The baby business, like pet adoption campaigns or the J. Peterman catalog, creates exchange value and public interest through narrative. Like Popeye's not-so-laborious unwrapping of the surprise package nestling Swee'pea, a key function of narratives that enhance adoptability is an erasure of the biology of birthing: "Running counter to open adoption, both safe haven and international adoption processes share a legal fiction about the baby as a parentless orphan, and subsequently advance a rescue narrative" (Oaks 180). Such narratives also tend to erase the economic crises that leave abandoning parents little choice or ability to parent their children: extreme economic inequity, or poverty, poverty, poverty.

So in a market based on wealthy parents' demands, supply comes at a cost to the unchosen children and their biological parents, whose needs are obscured by the seemingly necessary but inequitable solution. My own state's naïve, sweeping, and short-lived experiment in child saving will help me to make this point. In 2008, Nebraska was the last state in the United States to adopt a "safe haven law" providing designated safe spaces where minors can be dropped off for state sanctuary, resulting in the anonymous, voluntary termination of biological parental rights and responsibilities with legal immunity. Like baby boxes around the world, such surrender sites were usually intended, and specifically indicated in the laws adopted, for infants. But when Nebraska extended its version of the law for any minor up through seventeen years of age, a much needed eye-opening occurred. Although we are one of the least populous states, with a total state population of less than 2 million (half of the population of any major city), we nonetheless had thirty-three minors surrendered at safe haven sites in three months, five of them from as far out of state as Michigan, Washington, Georgia, and Arizona (Eckholm). None of them was an infant—many were teens, often with mental illness or behavior problems that their parents couldn't handle without proper support. Whether or not one believes surrender sites like safe havens and baby boxes to be a tolerable solution, seeing the numbers of parents who feel they have no other recourse should at least be a wake-up call. Laury Oaks agrees: "Events that unfolded in Nebraska demonstrated the need for a reproductive justice framework that emphasizes the importance of understanding safe laws as a strategy that works against addressing the social injustices that compel infant, and even child, abandonment" (152). Such instances give us a more realistic idea of the pressures parents and their children often have to face in isolation.

Detractors from such policies suggest that the opportunity for anonymous surrender reduces accountability and so makes it too easy, thus increasing the number of children abandoned: "The radical adoptee advocacy group

Figure 3.4. Author photo. Nebraska safe haven policy updated.

Bastard Nation has been particularly critical of U.S. safe haven laws, which it has opposed unequivocally" as "baby dump laws" (Oaks 22). I'm not sure what alternatives Bastard Nation might have recommended in desperate cases. But their propaganda repeats a panic-provoking trope that was influential in creating safe havens: the baby in a dumpster. Laury Oaks writes, "The character of the desperate teenager who conceals or denies her pregnancy, gives birth unattended, and might dump her newborn was a prominent feature of rhetoric surrounding the passage of safe haven laws" (77). As with Skinner's "baby box" the panic centered on a containment motif: "The dumpster itself often was used as a shorthand for all abandonment locations, conjuring the treatment of a newborn by irresponsible mothers as disposable trash" (78). The Nebraska safe haven fiasco unfortunately seemed to confirm another way of scapegoating minors through the "babies having babies" stereotype in one case: a sixteen-year-old mother who surrendered *herself* with her 10-month-old baby. In this curious inversion of teens "stealing ourselves" as in *Unwind*, media focused more on her act than the fact that she herself was a "throwaway" teen: "The teen and her son arrived at an Omaha hospital after being displaced from the teen's mother's home, and both were placed in foster care" (151). This was at a time when antiyouth rhetoric had dominated the news for at least a decade, with teen pregnancy as a potent red herring in spite of its decreasing incidence: "Teen pregnancy itself is politicized and stigmatized as a social problem, while at the same time experts observe that its incidence is decreasing" and "the birth rate for teenagers reached an historic low across all ethnic groups" (80). Mike Males has debunked the myth of teen pregnancy in both his *Framing Youth: 10 Myths about the Next Generation* (1999) and, in greater, updated detail, in *Teenage Sex and Pregnancy: Modern Myths, Unsexy Realities* (2010), where he argues that "'teenage sex' and 'teenage pregnancy' do not exist as distinct teenage phenomena, but are straight-line functions of economic conditions and the sexual behaviors of adults" (10). And whereas the stereotyped teen mother has been ubiquitously racialized, Males points out that "*teen birth rates track not racial composition, but poverty levels*" (117).

In *Unwind*, teen pregnancy is depicted as a prominent cause for abandonment, and children are only valuable in their exchangeability, but like the safe haven laws, there is an out for unwilling or incapable parents called "storking." Law protects the abandonment of infants on doorsteps, as long as the parent abandoning the infant does not get caught in the act, leaving the responsibility to those who've been "storked." One character, Lev, reminds others with whom he is on the run, that "Moses was put in a basket in the Nile and was found by Pharaoh's daughter. He was the first storked baby" (Shusterman 72). (Incidentally, the first state to adopt a safe haven law was Texas, where it has been called the Baby Moses Law.) The protagonist, Connor, has "seen a storked baby twice on his own doorstop," explicitly revealing the neighborhood's disturbingly believable secret of passing off the responsibility (61). He understands the dire consequence of the community's secretive actions, telling Lev and Risa that when he was seven, his parents, who had already raised two storked children, found another arrival but left it very early in the morning on a neighbor's doorstep instead of raising it as required by custom: "My parents figured, who's gonna know? My parents swore us to secrecy and we waited to hear the news from across the street about their new, unexpected arrival . . . but it never came. They never talked about getting storked and we couldn't ask them because it would be a dead giveaway that we'd dumped the baby on them." No one claims the baby, "and then two weeks later, I open the door, and there on that stupid welcome mat, is another baby in a basket." But it is not another baby; it is the same baby: "It turns out that the baby had been passed around the neighborhood for two whole weeks—each morning, left on someone else's doorstep . . . only now it's not looking too good" (73–74). Irresponsibility for other people's children, lack of accountability, secrecy all conspire in this story with disastrous results. Not only does the baby die, but "[p]eople were crying like it was their baby that had died . . . And that's when I realized that the people who were crying—they were the ones who had passed that baby around. They were the ones, just like my own parents, who had a hand in killing it" (75).

Shusterman does not let his readers get away with sentimental masking of responsibility or accountability, drilling in his point through Connor's commentary: "In a perfect world mothers would all want babies, and strangers would open up their homes to the unloved ... But this isn't a perfect world. The problem is the people who think it is" (75). Actually, in a perfect world, dads would also want their babies and characters in young adult novels would hold parenting gender equity as an ideal, but I quibble. Connor's first two statements are beloved clichés of young adult fiction, but the last requires some unfolding—idealism about communities coming together allows and shrouds unthinkable thus deniable individual actions. Actualizing such ideals requires the kindness of strangers and the ability of communities to support each-other interdependently with transparency. After all, the group of "other people" needing to recognize social imperfections and take responsibility for child welfare includes you and me. Passing along the problem isn't progress; it is turning your back on it.

Even during the adoption craze of the 1920s, so popular in newsmedia, there were signs of our duplicitous lip-service toward cherishing children in order to mask communal lack of commitment and family isolation. With the introduction of Walt's foundling son, Skeezix, to Frank King's *Gasoline Alley* (1918–59), we can see the standard trope of the baby in a basket on the doorstep. Like Popeye, Walt Wallet is "gifted" this abandoned baby personally, by someone who knows he is "kind hearted" (see figure 3.5). In the dailies version of this discovery from February 14–15, 1921, Walt, much like Popeye, reveals his genuine care but cluelessness about how to handle a baby (2005, n.p.). But in the Sunday version introducing Skeezix on February 20, 1921, another dimension is added. Neighbors drop in to see the new baby and offer their sentiments, with praise, baby talk, and admonishment for the abandoning parent: "Isn't he grand! I'd give anything if I had a baby like that!" and "Who in the world would leave such a sweetie? If I had 'oo I'd love 'oo to pieces!" (see figure 3.6). But in the next frames, when Walt offers the baby to the fawning couples, the tone and body language instantly change: "One is plenty! Oh, no, we couldn't possibly!" (2007). Through humor, King demonstrates the disconnection between sentimentality and commitment surrounding child care.

Protectionism allows us to do just that by downplaying the girding self-reliance of actual children in crisis and hiding the extremes of conflicts they face. Although Theodore Dalrymple's rhetoric tends to be reactionary, I appreciate his unsentimental clarity on this process: "Sentimentality is the progenitor, the godparent, the midwife of brutality" (50). It allows us to refocus our fear and anger in a compensatory and counterproductive manner. Dalrymple even claims, "Sentimentality has been the forerunner and accomplice of brutality

Figure 3.5. Gasoline Alley, by Frank King. February 14–15, 1921. Public domain.

wherever the policies suggested by it have been put into place" because the "cult of feeling destroys the ability to think, or even the awareness that it is necessary to think" (231). Within the context of the cult of sentimentality, an insistence on seeing castaway children as either damaged beyond repair or products of miraculous conception with erasable origins often diverts our compassion, offering through conjecture a simple identifiable party to blame. We can imagine someone else responsible and scapegoat, rather than revise policy, wallowing briefly then retreating into the solace of delusional denial in order to think the world just perfect enough to tolerate without action. Or we can dare to reflect a bit longer on our own obligation to help—better yet, even find a practical solution.

Although I'm not suggesting there is any totalizing solution through grassroots action alone, a pertinent example to both containment motifs and hopes for community commitment can be seen in the "Baskets for Babies" project—a kind of neighborhood inversion of storking. In response to a media story on a girl "dumping" her baby behind a Pittsburgh church, one of the congregants, Gigi Kelly, a local nurse, "found an old laundry basket, lined it with a warm blanket and put it on her front porch. Then she called reporters with a plea for young mothers to bring their babies to her. I'll take it from there, she promised.... With only a manual typewriter and a fax machine, she turned her Baskets for Babies program into a public-awareness campaign for young moms who think they have nowhere to turn. Now when night falls on Pittsburgh, 608 families leave their porch lights on and have their baskets ready" (Roche).

Figure 3.6. Gasoline Alley, by Frank King. February 20, 1921. Public domain.

Although no one had used Kelly's service at the time of media reporting it in 2000, "the project served as a platform for a future safe haven policy" (Oaks 50). In this way Kelly at least modeled effectively for her community that "other people's children" aren't just other people's problems.

Lenore Skenazy, proponent of "free-range parenting," calls out "shamers and blamers" who troll online over the supposedly finer (but often asinine) points of parenting, pointing out that "the real impulse behind that reaction is our own fear" (55–57). Blaming other people's children and "interparent swiping" only fuels more fear, accomplishing nothing constructive, instead merely tucking real problems out of public view, so community members can take a pass on sharing responsibility (110). And the popular culture we create and consume reflects this habit. Maggie Gallagher recounts her father-in-law's reaction to pervasive narratives like *Romeo and Juliet*, *Fiddler on the Roof*, and *Bend It Like Beckham*: "Why is it that parents are *never* right?" (167). It's true that dysfunctional families make better copy and get more screen time.

Likewise, pop psychology (or the public consumption of self-help reading quite remote from legitimate practice) actually thrives on blaming parents, or as my partner's mother used to often complain in exasperation, "It's always the mother's fault." She was right—it's simply reductive logic, unfair and untrue. Blaming parents just gives an excuse for community inaction, whereas solidarity between parents and recognizing children as a group with unique political interests that can't be met in the private sphere alone might create empathy, cohesion, and positive results.

When we keep children, like private property, segregated from the public sphere as part of "homelife" only, we are less likely to see where our protections imprison them. And when we allow sentimentality to cloud our compassionate thought with emotional dismissals, we are bound to make poor decisions for others as a group. As early as 1900, Charlotte Perkins Gilman argued, "The one main cause of our unfairness to children is that we consider them wholly in a personal light. Justice and equity, the rights of humanity, require a broader basis than blood relationship.... One's own child and one's neighbour's child grow up and pass out of childhood, and with them goes one's interest in children" (118).[25] This rotating community investment further islands children while in the temporary confines of childhood. Gilman explains, "We should bear in mind in studying children that we have before us a permanent class.... As members of a society, we find that they received almost no attention. They are treated as members of the family by the family, but not even recognised as belonging to society" (119). Counter to recognizing children as a "permanent class" that simply cycles members in and out as they age, we atomize their identities as reflections of parents, or the nuclear family, without providing ample opportunity for them to discover a larger group identity and find solidarity with others of their current "class," forming their own publics when needed. There is, then, unfortunately nothing new about this problem, but scholars from multiple disciplines and activists from multiple perspectives seem to agree that the shrinking, controlled sphere of childhood has intensified with the rise of consumer capitalism. According to Danah Boyd, minors in the digital age have the same "limited geographic freedom" that their parents may have had but even less "unstructured time," and "socializing is also more homebound," thus limiting the potential of sustainable publics forming through school (21, 1). Rather than affording them greater privacy and autonomy, the crunch of older politicians' fears prohibits access to unsurveilled publics with age peers (19). As a result, even social networks online are inadequate for the privacy of a young person who needs to "carve out an identity that is not defined solely by family ties" (17). The dimensions and contours of the island have changed, but it is still a very controlled space.

Another detriment to community interdependence when it comes to parenting is the trend in recent decades toward extreme, individualistic protectionism. Hara Estroff Marano and Lenore Skenazy both call out the growth of "mommy (and sometimes daddy) Web sites" for parents "who delight in taking potshots at each other's parenting. The rise of these sites began in the mid-nineties ... which dovetails almost precisely with the spike in helicopter parenting" (Skenazy 109–10). National rhetoric somehow made oxymoronic sense of every child being "exceptional" in his or her own little nuclear family, which is of course statistically impossible in the larger picture, which is thoroughly obscured in rhetoric of privatization. Gaia Bernstein and Zvi Triger call this new extreme of the old "selfless" model "intensive" overparenting; Hara Estroff Marano calls it "invasive" parenting. This process of deeming individual children "exceptional" rather than children as a group, the epicenter of parental focus gained dominance in middle-class practice, belief, or at least discourse, in the 1990s reflected in such scholarly, popular, and consumer campaigns as Baby Einstein, Baby Beethoven, and Baby Mozart—promoting exceptionality with earlier and earlier educational interventions to enhance baby's future intellectual performance and provide educational advantages. The resulting "Mozart effect," seen in research on child development indicating improvements in spatial and math skills demonstrated by babies who listen to his music, was reflected in the market by consumer goods designed to enhance baby's "exceptional" brain. Diane Ehrensaft describes the expectation of toddlers "following in Mozart's footsteps" as a self-deluding imposition hiding monetary expectations: "We become fairy godparents who shield our children from any bad feeling and wave our magic wands filled with stickers and stars so that as in the fairy tale, our sons and daughters can believe that anything they touch will turn to gold. But we never lose sight of the fact that it is gold that we want for them" (128). Instead of actually providing these advantages, such approaches actually presume "children, irrespective of their age, as vulnerable and helpless," deincentivizing independence up through one's twenties (Bernstein and Triger 1275–76). Not every child can become a child prodigy—a baby Mozart—and apparently the trend in overparenting proved that point saliently. This pedagogical and consumer hype would ultimately backfire: "It appears that while in the past the job of the parent was to expose the child to the outside world, today's parents seek to protect their child from the outside world. An emerging body of research, in addition to significant anecdotal evidence, suggests that current trends of Intensive Parenting can in fact be harmful to children" (1275). But this impossible impetus that encouraged parents to be in competition with each other through their children's accomplishments revealed a great deal about how we perceive and *use* children.

Why should we want our own child to be exceptional, which by definition connotes "standing apart," in disconnection from others? Would you really want your kid to be like Mozart? He was kind of a young twerp who turned into an overgrown twerp (no disrespect—love his music, and his letters, but come on—this is not a person I'd want to have to clean up after or tend). No doubt some of Mozart's less attractive traits had some connection to being a child prodigy, dare I even say spoiled (or damaged like so many child celebrities?).

We have to be able to distance ourselves from the actual selfish motives involved in selfless parenting. Rebekka Habermas argues that in the first quarter of the nineteenth century (coincidentally, in the second and third decades following Mozart's death), with the growth of industrialization in Western countries, the ideal clearly emerged of parents holding each other to "new standards of selflessness" (48). While middle-class families became nuclearized and property privatized, so, of course, did childhood, but with benefits for so-called "selfless" parents: "The more children came to be regarded as objects deserving of care and affection, the higher the status they attained in the marital relationship" (50). Likewise, in what Dalrymple calls the "toxic cult of sentimentality," parents consider children, to some degree, as a reflection of themselves. Even syrupy representations of "other people's children" down on their luck can "evoke instead, and are appeals to, a warm and self-congratulatory feeling of sympathy, that assures the person experiencing it that he is a moral person capable of empathising with others, but requires nothing more of him. The comforting and unearned warmth of feeling is an end in itself." As a result, very little actually changes except for slight variations in a recurring performance of pity that permits detachment. In fact, "Sentimentality then becomes coercive, that is to say manipulative in a threatening way" (Dalrymple 92). In such a context, if your reaction is to insist that the problem indeed exists and something better must be done, you are at best considered a killjoy and at worst accused of being unfeeling for not conforming to "higher" sentiments.

In the threat of the Gobblers, Philip Pullman highlights an uncomfortable parallel between child abduction and the extremes of unchecked protections cloaked in secrecy, and through storking, Neal Shusterman demonstrates a breakdown of community interdependence associated with the extremes of isolating children in nuclearized families and excessively privatizing control over offspring. Coercive sentimentalism puts a great burden on those sentimentalized as well. It's not like children's authors can't grasp this reality; many do, and profoundly. Another example, from Maurice Sendak, bears mention for its poignant contribution to understanding the issues discussed in this chapter: *Outside over There* (1981). A changeling tale in picture-book form, it was Sendak's favorite, and perhaps most personal. It also has a subtext that is revealing about how protectionism can operate psychologically. On a straightforward level, it is about Ida, who doesn't watch her baby sister closely enough although it is her responsibility, and as a result, in true cautionary form, the baby is kidnapped by goblins to "be a nasty goblin's bride!" Like Orpheus, Ida uses her music to beguile the captors. She succeeds at rescuing her sister, and the book ends with her father's remote reminder that "Ida must watch the baby and her Mama," demonstrating that Ida's responsibilities also include reciprocity as part of her relationship with her parents: as a family they are interdependent.

In the opus of an artist who created picture books heavily layered with enigmatic meanings, this one requires the most explanation, like the multiple appearances of Mozart. Sendak claimed, "In some way, *Outside Over There* is my attempt to make concrete my love of Mozart, and to do it as authentically and honestly in regard to his time as I could conceive it, so that every color, every shape is like part of his portrait" (qtd. in Cech 218). Certainly, the aesthetics of Mozart's time are present, as is the infantilization of Ida's mother, reminiscent of Bernardin's Virginia, who like Virginia's love, Paul, is reading a missive from her beloved who is at sea, in this case, Ida's father. John Cech contrasts Mozart in Sendak's personal symbology to Ida's father: "Mozart is the reliable father who offers access to the powerful, healing world of art—not the one who carelessly 'dumps' responsibilities on a child in his absence" (237). Here, Cech is speaking of Sendak's personal connection with the historical figure of Mozart—his history as much as his music. It is certain that Mozart, as a child prodigy (not just imagined father figure), would appeal to Sendak, for whom respecting kids as persons was a paramount concern. As a child, Mozart was not recognized as he should have been when he began his career composing at age seven. According to Mozart's father, "instead of encouraging such a heaven-sent talent" the public failed to take his work seriously because of his youth, and "the persecutions of my son began" by "the poor child's enemies" (Eisen 78–79). Arguing that a child (at this point he was twelve) "is incapable of writing such music," jealous and condescending performers sabotaged a production of his work (80). The life of a prodigy hardly sounds easy.

But I am interested in the kidnapping theme of *Outside over There*, especially the cloaked references to the Lindbergh baby. Like the Lindbergh kidnapper(s), the goblins enter through the window, and Ida backs out the same window and falls, although of course the book has a happy ending, whereas the famous kidnapping of Charles Lindbergh Jr. did not (the kidnapper's fall from the ladder killed the child). As narrated in the media, kidnapping stories are modern-day versions of changeling tales, which often only involve a one-way swap. John Cech explains, the Lindbergh kidnapping "terrified Sendak as a child, especially as the search for the child dragged on for months" (231). It was clearly a defining moment in his childhood that shaped his view of children—notably not as victims, however. A closer glimpse in his later life explains how and why.

During his final interview, with Gary Groth, Sendak spoke at length about his experience on seeing a newspaper photo in which the Lindbergh son's dead body was clearly visible. When then four-year-old Sendak tried to point it out to his mother at a newsstand, she chastised him: "You didn't see that, that's disgusting! Why do you think of such things?" And his father said later, "I don't want you to talk about that!" These denials (more like calling him a liar, really) had a lasting affect: "I was convinced that I was crazy and that I saw a dead baby in the newspaper.... It's only in the past few years that I realized Colonel Lindbergh was enraged that that picture was used and it was taken off the afternoon edition; I saw the morning edition" (Groth 79). So his parents' gaslighting on the issue stayed with him until his final years. Whether or not it was their intention, he was punished for innocently speaking about something he plainly saw—strong evidence of the selective ignorance we impose in the guise of innocence.

An older, wiser Sendak observed the same kind of vehement denial in discourses following 9/11, and he uses one example to indicate children's need for reciprocal understanding and responsive protectiveness toward parents who insist they maintain appearances of safe, selective ignorance. A friend whose daughter went to school near the towers witnessed the attack and hurried to get her from school. The child told her father, "Oh, it's wonderful, Daddy, we had a wonderful time. The smoke was all over and the butterflies were flying all over the place. We saw butterflies!" (Groth 80). After a day of games, ice cream, TV, and "everything they could to obliterate the day," the daughter confessed at bedtime, "Daddy, I didn't really see butterflies. They were people." Sendak would later tell his friend, her father, "Do you realize she was protecting you?" (81). Sendak makes clear that protection must recognize the reciprocity of its dynamics.

In social work, this kind of role change, in which kids protect their parents' emotional stasis (or physical well-being) is called "parentification"—like Ida's charge from her father, having the responsibilities of a parent without the power of being adult. It is often interpreted as one indicator of neglect—but it actually happens on subtle levels in happy, secure homes as well, because as much as we like to believe we can shut our happy little homes off from harsh realities of the larger world, we are part of it, and so are kids. In Sendak's first anecdote, we hear of his own parents trying to protect him but actually distressing him with destabilizing doubts that could have been honestly discussed instead and so more easily forgotten. In his second anecdote, we hear him identifying with a contemporary child who feels she must take part in protectionist pretense with her parents. It doesn't matter that her parents are acting protectively when their child's empathy prompts her adopting the pretense they themselves are wishing to uphold. As a result, the child maintains the pretense to protect their emotional vulnerability, in spite of the fact that her own experience was more traumatizing than theirs in the first place (more on breaking such pretenses in chapter 5). Children's authors can and do at times recognize the need to process distressing realities such as this one, but the inertia of traditional denial has remained powerful in formulaic books for young audiences. As in Dalrymple's argument about the "toxic cult of sentimentality," we can vicariously witness the weight of pretense and the startling reality that it can actually put the burden of protection on (parentified) kids it's meant to protect. But denial can't bring Lindbergh's baby back to life, change falling bodies into butterflies, or make untenable family life completely untraumatizing. We are the grown-ups, so we should know that.

In her memoir on foster care, Victoria Rowell offers a positive spin on the concept of parentification from interpreting it as a sign of crisis (that reveals a child's having too much responsibility for her own parents in a burdensome role reversal) to instead recognizing resilience (indicated by a young person taking responsibility for herself). She calls this self-nurturing through self-reliance "becoming my own daddy," explaining, "After all, the priests had me calling them my Father and the drunks called themselves my Daddy; hell, I might as well fill the slot myself" (171). And godspeed, sugar daddies.[26] Rowell's experience provides one example of how raising oneself by default as self-possessed "owner," like the boy in *Mister Dog*, belonging to oneself only, has its perks: "One of the things I could appreciate about being a former foster child was that there was no family to answer to or seek approval from.... [W]orrying about not living up to expectations, I never had any of those limitations." Where others "had the security, they did not have the freedom to explore who they really were; rather, it was dictated to them. There was a family protocol, a mandate to uphold the distinguished pedigree, forcing them to give up their artistic dreams" (262). I am, of course, not suggesting that all children should or even could self-parent or that all children should emancipate themselves as soon as they can handle independence. I'm simply reasserting what should be obvious: our top priority should be educating toward that goal of independence regardless, prioritizing participation as one part of that preparation.

Rowell's rocky but successful transition into independent adulthood was especially aided by two fortunate though hardly representative strokes of luck: she had "many mothers," and one of them stressed and modeled the importance of the economic self-reliance that becomes so critical for the kinless but also for girls, who are less likely to be taught this lesson: "[O]ne of the reasons Agatha encouraged me to become close to her sisters was because of the extremely positive influence their Aunt Cash had on them.... [E]ach of the Wooten sisters was ultimately self-made, and all four were property owners. Very early on, that stirred something profound in me. Proprietorship was power" (88). This is a lesson that could be impressed upon not just kinless minors but all children, especially girls, who "may intuitively figure out that the price of Daddy's care is her own frailty" (Victoria Secunda qtd. in Perle 70). But the good fortune of finding not just many mothers but true nurturers is even more difficult to guarantee.

The inequitable distribution of "exchange value" among kinless or alienated minors leaves many in more vulnerable straits. Some forms of survival can depend on who can claim you or whether or not you are strong and experienced enough to claim yourself. David F. Lancy provides a realistic reminder that we can't just snap our fingers to instantly recreate some nostalgic past norm for childrearing in larger, extended families: "Unfortunately, childrearing can no longer follow the village model because, today, being raised by your older siblings probably means you're on your way to becoming a gang member" (156). But our denial doesn't work either. The kinless and the voluntarily kinfree can at least rebuild their own kith, through public identity and engaged community care. Middle-class parents and elite policy makers will have to take their class blinders off.

We need to revive public roles for nonbiological nurturers and esteem those who fill them. Looking over millennia for models proving this possible, John Boswell recounts both negative and positive evidence. Like controversial baby boxes, safe havens, and "storking" in *Unwind*, Boswell found that

> "fostering" of various sorts appears to have had an intricately ambivalent effect on the position of children, somewhat like that of oblation: while it might establish a powerful bond between the foster family and the child, making up in many ways for the distance or absence of natal parents, this very fact probably encouraged parents to resign children to foster care more casually, more completely, and on a wider scale than they would have otherwise, just as oblation, by removing the more troubling aspects of anonymous abandonment, subtly promoted its more structured form. (359–60)

Where we provide anonymous opportunities for safe surrender, we may, in fact, permit it, which might increase abandonments but still cut down on neonaticides. Larger social implementations can sanction abandonment, but dire circumstances on the microsocial level are what motivate the desperate act in the first place. One cannot deny that by putting such structures in place, and creating models for willing community care, fostering children once "contributed to an atmosphere in which 'foster' relationships were idealized as great and ennobling rather than makeshift or second-rate, thereby greatly offsetting disadvantages 'foster children' of any sort—abandoned or not—might have suffered" (360). Perhaps the difference in these interpretations—dangerous permissiveness as a social sanctioning of abandonment or reaffirmation of public responsibility—depends on whether you are looking at structure or superstructure. Either way, much could be done on both ends to bolster community care and encourage each of us to value not just caretakers but other people's children.

4

The Prison House of Comics Censorship and Participatory Resistance

Heaven lies about us in our infancy!
Shades of the prison-house begin to close
Upon the growing boy
   —William Wordsworth (1804)

If you are going to buy a playpen, do it before the baby is used to the freedom of the open floor, otherwise he may object to being put behind bars.
   —Dr. Benjamin Spock (1946)

Histories of American childhood and comics are fascinatingly entwined. While the youth demographic as a consumer class grew in the 1930s and 1940s, so did the use of this medium associated with them. Patricia Crain points out that even the earliest books marketed to kids signified their entry into a consumer class, even when parents or relatives technically did the purchasing: "The book is one of the first consumer objects addressed specifically to children, marketed and advertised especially to them." This significance is demonstrated by inscriptions: "Some inscribers note that the book was 'bought,' sometimes with the price."[1] With the rise of pulps and comic books, such ownership was far more cheaply accessible—and these new owners became proud custodians and promoters of the medium. Any child with pocket change could frequent the nearest drugstore to peruse the huge turnover of titles, then buy, share, or recommend their favorites. Such an act, according to Crain, "represents one of the child's first encounters with private property," and "a claim of ownership would be served by signing the book.... One might say that the modern child is positively identified as one who owns—or more strictly, one who performs the rites of ownership," thereby asserting "a right to property, and implicitly mak[ing] a claim for one's status as not owned oneself" (115). Making these rites of consumer choice, ownership, and symbolic self-possession more widely possible and appealing for young audiences, comics would provide the "permanent class" of minors with a public forum during following decades, but they would also lead to counterefforts as that outlet threatened the recently tightened controls of the middle-class nuclearized family. Some adults were concerned about their loosening grip on the flow of information as well as the growing industry and medium through which it was flowing. Fears spread these worries to vendors, librarians, and parents, propagandistically to keep children in the little boxes safely allotted them within a private sphere.

Mass popularity and a double punch of visual and verbal content gave comics immediate, affective power some thought too dangerous for young minds.[2] Certainly, like any medium, it had its tasteless, unsavory, scandalous, indoctrinating, or simply high-turnover/poor-quality art and writing. Bradford Wright has demonstrated how various publishers promoted the war effort during the 1940s through a hideous vilification of ethnic others.[3] J. Edgar Hoover saw comics as a powerfully persuasive medium for promoting the necessity and reputation of his Federal Bureau of Investigation: "J. Edgar Hoover loved crime comics. He said they were 'highly important influences in creating a public distaste for crime.'... One of his favorites was *Dick Tracy*" (Powers 138). But when it came to blaming crime on "juvenile delinquency," he was more than happy to throw young people under the bus and blame their supposedly rising role in crime on their parents. By 1945, he was directing more attention to pulp publications and a radio show called "This Is Your F.B.I." In the final episode in 1953, a virulent antiyouth, antiparent approach dominated the framing narration: "Youth has been the vanguard of the criminal army in this country. The basic cause of juvenile delinquency is a lack of moral responsibility and for this the blame rests squarely on the parents of the country for it is in the home that the child must learn that others besides himself have rights and must learn the values that help him grow into a decent, law-abiding citizen—a public servant and not a public enemy" (230). Such pronouncements would be very consequential for mid-century children and teenagers.

Popular mediums could be used to indoctrinate readers nationalistically, and to believe the scapegoating of young people was legitimate. But comics additionally had a liberatory capacity for the young, by being accessible, offering at times a staggering array of choices, catering to diverse tastes, and welcoming audience participation. Even *Little Orphan Annie*'s creator, Harold Gray, used the comic strip to mobilize kids in the war effort: "The Junior Commando movement sent thousands of youngsters scrambling through junkpiles and knocking on doors to round up newspapers, scrap metal, old tires, kitchen grease—all the raw materials needed to feed the factories that were manufacturing war products" (Smith 49).[4] Operating somewhat like an Annie fan club, children wrote to Gray to enlist, like one reader from Erie: "This is our war, too, and we want to give all we can to help the soldiers who are giving all they have" (49–50). Like Hoover, however, Gray was quick to find a new target for his reader to unify against a decade later: "It often seemed that Gray's ultimate goal in his life was to offend everybody at once. If that was the case, he came close to success in 1956 with a sequence on juvenile delinquency. The bellowing of outrage reached hurricane proportions," provoking "angry editorials in union and religious publications, the syndicate's mailing bulging with letters, and—most serious of all—a number of papers canceled their subscriptions to *Little Orphan Annie*" (68). Casting teenagers as the latest American problem, he depicted them as out-of-control punks, thieves, and gang members, but his audience resisted buying into it as they had the wartime calls to action. You can't really create a child character who tugs at readers' heartstrings about children and then turn right around to blast them with antiyouth propaganda.

This is not to say that persuasive propaganda and this limited public forum were particularly distinguishable at all times. The proliferation of clubs to join and campaigns to follow certainly read as transparent gimmicks. Although certainly influencing public views, comics would eventually, at least, offer a semipublic outlet for minors to express themselves, critique, and debate matters of taste. Even where advertising and manipulation are rampant, comics could provide a rallying point in which community members could define themselves as a group.[5] Young readers could indulge in fantasy of full participation or actually subvert the efforts at controlling them. Mickey, Herbie, Jeff, and Ken, of Elmira, New York, wrote this lovely combination of stretching the permitted activity of innocent child's play and exercising ironic skill with the little leverage allowed: "Dear Mr. Hoover, Please help me and my friends start an F.B.I. club. We need guns, bombs and other things to surprise the crooks. If you don't let us have this club, it would be like having a choice between law and crime, and saying you want crime" (qtd. in Powers 189–91). Another indicates the extent to which one fan from Lansing, Michigan, still viewed ultimate power as belonging within the private sphere: "Dear Mr. Hoover: My name is Reggie and I am 11 years old. I would like to start a junior FBI, and you and me will be boss. It will be easier to boss the Junior FBI than the real FBI because if the Jr. FBI men don't want to do what you tell them, you can always call their Mother." One downside of presenting the FBI as an alternate but legal gang was that it also promoted distrust and spying on others in your community, as in this letter from Mary K. of Birmingham, Michigan: "Dear Mr. Hoover, There is a boy I know named Red Hopkins. He found a picture of you in a magazine and he cut it out. Then he took your picture and put it on a poster and wrote WANTED below the picture. I am not a squealer, but I think you should know about Red Hopkins" (197).[6] Less humorous examples reveal a rhetorical division of youth into limited types: delinquents or informers, criminals or squealers. Raymond J. of Seattle unwittingly reveals this rigid bifurcation: "Dear Mr. Hoover, In our neighborhood we have started an FBI club. So far we have caught 8 people stealing out of stores. When we catch a person shoplifting we just tell the manager of the store. Some kids think we are squealers but they are definitely of the criminal type" (qtd. in Adler). Another letter writer reinforces the typing but suggests the subversion it might allow: "Dear Chief of FBI, Have you ever heard of a child FBI man? If you could give me a gun and a badge, I could be one—Burglars wouldn't suspect a boy of 9. I know this is sneaky but I think you should try anything to catch crooks. Your friend, Mark H., Dayton, Ohio" (Adler). Modeling a supposedly legal version of spying, like all in-grouping, this rhetoric also encouraged inherent out-grouping from others, potentially eroding youth solidarity.

Such in-grouping and out-grouping at least occurred in a public sphere, outside of the influence and control of the private family.[7] As a participatory medium, comics had the potential to provide a vehicle for promoting rights to privacy, consumer choice, access to information, and rhetorical reciprocity. Many comics fans wrote and drew their own for entertainment. One impressive example of war comics by a young fan can be seen in Michael Kugler's "A Nebraska Boy's Comic Strip Narrative of World War II," which demonstrates the boy's sophisticated understanding of how to frame, create movement, and pace action through emphatic perspectives and shifting scales. James ("Jimmy") Kugler was responsive to the wartime pop culture surrounding him, repeating some "stereotypes about the Japanese and Germans in ads for films, bond sales, and editorial cartoons. Jimmy followed their lead. He included maps to help orient the reader and provide a factual, official tone that resembled the charts of the South Pacific featured in Milton Caniff's *Terry and the Pirates*, local papers, as well as film serials" (Kugler 10). The format in general, not the sometimes shockingly xenophobic content, would inspire many to try their own hand, but also would play a consequential role in censorship to come.[8]

Northwestern artist Duane Pasco recognizes Milton Caniff as a central influence to his craft: "From an early age, I started drawing the characters from *Terry and the Pirates*.... I got deeper into drawing scenes from *Terry and the Pirates* until I could produce any expression" (13). As with so many other comics fans, Pasco would also be inspired to correspond with his idol when he was fourteen: "One day I sent a large envelope to Milton Caniff" including "drawings of a couple of his characters" (13–14). Caniff's unexpected reply testifies to the respect and mentorship many comics artists granted young readers: "He had written in longhand a two-page personal letter, complimenting me on my drawing skill but suggesting that I try to develop my own style and not copy another artist. He included a lot of printed material with instructions on how to get work, syndicated pitfalls to watch out for—lots of stuff. I was grateful and overwhelmed. Never again did I copy Caniff, although I continued to read his strips and admire his artwork" (14). The medium and industry would encourage artistic development, critical analysis, career goals, and interactive participation, demonstrating a reciprocity rarely seen in the marketing of stories to young people.[9]

In a title that also demonstrates lesser-known realities (like that girls made up a significant share of comics readers at the time, and they responded to hybrid comics like romance and crime), two fan responses to the 1949 comic *Guns without Gangsters* are worth noting: both are representative of common issues addressed in letters to the editors. Anna Travis of Pennsylvania wrote: "I also wish to congratulate you on the fine spirit in which you take criticisms," clearly demonstrating her appreciation of the reciprocity of the medium but also her sophisticated understanding of the democratic process letter columns encouraged. Another fan, Shirley Storm of north Hollywood, revealed her father's approval of the title: "My father surprised me very much. You see, he usually hints about me bringing home silly, unbelievable comics, as he calls them. But this time I caught him reading your comic, GUNS AGAINST GANGSTERS. He said it was the only interesting comic I had ever brought home. So keep up the good work" (Urban and Wheeler). Such intergenerational debates on matters of taste, however, paled in comparison to public debates.

In the 1940s and 1950s, well-meaning Americans from religious, academic, and mental healthcare backgrounds had already launched a crusade against comic books, claiming they were to blame for failing literacy, moral corruption, and ultimately juvenile delinquency.[10] Among the many who have recontextualized psychiatrist Fredric Wertham's anticomics crusade from the vantage point of the twenty-first century, Carol Tilley emphatically isolates for consideration his rhetorical question from *Seduction of the Innocent*, "Is it *possible* to take a child's mind 'too seriously'?" (404). Jared Gardner has written, in his nuanced reconsideration of Fredric Wertham's role in the comics purges, that "the problem for Wertham was less that people were not taking comics seriously; rather it was that they were not taking the minds of the young readers seriously" (86). Although ultimately Wertham also failed to recognize the "creative agency" of his patients as comics readers, he is one of the few to have at least listened to and documented young readers' responses to comics during the decades of debate surrounding the supposed dangers of the medium. Often considered the culminating symbolic authority in the US conflict over comics and censorship, the Senate Subcommittee on Juvenile Delinquency, established in 1953, received hundreds of letters protesting comics censorship (largely in response to EC's call for such letters), yet, none of these, or any testimonies from comics fans, is quoted in the two-hundred-page report that resulted from the subcommittee's hearings (Pustz 41). The National Archives in Washington, DC, however, has preserved more than two hundred of these otherwise ignored letters, many of which were written by children and teens. I intend to take arguments from these letter writers and young comics readers seriously, gleaning what has been omitted or silenced in the documented history of this much-covered issue and time period.

Most comics threatened in the purges of the 1940s and 50s were crime, horror, and romance titles, through which producers were discovering and catering to a teen and adult market at that point still unrecognized by most publishers (consider the gateway example *Catcher in the Rye* came out in 1951, slowly revealing to higher-brow editors that indeed a younger market was responding to it). Adolescence was emerging as a new social and familial territory with disputed boundaries: young people were staying in school longer, prolonging their dependency, but they were also entering the workforce part time at earlier ages, thus gaining newfound if limited autonomy (Fass 7; Gilbert 20). James Gilbert has described the rise of youth consumption and resulting anxieties about youth mass culture of the 1950s as "a struggle in which the participants were arguing over power—over who had the right and responsibility to shape American culture. Although most participants invoked the name of all Americans, they probably thought of their fellow citizens only as the passive consumers of culture not its creators" (7). Many, undoubtedly, were especially unwilling to see children as active participants in mass culture, independent from family or school limitations to choice. This power struggle involved deciding when young readers became co-creators rather than passive consumers. Did the new generation of older youth with more pocket change earn the right to become participants in the creation of mass culture? How a person answered this question was likely to land them clearly on one side of the comics censorship debates from the late 40s to the mid-50s.

These "sides" could be easily categorized as reflecting adults' views on this "new life phase" of adolescence itself (although many other factors were involved). What rights to privacy and reading choice should persons in this liminal phase have? I studied the Senate Subcommittee on Juvenile Delinquency's collection of letters on comics censorship at the National Archives with this particular conflict in mind. In the following analysis, I will present archival material to concretely acknowledge the views of young readers who knowingly confronted censorship and restrictions to their consumer choice.

In 1948, Fredric Wertham called for the censorship of comics by specifically citing consumer choice as an absurd defense: "[C]hildren are bombarded with at least sixty million comic books a month. That is seven hundred and twenty million of them a year" (27). There is some truth to his critique. Anyone looking today at the numerous titles lumped together on newsstands would certainly deem most inappropriate for child readers, but we would be looking from a perspective hyperinformed by established codes of age appropriateness that were controlled then by librarians and today are prefiltered through marketing. Even Charles Schulz, who first made his fortune in an unregulated market, would mock the sight of a drugstore comics display in his June 22, 1952, strip featuring Charlie Brown ogling titles like "Mangle," "Slaughter," "Choke," and "Murder komix" (see figure 4.1). The Senate Subcommittee on Juvenile Delinquency contains a photo of a drugstore sign in Schultz's stomping ground of St. Paul, Minnesota, from the same time period declaring that "we refuse to handle Trash, Filth, or Junk to get the magazines you and we want" (see figure 4.2). Much of the resulting debates centered on matters of "taste" and who should dictate such matters.

Milton Caniff, creator of *Terry and the Pirates*, did so as well when he testified at the censorship hearings: "Insofar as deploring individual books ... that is a matter of individual taste. Some books I like which you wouldn't like. I can't say, blanketly, for instance, that I dislike all crime comics or I think they are bad. I think they are only good or bad as they affect you, the individual, and by the same token, the individual reader or any age group is affected relatively rather than as a group and cannot be condemned, I believe, as a group" (Harvey 2007, 670). Caniff's argument highlights the specific problem of targeting an entire group based on identity. Not only should taste be a matter of personal choice, but to selectively impose it on an entire group of people so defined based on the actions of individuals (if in fact juvenile delinquency had been on the rise) is clearly an encroachment upon assumed rights. Comics readers demonstrated a capacity for self-censoring in exercising their own enlightened

Figure 4.1. Peanuts, June 22, 1952. Copyright © Charles Schulz. Courtesy of Fantagraphics Books. (www.fantagraphics.com).

consumerism. For example, David Pace Wigransky, then fourteen years old, would respond to Wertham's *Saturday Review of Literature* article in the same venue by arguing, "It is high time that society woke up to the fact that children are human beings with opinions of their own, instead of brainless robots to be ordered hither and yon without even so much as asking them their ideas about anything.... The comic-book publishers know what the kids want and try to give it to them. This is not only democratic policy but good business sense" (20). Wigransky's argument (and several letters discussed below) ties the debate clearly to private matters of taste being publically determined and enforced.

Comics producers, however, largely ignored "democratic policy" in exercising their "good business sense," knowing that ultimately adults could curtail child choice. For example, Fawcett Comics Group, the publisher of *Captain Marvel* and many romance and Western titles especially popular with a teen market, directly addresses parents and advertisers, not its readership, in its 1949 pamphlet entitled *Kid Stuff Is Big Stuff a Primer of the Youth Market* defending itself against censorship: "Only the comics magazines cover this market thoroughly" and "nearly half are introduced to the comics by parents ... convincing evidence that they approve of the comics for their children's reading" (Starch and staff). This nod to parental authority, however, obscures

Figure 4.2. Photo from Senate Subcommittee on Juvenile Delinquency. National Archives.

the fact that contested comics were primarily purchased without any parental input to older minors. Their own graph comparing the age of children to their consumer autonomy and self-determination more accurately reflects that around the ages of eight to nine years, children emerge as the consumers making purchasing decisions (see figure 4.3). Just as child participation is inversely proportionate to their protection, child purchasing power and consumer choice is negatively correlated to parental discretion.

Only EC comics, the company most likely to suffer from curbing the market for "weird" and horror titles, addresses youth directly to appeal to would-be censors in its "E.C. Fan-Addict Club Bulletin," which was usually only mailed to the nine thousand members of the club, but this special bulletin was delivered to all seventeen thousand subscribers of EC titles (Nyberg 120). This "appeal to action" warns that "do-gooder groups" are arguing that comics cause juvenile delinquency and advocate censorship that will threaten the "whole comic

WHO BUYS COMICS MAGAZINES?

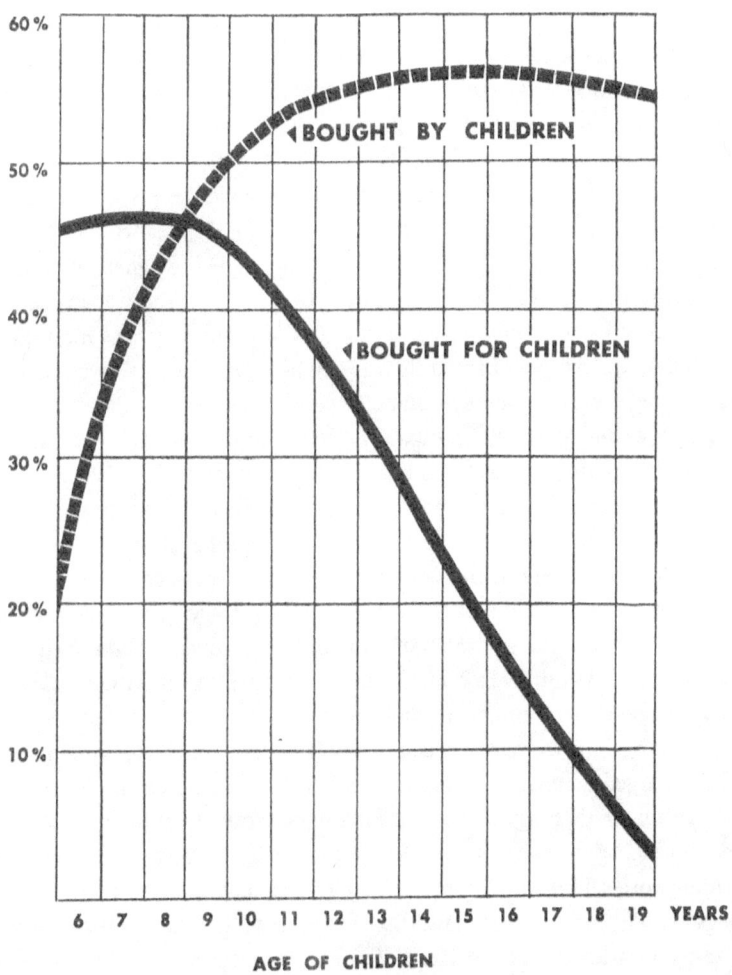

Figure 4.3. "Who Buys Comics?" from Kid Stuff Is Big Stuff, by Daniel Starch and staff, 1949, 10. National Archives, Washington. Open Access.

magazine industry," requesting that its readers join a letter-writing campaign in protest. Even so, the call for letters appeals to parental authority: "Make it a nice letter! In the case of you younger readers, it would be more effective if you could get your parents to write for you, or perhaps add a P.S. to your letter, as the Senate Subcommittee may not have much respect for the opinions of minors. Of course, if you or your parents disagree with us, and believe that comics ARE bad, let your sentiments be known on that too!" (National Archives). The more than two hundred letters still stored in the National Archives do include some from adults in support of censorship, but the EC call for letters that circulated in the subscriber newsletter was also reprinted in their comics, so for the most part it met a larger audience, including minors who were already committed to reading comics. In fact, according to a "Survey of E.C. Fan-Addict Club Letters" in the National Archives, of the 217 letters logged by the Senate Subcommittee on Juvenile delinquency, only 27 opposed comics, and of these, many specifically agreed to censoring only horror and true-crime titles, genres more liminally situated on the fringes of an audience with new purchasing power only emerging as a separately recognized market: teens.

Letter writers in the EC campaign directly countered the hypocritical hype by simply turning accusations back on censors, as in A. J. White's "You are protecting adult delinquency and tearing down the ideals of youth." Some tried to educate by providing nuance to correct misapprehensions concerning genre and audience, like eighteen-year-old Bobby Lee Jones's equalizing statement: "An adult is only a child that is older." Bob Stewart, aged sixteen, reasoned economically, encapsulating much of what has been repeated *ad infinitum* since, that almost all youth, delinquent or not, were reading comics, thus Wertham's logic that so many young criminals being comics readers hardly represented a correlative, not to mention causative, factor; but he also explains the less-acknowledged issue of an emerging teen market: "the Entertaining Group is *not* publishing comic books for children! You can look at an EC yourself and see this fact. EC has acquired the finest comic artists available and prints maturely written stories. I know of many teen-agers who have stopped reading all comic mags but EC because they have discovered that the other comics are directed at those of a lower age level. . . . When they mature they will find that they can only find real entertainment in EComics just as I did when I was twelve years old."[11] But, in the meantime, entertainment is just that. Charles Casady, "an average American, fourteen year old boy," reminds the subcommittee that comics are meant for leisure: "I admit I would rather read a comic than do my math any time but then I would rather do anything rather than math."

Were the young simply parroting adults, impressionable and in need of the proposed protections imposed through censorship? Or do the voices of youth protesting comics censorship in the 50s constitute a rightful expression of participation? It is true that many of the letters parrot suggested claims from the EC call for letters that comics simply incorporate the same level of violence and fear that pervade common fairy tales. But at least their humor is uniquely concrete. For example, Charles Lane (age fourteen) and Irene Lane (age eighteen) say they "don't expect" to commit crimes in the near future and compare comics to fairy tales like "The Ugly Duckling," "Jack and the Beanstalk," "Hansel and Gretel," and "Little Red Riding Hood," asking, "Now if comic books are bad for teenagers and adults, why do they read such horrible stories to children?" The comparison with fairy tales is more apt than trite. Censors who would seem to be advocating more didactic reading for minors were in fact willfully forgetting one of the oldest forms of didactic storytelling, the cautionary tale, which instructs by assigning punishing consequences to undesirable behaviors. Eleven-year-old Maurica Osborne calls out this disingenuous logic: "[Y]ou are wrong about horror comics hurting we children! Something horrible always happens to the killer, robber, etc" (see figure 4.4). Children and teens are just as capable of learning through negative examples as they are through positive models. John Brill likewise suggests the insincerity of censors: "Unless you can find some other reason for juvenile delinquency I know it is not comic books. I will be forced to think you are still very, very stupid."

One could argue that contributors to the letter campaign are simply repackaging the arguments made well known through advocates like Lauretta Bender (psychiatrist) and Josette Frank (literacy expert) in the 1940s. Or are they also expressing preference—a matter of taste? Diane Sherry is clearly indicating personal taste, I believe, when she writes, "If the world did not have comic books there would be nothing to arouse the reading interest of school children, except these terrible 'Dick and Jane' books." Her letter also reveals awareness that not trusting children can encourage duplicity: "I have a girlfriend whose mother forbids her to read them and so she goes down to the drugstore and reads them anyway. Maybe the children whose parents forbid them feel guilty so they act out the script" (see figure 4.5).

Fourteen-year-old Robert Ramos, who looks "forward to a cartoonist's job in the comic book industry," exposes a hidden class bias in the censorship movement by explaining the importance of comic book accessibility to lower-income families: "[W]e're not rich enough to buy a TV." The 1949 Fawcett study on marketing through comics confirms that comics ownership is most pronounced in families of workers in the lower middle class and upper working class (see figure 4.6). Inexpensive entertainment for all ages is prioritized by comics defenders. And the protest letters also express awareness of the escapist role of fiction and scapegoating of targeted groups. Eugene R. Masters,

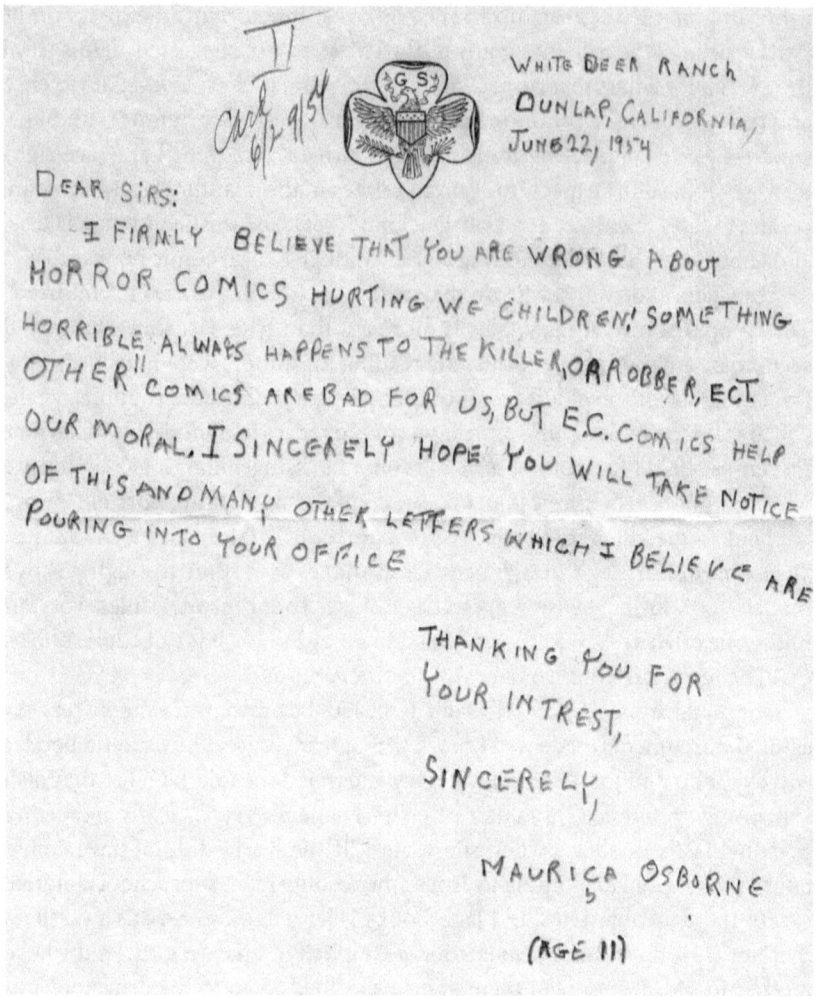

Figure 4.4. Letter from Maurica Osborne, age 11 to Senate Subcommittee. National Archives.

then fifteen, would write, "You have been urged to do this [censor] by certain groups of people who are ignorant enough to believe that if you hide crime and horror from the young reading public you can stanmp [sic] it out among that group. This is plainly ridiculous ... Are you capable of believing that simply reading about crime can lead an intelligent American youth into a life of delinquency?" And if so, many concur; violence still would be modeled by the political example set by adults. D. W. Hurst writes, "If you have to crack down on something, crack down on the parents." Perhaps sixteen-year-old Don

> June 22, 1954
>
> Dear Sirs:
>
> My name actually isn't too important so I'll get right to the point.
>
> Comic Books are not, in my own opinion harmful mentaly. Some times you hear about the grusome slayings that were acted out to follow the script of a wierd Comic but this rarely happens. If the world did not have comic Books there would be nothing to arouse the reading interest of school children except these terrible boring "Dick and Jane" books which I was not in the least bit interested.
>
> Comics are found in the home everywhere and if the Parents forbid them the Children will have even more curiosity and always find other ways to read them. With comics the children can catch the meanings of the words by the pictures. I, at this moment am subscribing to 3 comic books. The word Weird arouses most childrens interest and even right now
>
> I have a girl friend whose mother forbids her to read them and so she goes down to the drugstore and reads them anyway. Maybe ~~because~~ The children whose parents forbids them feel guilty so they act out the script.
>
> I hope I've gotten my point across to you and Thank you very much for your kind attention.
>
> Yours very truly,
> Diane Sherry
> 1333 Norino Drive
> Whittier, Calif.

Figure 4.5. Note card from Diane Sherry to Senate Subcommittee. National Archives.

Cunningham has a similar idea with his point that any problems were part of the larger culture, not that of children or teens alone: "I read in a magazine on how to make your own 'Atomic Bomb' and this was *not* a comic book."

Between these voicings and the rhetoric used to silence them, one can directly discern the hypocrisies of American protectionism toward the young, which would increasingly predominate by the end of the century. Relatively

BY INCOME GROUPS:

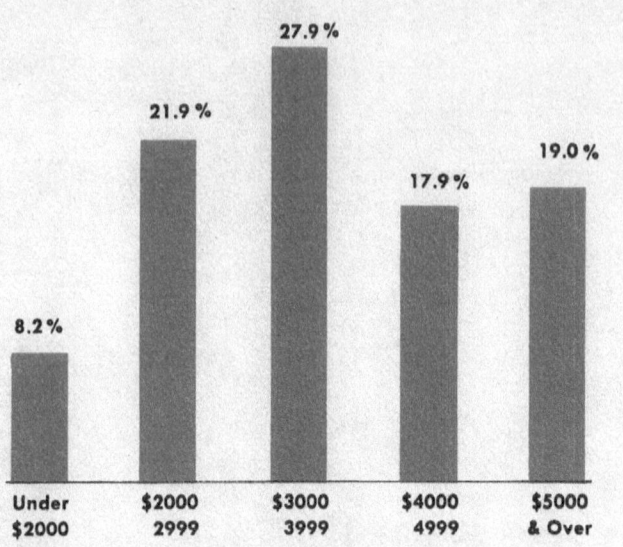

BY HOME OWNERSHIP:

BY OCCUPATION:

Professional and Semi-Professional	11.7%
Major and Minor Executives	8.5
Proprietor and Small Business	8.4
Salesman	8.9
Clerical and Government Employees	10.9
Skilled Worker	31.7
Semi and Unskilled Worker	14.2
Miscellaneous	5.7
Total	100.0%

Figure 4.6. Family consumption of comics by income group from Kid Stuff Is Big Stuff, by Daniel Starch and staff, 1949, 13. National Archives, Washington. Open Access.

unrecognized in our culture, children's participatory needs for self-determination are easily disregarded in the name of protection, seemingly shielding children while curtailing their participation and choice. The larger child-rights context surrounding this particular era is important to recognize, especially as it concerns a medium so often praised for encouraging a "participatory, inclusive model" of "active readership" (Royer, Nettels, and Aspray 277, 287). My favorite letter in the collection at the National Archives, and perhaps the strongest protest voice in the spirit of active readership and participatory rights, came from fourteen-year-old Philip Proctor, who seemed aware that most censors don't actually read what they censor: "We don't buy these mags because we have a thirst for blood, we buy them for the stories, the snap endings, the artwork, and because they deal with the unknown. . . . Read one, you asses." Proctor, later famous for his voice acting, assured me that he had been aware of having a political voice when he wrote his protest letter in 1954: "Regarding my thoughts about my letter being actually read and entered into evidence—my father, Thomas G. Proctor, was a lawyer but deeply involved in the Democratic Party in New York at the time, and his father, Robert E. Proctor, from Elkhart, had been an Indiana State Senator—so, yes, I was very serious about the issue and expected to make a statement that would be recognized." Although Proctor was confident as a participant in a democratic process, plenty of the protestors anticipated infantilizing responses, perhaps most ironically expressed in all caps across the top of Glen Double's letter: "PLEASE READ BEFORE THROWING AWAY." I'm heartened by the fact that it was not thrown away—instead, the writer takes a small place in history, his letter stored now for more than sixty years for the American public to see. It will be preserved, but have the contents been heeded? In scholarship about children's literature and culture, we need to rigorously seek such evidence of actual youth participation and devise methods of analysis that recognize young participants' nuanced, diverse, and individualized perspectives. We need to untuck these minority voices from the unexpected but quotidian ways they are hidden but preserved.

George Royer, Beth Nettels, and William Aspray go as far as to say that with the rise of comics one could witness "the transition of the comics reader from the passive consumer to an active participant in shaping both the future of the medium and a participatory reading culture" especially in the 1950s (277, 285). Through letter columns, contests, and sharing copies, comic book readers not only exercised choice as a new consumer base but preserved copies as stewards of the form through custodial rituals like carefully finessing slipcovers. David Serchay calls such collectors "librarians of the home." Their role was absolutely participatory, including critical analysis of plot inconsistencies and sophisticated appreciation of formal elements; and collecting was crucial to the preservation of youth voices, as reproductions rarely include letter columns in reprints and anthologies.[12] Many letter writers express that these qualities interested them in a career in comics, to participate in their creation. The fact that many of the letter writers joined fan clubs, wrote fanzines, or engaged in appreciative explication indicates how active they were as readers. One, E. Nelson Bridwell, would ultimately work for EC and DC comics, gaining occupational education through following some of the "better crime and horror comics," explaining, "I have read so many malicious falsehoods about comics I wouldn't believe a word these self-appointed censors say." Disingenuous critiques discredited concerned adults, and their threat to the medium may have galvanized sophisticated readership further.

The history of comic books in the twentieth century signaled the rise of child culture as a market-recognized demographic with consumer power, but censorship of child reading also reveals the restrictive force of an adult-generated reactionary backlash. Without encoded and enforceable rights to participation and self-determination, such protectionism continues to invisibly confine young American citizens. But we can learn by retrieving otherwise lost voices that testify to participatory ideals. Too often the default in our discipline is close reading as an end in itself, and our theoretical preoccupations often take us even further from situated experience. In the letter campaign, letter columns, and by interviewing former fangirls and fanboys now in their twilight years, we can more accurately celebrate their active readership.

Comics have been called "the folklore of the times," "the literature of the playground," and even "the weaponry of the schoolyard" (Hajdu 44, 215, 217), phrases that especially apply to serialized comics (like daily strips, comic books, and even single-panel cartoons) that are produced rapidly and steadily, often following or embedding quotidian ephemera, capturing daily or monthly preoccupations of their culture.[13] In the context of literary study, Philip Nel writes that "comics' seriality (whether in comic books or daily strips in newspapers) creates a different narrative experience. . . . [T]he storyline often continues from issue to issue or day to day. . . . [S]eriality places distinct demands on the comics genre" (452). Nathalie op de Beeck adds that commercial and historical contexts are less transparent in picture books than comics, because "unlike comic books—they generate anticipatory nostalgia" (2012, 475). Instead, comics can have "a counter-cultural function" (476) and reflect small-scale concerns that might at the time be considered historically unimportant but are relevant to readers' lives. And, as if to confirm that relevance, historically, kids' comics have incorporated child readers' own voices as well, not just in letter-writing campaigns, but throughout the pages of comic books themselves.

One comic series that epitomizes this layered, folkloric, and polyphonic historicity is the acclaimed *Sugar and Spike*, by Sheldon Mayer, that ran from 1956 through 1971, an important transitional period in the history of children's reading in the United States because it directly followed heated censorship debates that peaked with 1950's hysteria concerning juvenile delinquency. *Sugar and Spike* seems unaffected by and unreflective of the cultural tempest surrounding the industry at the time of its inception, but that very conflict is present and effectively counterbalanced through the comic's heightened interactivity with actual readers from the minority group being discriminated against: the young. The series also captures less sensational but nonetheless fascinating cultural realities that were affecting children: restraints (material or linguistic), the pictorial turn of the media, and the resulting expansion of literacy skills. In spite of its historical context of increasing protectionist restrictions on the young, Mayer also conveys liberalizing views of children as resistant consumers, interactive readers, users of new technology (especially the television), agents in need of greater autonomy, and preverbal thinkers (capable of more sophisticated thought than they can articulate in the adult-serving modes of written, and even spoken, language). In the series, Mayer circumvented the constraints of the Comics Code by focusing on two prelinguistic babies;[14] he also thematized the importance of escaping restrictions like the "prison-house of language" through visuality and visualcy, and the sometimes necessary but imprisoning aspects of childhood itself. In *Sugar and Spike*, visuality becomes a means of bridging gaps caused by age, differing development, ability, language, and traditional word literacy. As in the containment motifs of ships in bottles, babies in boxes/baskets, and the islanding of children, Mayer's enclosed spaces often contain the adventures of his title characters, who then escape and solve all of their problems from outside the prison house of adult language through their own prelanguage. By focusing on abstract "imprisonment" he was able to subversively comment on more structurally observable phenomena that were affecting his readers.

Before the purges of the 1950s, comics were particularly popular with children, who formed a new consumer base,[15] but the heavy censorship of the 50s, and continuation of the code through most of the 60s, cost the industry many of its readers (some of whom had been co-opted into burning their own comics collections in public demonstrations), and the result was that parents regained much of the consumer power behind choosing what youngsters would read.[16] As Stephen Kline has explained, "The comic book marks an important transition in this growing market for children's fiction. The comic-book industry clearly demonstrated the viability of a children's market by turning out a product that children could buy with their own hard-to-come-by pennies. Comic books also inspired a new set of literary formulas that could sustain a mass audience" (102–3). In perhaps the most convincing example from the National Archives collection of letters protesting comics censorship is the petition signed by a group of young neighbors from Elmont, New Jersey led by Ann Carnevale, who tells the Senate Subcommittee on Juvenile Delinquency debating comics censorship that she and her cosigners are "hoping you will use your common sense and change your ideas about these interesting comics" (see figure 4.7). Such collective action, which goes far beyond the personal letters called for by EC suggests that, indeed, comics had already begun to mobilize solidarity and awareness in their readers by encouraging "the development of critical and political literacy" that Hatfield and Svonkin attribute to the medium (434).[17] Nathalie op de Beeck goes even further, arguing, "For children to choose and prefer comics, then, is a sign that older generations do not determine children's memory making, identity formation, political leanings, and erotic proclivities" (2012, 476). Whether or not censoring advocates acknowledged these child publics, they found a forum and freedom in comics not documentable in library reading rooms or schools.[18]

Sugar and Spike was created at a time when the Comics Code Authority (formed in 1954) had to limit what could and could not be printed in comics, putting complex pressures upon all comics producers, but especially on those addressing young or transitional readers.[19] The series exemplifies the tension of writing to an audience whose freedoms are being limited and attempting to respect them and give their voices a public forum. The series focuses on Sugar and Spike, two early toddlers (variously called "infants" and "babies") who never age and speak their own language (to which readers are privy), leaving them mystified by the adult world. Readers are asked to "put yourself in a baby's place for a minute, and see how things look to you then! Right away, you're a stranger in a foreign country. You don't speak the language and you don't know the customs. You can't move around very well by yourself, so it's hard to find out about things. Probably the first thing that strikes you is that being behind the bars of this thing called a 'crib' is pretty much like being in prison!" (*Sugar and Spike*, April–May, 1956).

This fictional device, whereby the audience can understand two babies who can communicate clearly with each other (and occasionally the young of other species), is not a particularly novel one today. It's been used in texts like *Mary Poppins,* and many others since Mayer's creation, like *Free to Be You . . . and Me* (puppet scenes), *A Series of Unfortunate Events, Rugrats,* and *Baby Geniuses* to suggest the extent to which (preverbal) young people can be isolated by language and might require more active listening from adults. But *Sugar and Spike*'s creator was also subverting the 50s censorship that threatened his medium and livelihood as well. It is no coincidence that when David Pace Wigransky, the fourteen-year-old editorial writer defending kids and comics against the rants of Frederic Wertham, decried the double-standard that threatened his own freedom of reading choice, he did so by also invoking the prison: "Dr. Wertham seems to believe that adults should have the perfect right to read anything they please, no matter how vulgar, how vicious, or how depraving, simply because they are adults. Children, on the other hand, should be kept in utter and complete ignorance of anything except the innocuous and sterile world that the Dr. Werthams of this world prefer to keep them prisoner within from birth to maturity" (19–20). The Comics Code hindered artists and writers, but it may have also forced them into more subversive methods of addressing child-readers from a compassionate and surprisingly similar prison.

Mayer used his highly successful personal style to respond with humor to the constraints of the Comics Code, the traditional restraints of language and literacy, and the containment of childhood itself (analogized through cages and comparisons between babies and nonhuman animals). Part of Mayer's success in attracting child readers was to exploit the full potential of the medium for incorporating their actual voices interactively.[20] While librarians and parent groups rallied against children's rights to choose and to buy comics, the medium directly addressed their market. Stephen Kline explains that "[i]n the immediate postwar period and the early baby-booming 1950s, comic books established themselves as the most important medium of direct communication with children" (102). By acknowledging that story ideas came from readers, *Sugar and Spike* maintained an image of representing what a young reading community wanted (rather than corrupting future delinquents). Matthew Pustz writes that "As comic books grew in popularity in the early 1950s, publishers began to transform a text page mandated by postal regulations from an infrequently read story to a compilation of readers' comments.... Fans could make announcements about clubs, advertise for pen pals, comment on stories, argue with other fans, and participate in contests" (166–67). Often this space invites reader input on the course of developing plot and technique for future stories, as in this note in the letter column: "In a recent issue we printed a letter asking whether we'd ever show Sugar and Spike grow up. We asked for letters on that subject, and the mail has been flooded with them. The majority, especially Cynthia Streeter of MacDonald, Ohio, Karen Sarant, age 9 ½, of Vidor, Texas, Eileen Kelly, age 10, of Worcester, Mass., were emphatically in favor of keeping Sugar and Spike as they are—babies—so we guess that's that—Keeping writing" (letters column, no. 12, December 1957). Fans who suggested plotlines they'd like to see were recognized within the stories themselves as originators by name. Not only was it routine to recognize letter-writers' contributions, but their

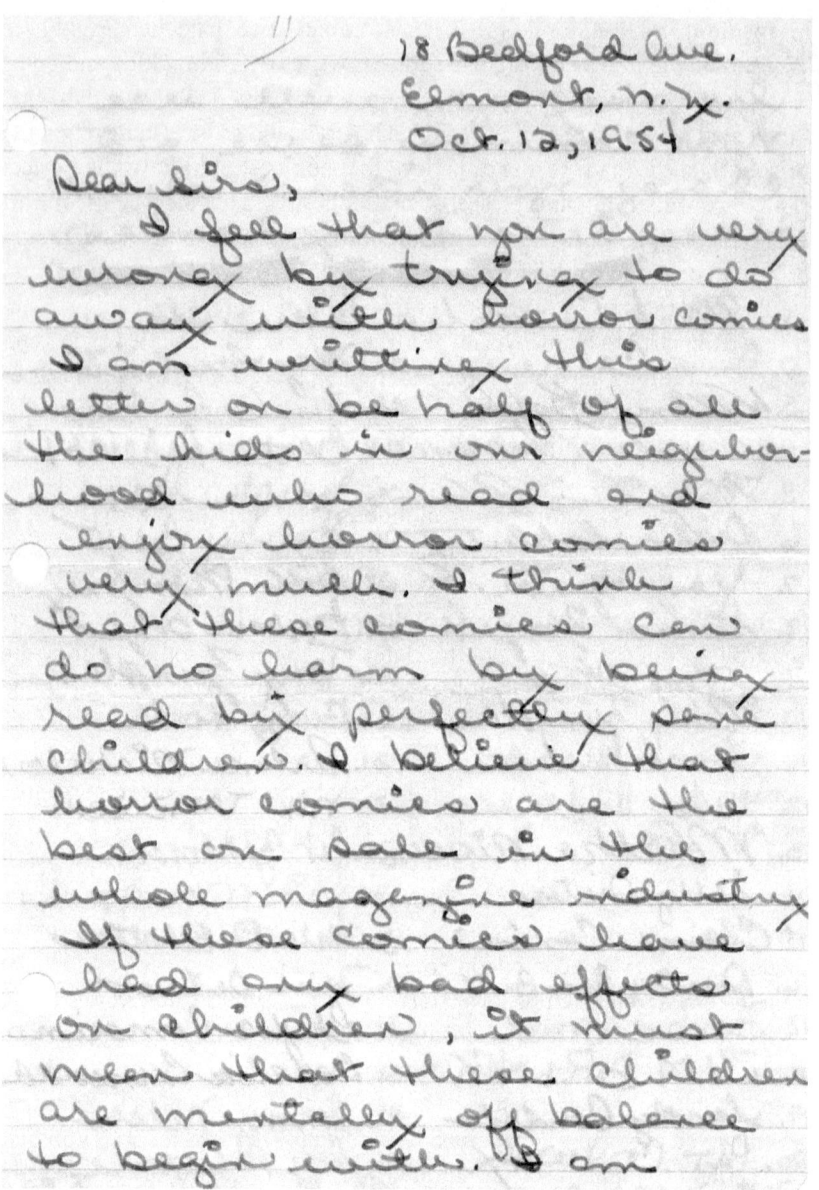

Figure 4.7. Petition to Senate Subcommittee on Juvenile Delinquency from "the Elmont children" (Elmont, NJ) October 12, 1954. National Archives (Washington, DC).

hoping you will use your common sense and change your ideas about these interesting comics.

~~The Great Writers~~:

1. Mark Carnevale
2. Ann Carnevale
3. William Kozel
4. Carolee Cochrane
5. Mary Janie Gabriel
6. Dick Schlutz
7. Jean Hunter
8. Richard Mangelt
9. Greg Stinger
10. Mary Zingola
11. Janet Nesblac
12. Judy Andersen
13. Martha Nissen
14. Sally Dieter
15. Claine Canine
16. Dorothy Ann Bull
17. Bobbie Brink
18. JIM BRINK
19. Sandy Condolo
20. PAT CONWAY
21. Dolores Idd
22. May Porchintera
23. Vinie Primeo
24. Berta Roberson
25. Joseph Dext
26. Bobby Bayo
27. Bill Morgony
28. Barbara Boyle
29. Tony Zingola
30. George Kovar
31. Arlene Nicholson
32. Nix TAMBORONI
33. Pat Zahlmann
34. Gil Mangoni
35. Gale D. Echotier
36. Niel DeLeo
37. Phylis Comorino
38. Dedalia Carnevale
39. Sonny Nelson
40. Roy Alagonia

P.S.* We are sane, normal, fun-loving kids!

contributions influenced compositional decisions. This interactivity is fully evidenced in the paratextual matter of each issue of *Sugar and Spike* (much of which, unfortunately, are not included when issues are anthologized, as in the DC Archives edition of the first ten issues): the letters page, "write your own comics" page, acknowledgements for readers' story ideas, cut-out greeting cards, drawing contests, and "Pint-Sized Pin-ups"—paper dolls with fashions designed by readers. Some of these could be highly original—my favorite one is a "THINKING suit" for Spike by twelve-year-old Carole Comley that says "Quiet! Genius at Work" and is shown with a matching mortar-board hat that has a glowing lightbulb on top (no. 18, September 1958). Others showed aesthetic promise. Trina Robbins writes of the widespread interactivity of kids' comics in the 1950s: "Among the many readers cutting out the paper dolls and mailing in clothing designs during this period were fashion designers Betsey Johnson, Willi Smith, Calvin Klein, and Anna Sui" (16). And one such interactive reader, Nell Rose Kottal, would become Sheldon Mayer's obvious favorite, reader and fan (one of her contributions can be seen in no. 7, 1959).

Nell wrote her first letter to Sheldon Mayer for the letters column after reading the first issues when she was eight and received her "first mail" in response (Wall).[21] In the July 1957 issue number 8 letters page, appear Kottal's second letter, thanking Mayer, and Mayer's reply: "Sometimes after a hard day at the drawing board, I feel a little too tired to answer more than ten of them. When I got your letter I was reminded of how much an answer meant to me when I was little and wrote letters to magazines. So I have hung your letter on the wall in front of my desk, and whenever I think I'm too tired to answer any more letters, it catches my eye and I tackle ten more before I give up." In an interview with Sheldon Mayer's daughter, Merrily, Bill Alger asks about Mayer's fans, and she responds, "He had one I'll never forget: Nell Rose Cottal [sic], a girl he drove to see with her mother and brother. They met and had lunch together. They didn't come to the house. He'd go visit them. He talked about her a lot. He loved the fact that she loved his work" (22). Kottal and Mayer's conversation began on the letters page of *Sugar and Spike*, where Mayer encouraged Kottal's artwork and clearly enjoyed having a fan who appreciated the comics form with such a sophisticated understanding. And at a time in which many young comics readers were being vilified as potential juvenile delinquents, Mayer kept the comic squeaky clean, but not condescendingly sweet. Nell reports, "We corresponded, and he wrote to me as if I was an adult, never talking down to me" (interview). This respect and curiosity toward youth surfaces repeatedly in the *Sugar and Spike* letter column, whenever the author/artist has to defend the premise of the series—that just because we can't understand what preverbal babies are thinking doesn't mean they aren't thinking.

Sometimes in the *Sugar and Spike* letter column, one will find fans referring to letters in past issues, playing practical jokes, even providing drawings of their own (reinterpreted by Mayer's pen). A common topic of conversation is the point of view in which Mayer rarely shows the faces of Sugar's and Spike's parents. Readers frequently inquired about this technique, and sometimes sent in their own drawings of the parents' faces to great humorous effect (of the let's-laugh-at-grown-ups variety). Of course, the real reason Mayer didn't show the parents' faces (that is, until readers voted to see them) is to keep the focus on the title characters—their world, their words (of course, a "baby's-eye view" impossibly translated from baby talk). It is narratively necessary for the readers' view to be restricted so that we might understand how confusing the otherwise simple problems they solve are: How did those small people get in that box? (TV); are people disappearing in a "loozum door"? (revolving door at department store); what is wrapped in these covered boxes? (presents); why is the lifeguard in a highchair even though he's big? As Sheldon Mayer explains in the letter column of issue 69, "I pretend that I'm a baby, a stranger to the world, seeing things for the first time" (February–March, 1967). For the most part, he traces how children are excluded from language yet possibly think more freely because of their exclusion. But the most common conflict that occurs at least once every other issue is that Sugar and Spike, or "doll-boy" as she calls him, get put back "in the pokey." And I believe this constant theme of imprisonment corresponds to the linguistic isolation that is foregrounded between adults and children, constantly provoking the question, who is trapped by language—those who are inside it or out?

From 1956 to 1971, Mayer found endless ways of imprisoning the toddler twosome, and usually Sugar masterminds a way out. This regular theme, whereby the toddlers are trapped in playpens, halters, animal cages, overturned cribs/wastepaper baskets, and pretty much anything with bars, reminded me uncomfortably of the "captivation emotion" that behavioral psychiatrist and comics creator William Moulton Marston identified as a key experience of child development and gaining a sense of mastery—practicing dominance over others and experiencing the "pleasures" of overcoming submission—a sort of process of bondage and release.[22] (If Mayer's characters enact such a process, the gender roles of Marston's *Wonder Woman* are reversed, however.) Following the 1920's research of J. B. Watson in which a "rage" response was provoked by "holding the infant's head tightly between the hands, pressing the arms to the sides, or holding the legs tightly together" (120), Marston concluded,

> The observed increase in strength of the child's muscular contractions runs closely parallel to the increase in weight or other types of antagonistic pressure

which the child is compelled to overcome in trying to carry out his former movements. It may be noted in connection with this dominance response that opposition pressure sufficient to stop all movement of the child's arms and legs does not suffice by itself to evoke motor stimuli of superior intensity to the child's motor self. (126)

This appears to be Marston's way of saying that a little restraint goes a long way, but "hampering" an infant's movement too much defeats the development of the "motor self." Although Marston based many a *Wonder Woman* plot line on this very process of restraint and supposed empowerment through provoking escape behaviors, it wasn't original to his work. It is played out in comics that predate his, where superheroes are bound and break out, including the earliest Superman comics. But Sheldon Mayer centralizes the conflict—allowing his protagonists to overcome entrapment, represented through cages instead of being tied up (unless, I guess, one considers the beach episode in issue 29 from 1960 in which the duo is actually put into harnesses, but these only temporarily restrain them before the predictable escape).

When Sugar and Spike are put in a folding playpen when traveling with their fathers, they realize "this is a new kind of pokey!" Even a gift erector set they build around themselves is briefly seen, in a moment of panic, as a prison: "It's a pokey! Your uncle Charley tricked us!" (no. 19, October 1958). In the cityscape cover of issue 70, confinement and escape are a visual theme again as the toddlers, now giants, are contained yet bursting from buildings they've outgrown. The pattern vicariously celebrates overcoming restraints and escaping the prison of isolated dependency. Playpens become so synonymous with prisons in the comic that when Sugar and Spike reappeared, in a 2009 issue of *Batman: The Brave and the Bold*, and the title hero captures the villain Faust, he proclaims, "Now *you're* getting a playpen, all to *yourself* . . . in *jail*!" (no. 4, June 2009).

At the time Mayer was creating his comic, there was publicized debate about playpens. In 1957, a writer from an article in the *Chicago Tribune* would refer to "the great hue and cry raised against the play pen a few years back" (quoted in Vanderbilt). In one of the more passionate examples, *Redbook* columnist Irma Simonton Black had written in 1952,

> The condemned criminals in Alcatraz are also safe. They are not likely to be run over by trucks or to slip on highly polished floors. But the life they lead is not envied by the more vulnerable citizens who are daily exposed to the pleasant hazards of freedom. I have seen enough irritated, complaining babies standing

and shaking the bars of their tiny cells to be convinced that they do genuinely resent severe limitations on their freedom. (73)

But Dr. Benjamin Spock's guides have always assumed the playpen to be a normal part of early child rearing, though his language reveals a similar surface qualm: "If you are going to buy a playpen, do it before the baby is used to the freedom of the open floor, otherwise he may object to being put behind bars" (151). Later, Spock adds, "Let him out of the play pen when he insists. One child will be willing to stay in the play pen, at least for short periods, as late as a year and a half. Another thinks it's a prison by the time he's 9 months" (205–6). Spock's advice on this and all things baby-care became available to a mass audience in 1946, and these entries on the playpen have changed very little in consecutive editions to this day. Sheldon Mayer exaggerated the imprisoning aspects of the playpen and other contraptions, not as part of the "hue and cry" that seems to continue about playpens, but as a celebration of release.[23]

The less explicit problem of containment in our sentiments about children can still be seen in the "hue and cry" against and repeated visual metaphor of playpens. The fact that they've been redubbed as Pack n Plays protests this discomfort just enough to remain traceable. Geographer Roger Hart says, "As cities develop, there is a tendency for children to be increasingly contained" (135). He argues that the "felt need to 'contain' children in order to keep them off the streets, safe from traffic and unsavoury influences" has motivated "the control of children through their spatial segregation" (135, 136). Certainly, playpens visually represent our historical tendency toward containerizing childhood. But, as with privatization and islanding, containment is not always so visible. As with my earlier example from *Lord of the Flies*, in which an older child throws stones at and misses a younger boy, the protective encircling of children can be quite invisible. Playpens are simply a furnishing that represents coerced boundaries: "Where little children are unable to conform, caregivers rely on exterior means, including material objects, to maintain the accepted images and ensure the desired behavior of their children. In fact, only a small part of children's physical environment deals primarily with their physical needs. A great deal, including much of children's furniture, is used to direct, contain, and control a child's behavior" (Calvert, 62). According to Markella B. Rutherford, such barriers explicitly define outer limits internalized through socialization: "[A]s a figurative image, the example of the play pen is significant" to both "literal physical boundaries" and invisible "behavioral boundaries" (56). From the discourse of parents she interviewed about changing perspectives of child supervision, Rutherford identifies an "image of the 'disappearing' play pen" that "signifies a fairly common cultural perception that children have more freedom over their behavior at home than in the past" (57). This impression unfortunately masks the wider truth that public freedoms have concurrently diminished. Composing in a context in which such changes were more explicitly visible, Sheldon Mayer provided his toddlers an outer architecture of contained childhood as a first playground—the terrain of their adventures rather than an unsurmountable obstacle. By using this imagery to concentrate on linguistic alienation, play, and discovery, he also successfully conveyed a cultural transition from physical to mental containment.

Friedrich Nietzsche wrote, "We have to cease to think if we refuse to do it in the prison-house of language." [24] Like Wordsworth, Wittgenstein, and Jameson, Nietzsche used imprisonment as an analogy for the cognitive limitations that come with language acquisition. Mayer follows in this tradition, but he also used it to stress the limitations imposed upon preverbal subjects by those already indoctrinated by language and its inevitable accompaniment with internalized ideology. *Sugar and Spike* demonstrates the ability of the comics medium to visually break through language/literacy barriers and generation gaps. One way such barriers are highlighted and transgressed is through the device enabling Sugar and Spike to communicate with baby animals. In "Poky Problem," Sugar and Spike escape their playpen only to feel a defeated pang upon seeing a caged bird: "You can't win," pines Spike, playfully suggesting they can equate their identities (themselves as toddlers and the other as bird) with imprisonment, or at least restriction (no. 18, September 1958). [25] Reading these comics constantly brought to my mind an old button I have from Americans for a Society Free from Age Restrictions, which pictures a toddler sawing his way out of a crib, inscribed, "Age shouldn't be a cage." *Sugar and Spike* consistently literalizes the idea. The protagonists' "escapes" repeatedly act out a process of resisting restrictions, even though they often wind up in a time out in the corner after their escapades.

When the toddling escape artists communicate with baby animals, they identify with their caged experience but also with their linguistic isolation. In "Children and Other Talking Animals," John Morgenstern points out that "animals are 'delightful' because they do not have language, do not trouble you" by appearing or behaving like humans, but adults can also "wish to be able to think that children have no language," for similar reasons. Erica Fudge argues in her 2002 work *Animal*, "Language has often been regarded as the domain of the human.... 'I can speak, therefore I am human: it cannot speak, therefore it is not human,' this logic would go ..." (117). Such categorization clearly indicates a common prejudicial linking between nonhuman animals and nonspeaking infants (its etymological source, "enfant," itself meaning "nonspeaking"). Sugar and Spike (no. 30, August–September, 1960), for example, confuse caged young chimpanzees as simply being in their "giant-size playpen," changing places with them out of a sense that their "punishment" is unfair. But Erica Fudge also remarks that "We don't want to know what these animals are thinking, because it is eminently possible that they are thinking about us" (90). Mayer's use of this theme even echoes Carroll's Alice being advised against eating any food she's been introduced to, when in issue 53 (June–July, 1964) the kids meet a talking baby crab and recognize that "it's impolite to call a crab seafood to his face." Mayer suggests that all babies understand that their dependence and restriction come from size or age. A caged baby elephant explains to Sugar and Spike, "If I was big I'd be marching in the parade with my mommie, instead of being stuck here in the pokey!" (no. 20, December 1958). Such interactions indicate the problematic but inevitable marginalization of infants and nonhuman animals based on speechlessness. Allying babies more closely with animal young than with older individuals of their own species forces the reader's recognition of the enculturated otherness of early childhood.

Comics have long been associated with voicing the muted voices of children—taken to a delightful extreme in the *Axe Cop* webcomic and series, written by Malachai Nicolle, who was five years old when the writing began, artistically rendered by his adult brother Ethan. In some comics, the barrier between the language of children and adults is foregrounded absolutely (think *Peanuts*, in which adult language is represented as unintelligible, and irrelevant). There is a *Calvin and Hobbes* strip in which Calvin is asked to "Explain Newton's first Law of Motion in your own words," to which he responds, quite literally within the parameters of the test question, "Yakka foob mog. Grug pubbawup zink wattoom gazork. Chumble spuzz" (January 9, 1995).[26] Such phonetic representations of childhood "gibberish" (which are also used when Mayer shows the reader what adults around Sugar and Spike are hearing) remind us of the subversion allowed from the exclusionary social spaces created by language users around those yet to be initiated into shared usage.[27] David Carrier describes how "[t]he word balloon, by externalizing thoughts, makes visible the (fictional!) inner world of represented figures, externalizing their inner lives, making them transparent to readers" (73). When word balloons are filled with "nonsensical" sounds, they at once enact the fantasy of access to the infant's thought while phonetically representing a more realistic linguistic boundary. Visual storytelling often functions as a greater bridge to nonverbal conceptualizations.

Charles Hatfield explains, "After the late 1950s, the educational literature on comics fell to a murmur, until the 1970s when teachers began guardedly endorsing comics as a means of reaching the 'reluctant' or disabled reader;

this is an endorsement still founded on the assumption that comics' visual/verbal nature makes them easier to read" (2006, 363). Most would agree that the pictorial turn of the twentieth century created generations of "readers" who are visually literate in some ways surpassing previous generations. This skill is no doubt partly due to films and the establishment of televisions in American homes (a rapid process which took place during the comics purges). Mitchell Stephens explains, "No medium or technology, before or after, 'penetrated,' as the researchers put it, our homes more quickly.... [I]t took only eight years, after the arrival of full-scale commercial television in 1947, before half of all American homes had a black-and-white television set" (6). This then-new technology is a frequent prop and subject of *Sugar and Spike*, subverting the imprisonment motif of being "boxed in." The "window-box toy" becomes a fascination for the toddlers, again indicating the interpellation and resistance of children through visuals. In one episode, Sugar and Spike are seen fully enthralled with a cartoon, but in the only panel with words, the commercials, they turn away to be completely engaged in their own play, resisting their interpellation as consumers perhaps merely because of the language barrier.

Again, Mayer reminds us of the power of visuals to communicate and recognize preverbal thought. And this power can bridge gaps in understanding, as well as motivate the young to make sense of language that eludes/excludes them. In my interview with Nell Rose Kottal Wall, a fan of Sheldon Mayer, she spoke of becoming a comics reader:

> I learned to read because of a Mickey Mouse comic book that my older brothers brought home one afternoon.... I SO desperately wanted to know what Mickey and Goofy were saying, but I could not read yet. I knew the alphabet, so tried putting the letters together while sounding them in a slur, and realized I WAS reading. It was the motivation of my desire to read that funny book that was the birth of my literacy.... So by age 7 in.... 1954, I was already a veteran of comics.

A feat of self-motivated learning, it does not, however, indicate that comics are necessarily easier reading.[28] I'm inclined to believe (and think Nell Wall would agree with) Gianni Rodari's account of comics reading: "[U]p to a certain point the child's principal interest in comic books is not determined by their contents, but is tied directly to the form and substance of the comics themselves. Children want to master the means of reading comic books," which is to say they are indeed a stimulating challenge rather than a nonthreatening path of least reading resistance (97). Below is an example of the difference between simple literacy-aiding illustration and the composite visualcy demanded from comics.[29]

Whereas traditional illustration implies a subjugated, redundant relationship between words and the images that simply represent them (or visually interpret them), comics usually prioritize the visual over the verbal, or at least make the visual essential to the conveyance of meaning. David Carrier writes, "What the ideal comic should provide is ... contact between image and word, to the point that the two form an ideal unity" (67). Consider Virginia Lee Burton's *Calico the Wonder Horse, or the Saga of Stewy Stinker* (1941), which Leonard Marcus calls a "gallant but futile gesture" toward the comics format (151). In it, Burton very consciously packed her panels with motion, but she failed to fully follow her own insight that "showed that the wordy, muddled, full color pictures and over-crowded pages were passed by in favor of simpler ones" (see Burton's "Symphony" 308). The wordiness of *Calico* interferes with the preference in comics for letting pictures speak in a condensed manner. If she had dared to leave her narrative wordless, it may have succeeded. After all, if anything is dispensable in comics it is the words. Perhaps this is a bit of an exaggeration, as when Italo Calvino muses about his preliterate appreciation of comics, "[B]eing unable to read, I could easily dispense with the words—the pictures were enough ... When I learned to read, the advantage I gained was minimal" (93). But more importantly to my point, the image and words are merely juxtaposed in Burton's attempt, seemingly kept separate, with no conceptual point of contact.

Robert C. Harvey has argued that "the essential characteristic of 'comics'—the thing that distinguishes it from other kinds of pictorial narratives—is the incorporation of verbal content. I even go so far as to say that in the best examples of that art form, words and pictures blend to achieve a meaning that neither conveys alone without the other" (2001, 75–76). While Nathalie op de Beeck rightly points out that to Harvey the words are central to the comic (2012, 471), I find his argument important because he is noting the importance of balance and the skillful interplay of meaning that can only result in tandem, combined with "all-at-onceness" (71), as David Carrier calls it, rather than simply through "juxtaposition," as McCloud insists. To also use Northrop Frye's term as applied by W. J. T. Mitchell, I use "composite text," which applies perfectly in some of Mayer's finest moments.[30] Unlike other creations by Sheldon Mayer, like *The Three Mouseketeers*, which had to be taken over by various other artists so that Mayer could concentrate on the talkative toddlers in high demand, *Sugar and Spike* remained thoroughly Mayer's work (although stories vary on the degree to which other artists were called in for supportive work when Mayer's eyesight worsened in the late 1960s). Nell Rose Kottal was very aware of the importance of Mayer's work remaining his own to preserve his composite creations: "The difference between a good and a great comic is when the artist is drawing his own creation.... I bet they didn't even think kids noticed things like that" (personal interview).

Creating meaning compositely also allows for subtle subversion or commentary not always easily gleaned by the light scan of a would-be censor. When Sugar and Spike go to see a Western with their fathers in "First Movie" (a story inspired by twelve-year-old Lynn Sinclair, of Woodside, NY), Spike's father gets worried during a shoot-out on the screen, proposing, "The action is getting heavy—the kids shouldn't see this! We'd better use our hats," which they promptly use to block the toddlers' view. Spike complains to Sugar, "They take us here to see that interesting stuff, and at the best part they hid it with their hats! (no. 23, June–July 1959). So they slip away, find scissors in the projection room, and cut holes in the hats so they can enjoy the rest of the flick.

When Victor Watson, a literacy specialist, worked with a reluctant prose reader who was a gifted picture reader, Ann, he realized that at times our emphasis on word literacy, our "process of trying to manage the syntax of sentences and the logic of letters did some kind of violence to Ann's ability to spin subtle narrative webs out of pictures," as if "being required to learn to read for her was analogous to the old practice of forcing left-handed children to use their right hands" (161). Not only does he credit Ann with keen and open insight as a pictorial reader, Watson recognizes that word literacy may dull our comprehension of visual storytelling. It is not so simple as getting to the right answer but also one of being able to "disrupt meaning" to create new sense as in Ann's reading of Maurice Sendak's *Outside over There*. When they "read" it together, Watson reflects that "it puzzles and irritates me that Sendak has included in one of the closing illustrations the figure of Mozart playing a keyboard instrument in a summerhouse. This seems bizarre, and I would like an explanation because I am an adult reader who dislikes loose ends. Ann, on the other hand, when I pointed at Mozart and asked who he was, replied calmly that it was Ida's grandad" (146).[31] Watson realizes that as a visual image reader, Ann has a keen ability to find "holistic sense" and "linking observations" that is quite satisfactory but often at odds with word literacy (148, 152). This insight might help us to consider more openly a young person's natural self-censoring process and co-existing possibilities for comprehending subversive subtext. Certainly, Sugar and Spike enjoy the movie they watch through the hats: guns are "bang-bang" toys "like the BIG boys play with," which they correctly interpret as "mean." In other words, the hats are not necessary.

As part of the pictorial turn of the twentieth century, comics carried out the shift from word-dominant flow toward visually driven narrative in composite texts. This trend is clearly reflected in highbrow children's books, like picture books, which Patrick Groff argues "increasingly are being purchased on the merits of their pictures rather than on the qualities of their written text" (298). Charles Hatfield ties this development to the direct influence of comics: "[P]icture book creators gravitate increasingly toward comic art techniques" (2005, 97). Certainly, the past two decades of Caldecott winners have shown a tendency toward compositeness (Eric Rohmann, Peggy Rathmann) and even wordlessness (David Wiesner, Jerry Pinkney)—escaping the prison house of language through image. Such "prizing," as Kenneth Kidd calls it, implies, in Nathalie op de Beeck's words, "how the picture book, comics, and other graphic work destabilized the conventional separation between word and image, how verbal-visual narratives gained prominence" (2010, 15–16).[32] This trend also seems to favor work in which the author and artist are the same so that they can actually compose compositely.[33]

Comics provide the model for escaping language-dependent literacy through constant experimentation in reversing the dominance of word over image. Some see comics as favoring and being limited to action over nuance, as Mitchell implicitly does in his earlier argument that "vernacular composite forms like the comic strip" can "defy the normal privileging of the visual image as the place 'where action is' on the cartoon page" (1994, 93). And if you take as an extreme the many wordless picture books on the market today (some by artists who publically acknowledge a comics influence, like Mo Willems and David Wiesner), the same argument has been made by Perry Nodelman: "Wordless picture books can easily depict actions, not so easily communicate feelings or meaning—and it is this that most distinguishes them from conventional picture books" (190). But once again, led by a more experimental comics influence, these limitations are also demonstrated as conventional, not absolute. One need only read Shaun Tan's *The Arrival*, or *The Red Tree*, to recognize the lack of truth to the idea that wordless or composite texts are limited to action.

Sugar and Spike are forever situated as outside of adult language and literate culture by being perennial infant-toddlers. They are aware of this outsider status as they metacomically quip on one cover in which, always escaping, they burst from a tall building as temporary giants: "I wish we could read! Then maybe we could find out how this happened to us!" (no. 70, April–May 1967).[34] This sophistication is the type of quality that drew readers like Nell Rose Kottal to Mayer's comics. The main theme of the comic seems to be that some of the more interesting and plotworthy events of childhood are linguistically inaccessible but visually and fictively imaginable, and, as such, *Sugar and Spike* is the perfect forum for investigating the ineffable, sophisticated, and subversive qualities of comics that Mayer celebrated. Subverting the censorship climate of the Silver Age with a conscientious voicing of muted childhood positions, and foregrounding awareness of the seeming impossibility of escaping the prison house of language, Mayer heightens his readers' appreciation of the comics medium as one in which visuals can communicate extralinguistically, and thus, more expansively than through verbal means. Ultimately, we don't want Sugar and Spike to unlearn baby talk, speak to their parents, or learn to read. Instead, we can fantasize that they exist in an endless but visually imaginable liminal social space that language and word literacy cannot contain.

In contrast, Sugar and Spike's real-world counterparts grow into language. How much easier, then, to look for their fledgling voices in accidental archives? If we recognize kids as emissaries of linguistically liminal literacies and subjectivities, and we actively listen, what else might we learn?

5

The Price of Protectionist Pretense

> We see children only as what they will do when they become adults. . . .
> In children most of all we deny illness
> —Arthur Frank (128)

Karen Sánchez-Eppler has written that the "sense of the dead child as the most powerful sign of right sentiment—for the family and for the individual—is itself one of the founding tropes of sentimentalism" (1999, 66). So it should be no surprise that the *dying* child becomes the rhetorical target of extreme protectionism. Just as the power of preverbal thought is considered in my last chapter, I want to turn to a darker example of child participation being thwarted by well-intended protective measures: adult emotion, especially anticipatory grief, blocking opportunities for informed consent and therapeutic honesty. Eva Illouz rereads the dimensions of capitalist culture to make embedded emotional controls a more explicitly influential part of modern development: "Far from being pre-social or pre-cultural, emotions are cultural meanings and social relationships that are inseparably compressed together and it is this compression which . . . confers on them their energetic and hence their pre-reflexive, often semi-conscious character" (3). In this light, Marxian "alienation" becomes not only an outcome of labor practices but also an internalized inflection shaped by "emotional hierarchies" in which fear and love are especially vulnerable to manipulation (4). In the emotional hierarchies of families, children can be easily alienated even by the most nurturing efforts. Some of the fallout seems unavoidable, because as we love and care for others, we sometimes necessarily burden them—thus, the curious and contextually shifting connotations of related terms like "caring" or "careful" and antonyms "careless" or "carefree." If caring didn't have costs, the latter two terms would be synonymous for not caring—but their connotations are opposing: one must not "carelessly" ignore nurture or empathy, yet to be unburdened of caring is freeing.

Our "higher" emotions don't just get the better of us; they get the better of those we love as well. In this chapter, I will explore one example of how those tendencies become normalized, even institutionalized, with unfair consequences, especially as the drama plays out in children's books about life-threatening illness. Barbara Ehrenreich, Samantha King, and Gayle Sulik have addressed the privatizing, gendering, and infantilizing already associated with some cancers. King points out that "the rise of the thon"—the craze of fundraising for a cure through events like the Leukemia and Lymphoma Society's Team in Training, keeps "the present-day focus of events on health within a strictly domestic context... quite far removed from their historical roots, which were entangled with the struggle to forge international cooperation in the post–World War II era and with issues of 'third world' development," poverty, and malnutrition with an aim toward better preventative medical practices (47). Like childhood, disease instead becomes a private matter domestically contained and operating on an emotional rather than radically restructuring level. For example, Sulik says of breast cancer in particular, "the culture surrounding breast cancer survivorship operates tyrannically, using cheerfulness as a form of social control to normalize and depoliticize the disease" (275). If a middle-aged woman diagnosed with breast cancer can't avoid "suffocation by the pink sticky sentiment embodied in [a] teddy bear," Pink Ribbon Barbie dolls, rubber duckies, and pink M&Ms when going for her mammogram, treatment, or counseling, imagine the dominance of cuteness and infantilization imposed on children diagnosed with potentially terminal illness (Ehrenreich 44; Sulik 373). In fact, I suspect that the ubiquitous "ultrafeminized" consumerism and "infantilizing trope... harder to account for" may actually have evolved from similar practices in pediatric oncology wards, but Ehrenreich makes clear that neither is fitting: "Certainly men diagnosed with prostate cancer do not receive gifts of Matchbox cars" (46–47). The gendering prevails in pediatric contexts, where "femininity is by its nature incompatible with full adulthood—a state of arrested development," but the tyranny of cheerfulness reigns over both boys and girls with life-threatening cancers (45).[1] Like the girl in Sendak's anecdote who played along with the pretense that bodies falling from the World Trade Center were just butterflies, children learn to follow the pretense emotionally demanded by adults entrusted with their care, especially their distraught family members. Like censorship, this pretense can become a prison house for ailing children.

Myra Bluebond-Langner, in her 1978 study of children with leukemia, *The Private Worlds of Dying Children*, depicted a range of denial, deceit and rare honesty she witnessed and rigorously collected, most frequently demonstrating "mutual pretense," with rare exceptions of "open awareness." Mutual pretense is defined by Bluebond-Langner as an unspoken consensus in which "each party defines the patient as dying but acts otherwise," resulting in hopeful expression only (199). Rather than encouraging child patients, such denial further burdens them with keeping up a masquerade while denying their own needs for "open awareness," which would allow discussing concerns, questions, and fears (220–21). Adults often actively withhold the truth from dying child patients, denying their rights to medical honesty, awareness, and agency. I will demonstrate how pervasively popular American children's literature about cancer mirrors the same relation—most often modeling "mutual pretense" rather than "open awareness," thus perpetuating a rights-suppressive discourse.

One barrier in adult-child relations is not so much trust as it is adult inability to see clearly that on health matters, kids can be penetratingly truthful, and parents can be quite deceitful. This paradox springs from the burden of care and responsibility—adults in part are protecting the young—but we also must realize where "protection" doesn't always justify concealing the truth. The most plentiful examples in this category are the lies parents tell about terminal illness, commonly expressed with phrases like "I just wanted to spare him the pain." In fact, parents spare no pain by lying about illness. Cindy Dell Clark advises: "Do not assume that a child can be spared pain or suffering by avoiding discussion of difficult issues" (161). I've always been surprised at how often parents, even in books for children that tend to idealize adult behavior, blatantly lie to inquiring child characters who are terminally ill or facing painful procedures, usually falling back on the brave-yet-pathetic sick-child stereotype that also imposes pretense on the young reader.

Myra Bluebond-Langner's ethnography of children with leukemia demonstrates this rhetorical tendency throughout—parents lying about procedures, many even withholding a diagnosis or the knowledge the illness is terminal from the patient, creating stifling dynamics in which parent and child are less honest with each other than young patients can be when alone together. Even nurses engage in a "mutual pretense" that nothing is wrong. We all have a subconscious filter resulting in subtle selectivity when it comes to the truth about dying, but it is never as simple as adults being more honest than children, or even the other way around. Bluebond-Langner argues, "Children are capable of choosing behavior so as to affect the way others see them. Children who know they are dying but wish to conceal this knowledge from their parents can, by doing some of the things that normal children do, momentarily change their parents' view" (9). The book documents the silences that adult caregivers and professionals impose on children with phrases like "When you're older I'll tell you why," even admitting, "I don't believe in telling my child everything" (36, 96). But concealing the truth about illness won't protect children from it, and assuming that they will accept sugarcoated explanations simply because the truth makes adults uncomfortable is detrimental to their ability to cope. In the most chilling revelation of this truth, where a child then has to protect his own parent from the truth she has made clear must be avoided, comes this moment: "Myra: 'Jeffrey, why do you always yell at your mother?' Jeffrey: 'Then she won't miss me when I'm gone'" (126). Jeffrey is emotionally protecting his parents as much as he can—a less recognized form of parentification. If we understand the personal resources that children have for emotional intelligence in facing illness, we might be able to foster their coping more effectively rather than saddling them with our vacillating anticipatory grief and denial.

Considered within the ethical parameters of child medical rights, texts as diverse in ethnic and historical contexts as Eleanor Coerr's *Sadako and the Thousand Paper Cranes* (1977), Virginia Hamilton's *Bluish* (1999), Cynthia Kadohata's *Kira-Kira* (2004), and David Small's *Stitches* (2009) enact the same denial and dishonesty, demonstrating the pervasiveness of a protectionism that in fact impinges upon children's participatory rights to full knowledge and self-determination about their bodies. Ultimately, "cancer books" tend to emotionally shield parents during their emotional struggle to support children rather than respecting young patients and readers by acknowledging their right to be informed and participate as knowing medical subjects. Imposing a pretense of "getting better" and "thinking positively," although sensible in the abstract, in fact simply imposes a greater emotional and social burden on a suffering child. Children's literature should instead foster open awareness, which the characters in Jodi Picoult's *My Sister's Keeper* (2004) and John Green's *The Fault in Our Stars* (2012) argue for consistently while foregrounding how difficult it is to achieve. That these rare exceptions occur in texts for older readers may suggest the increasing recognition of the maturing patient's right to knowledge, but they also in contrast expose the complete silencing in "cancer books" for younger readers, while excavating the deep, complex ways in which larger social forces reinforce silencing far beyond the context of home or hospital.

In John Green's 2012 novel, *The Fault in Our Stars*, narrator Hazel Grace Lancaster, a sixteen-year-old with thyroid cancer that has spread to her lungs, describes her favorite book: "[I]t's not a *cancer book*, because cancer books suck" (48). The main character of her favorite novel has cancer, but "Anna is honest about all of it in a way no one else really is" (49). Throughout *The Fault in Our Stars*, Green reminds his readers that dishonesty pervades popular discourse surrounding young people with life-threatening illness, and his novel invites us to consider not only how deceptive cancer books for young people can be, but also how dishonesty about terminal disease can dominate family dynamics, hospital conversations, even social media and public ritual. Green clearly positions his own novel against a traditional formula of sentimental denial—a formula so well known that *Saturday Night Live* did an off-color but on-point parody trailer of the film, *The Fault in Our Stars 2: The Ebola in Our Everything*, clearly referencing the formula even more than Green's novel. The schmaltzy mess made of Jodi Picoult's *My Sister's Keeper* in its film adaptation especially testifies to how pervasive the sentimental formula is in Hollywood. In short, we know the formula even if we haven't read many "cancer books."

Breaking with such a tradition is a difficult challenge—as is speaking honestly about anything an entire culture locks out of conscious awareness with taboos and silence. In traditional cancer books for kids, the wall of silence around potential child death is forcefully evoked, whether or not we are invited to question its fairness. Consider Eleanor Coerr's *Sadako and the Thousand Paper Cranes* (1977), in which Sadako is blocked from conversation with a boy, Kenji, who knows he's going to die and why, breaking the taboo of talking about it with Sadako: "I'll die soon. I have leukemia from the bomb" (42). When challenged by an adult who overhears and tries to halt the conversation, Kenji explains, "I can read my blood count on the chart. Every day it gets worse." The nurse responds, "What a talker!" and wheels him away (44). When Kenji dies, and Sadako asks if she'll be next, the same nurse responds, "Of course not!" (45). This is, of course, a conscious lie—one meant to console the adult as much as the child. When Sadako asks for her parents to put her "favorite bean cakes on the altar for my spirit" when she dies, her father silences her request: "Hush! That will not happen for many, many years" (55–56). Silencing a person making a dying request, diverting therapeutic conversation with a peer who has the same illness, and refusing to listen when a dying person needs to be heard would all be shocking if the person was older, but within the cancer-book context, it has a familiar, protective ring. Revisiting such conversations from the perspective of child rights foregrounds just how rare and difficult honesty is in practice, and likewise how inhumane denial can make adults who externalize the burden of care in spite of best intentions.

In American versions of the Sadako tale, another lie is repeated: that Sadako only folded 644 paper cranes. Following a Japanese legend that folding 1,000 paper cranes will grant a wish, peace, and health, the real Sadako managed to fold more than 1,500 paper cranes, but the novelized versions of her story change the number to an oddly consistent 644—eliminating the sad realization that Sadako's task didn't save her and that the child died with that hope deferred into a seemingly endless task (Ishii 63). The folk belief in holding up hope for dying children as a means of instilling a healthful resistance or at least a more peaceful resilience persists in fiction not fact.

In their study, "Does 'Telling' Less Protect More? Relationships Among Age, Information Disclosure, and What Children with Cancer See and Feel," Carol J. Claflin and Oscar A. Barbarin disprove the old adage that "what children don't know won't hurt them" (179). In fact, they conclude that "Even though young children were told much less than older children they reported similar levels of distress. This suggests that nondisclosure fails to mask the salient and distressing aspect of the illness" (169). And yet, Myra Bluebond-Langner would find that "American parents today are more open with their children about sex than they are about death and dying" (1974, 170). C. Knight Aldrich explains this avoidance is a primary trait of parental anticipatory grief: "Denial of the reality of the anticipated loss is probably the most common defense" (5). And so, understandably, one of the most consistent features of popular cancer books is their message of hope—from child-authored texts like Jason Gaes's *My Book for Kids with Cansur: A Child's Autobiography of Hope* (1987) and Christina Richmond's *Chemo Girl: Saving the World One Treatment at a Time* (1997) to adult/child co-authored books like Kate Gaynor's *The Famous Hat* (2008), and adult-authored books like Mary Brent and Caitlin Knutsson's *Chemo to the Rescue: A Children's Book about Leukemia* (2008) and Kim Chilman-Blair and John Taddeo's *What's Up with Richard? Medikidz Explain Leukemia* (2012), all of which focus on successful treatments and survival.[2] The emphasis is on providing useful information but stressing the more optimistic hopes over discouraging realities. Significantly, such works demystify procedures, like bone marrow aspirations, transfusions, radiation, and especially chemotherapy. For example, in the Medikidz series of medical comics for minors, peer-reviewed by medical doctors, superhero types take ill children to Mediland to learn about what ails them and what to expect in treatment. In one, a teen with leukemia, Richard, is told that white blood cells are "defenders," platelets are "fix-it guys," and red blood cells are "transporters." Bone marrow is a "garden" of "magic seeds" that will become either defenders or out-of-control "weeds" (15). Chemo, then, is a weed-killer, but when it doesn't eliminate the problem, radiation is necessary. The Medikidz chime, "MOST KIDS DON'T NEED TO HAVE RADIATION TREATMENT OR A BONE MARROW TRANSPLANT. IN MOST KIDS, THE CHEMO DOES THE TRICK ALL ON ITS OWN" (28).

There is a fine line, however, between emphasizing a few positives over preparing patients for many potential negatives—usually adults only *appear* not to cross that line while in fact doing so, by changing the subject or avoiding it altogether, a sin of omission at best. In Virginia Hamilton's *Bluish* (1999), Dreenie befriends Natalie, a classmate with acute lymphoblastic leukemia. When she asks her father, "Do . . . do kids get sick . . . and die, I mean, real easily?" her father responds, "No, not at all. Kids are tougher than anybody!" (46). He then changes the subject. Natalie's perspective is barely given, save for a few compassionate insights into her need to feel like a "normal" kid. The other children primarily see her as pale, inactive, and, at worst, someone who vomits in class—"It was gross, Daddy! I mean, e-ew!" (45). Dreenie's father compares Natalie's symptoms to the flu (46). Just for the sake of contrast, consider Dr. Michelle Au's description of a terminal case of acute lymphoblastic leukemia in a two-year-old child in *This Won't Hurt a Bit (and Other White Lies)*,

> David Barbaro is blasting off. Of course, this is a euphemism. "Blasting off" is just another way of saying that David is dying. . . . Over the past few days, his white blood count has skyrocketed from the relatively normal value of about 10 to the elevated 31, to the higher 44, to now the astronomical value of 91. Almost all of these white blood cells are the immature cells known in shorthand as blasts, which are the hallmark of ALL. Hence, in oncologic parlance, David is "blasting off." At this point, his life expectancy can be counted not in months or weeks, but in days. (246–48)

Dr. Au's description of this case (246–52) is full of all the drama, information, and compassion one might like to see in a children's book—but it also resonates with accuracy and respect. In contrast, finding precision and individualistic regard takes a bit of searching in the popular juvenile canon. Denial has a way of homogenizing fictionalized dying children into figures of pathos rather than persons, and it can blur a good deal more as well, socializing young readers into the role pretense demands.

Myra Bluebond-Langner published her landmark ethnographic study of leukemia patients a year after Coerr's *Sadako and the Thousand Paper Cranes* was published, and reading them together shows that conversations like the ones in Sadako stories (set two decades earlier) are quite typical in a ward of terminal pediatric patients. As in *Sadako*, Bluebond-Langner documents children following the adults' habit of avoiding even the word "leukemia," and the children internalize the taboo (34, 73, 96). Her analysis allows us to discern subtler effects of adult denial. Sometimes these include half-truths that upon reflection are straight-up lies, like the mother who admits, "Mary doesn't know what's wrong with her and she's not going to know. I don't even want to hear the word. Mary knows she has a serious blood disease, anemia—like me—and that's all" (96). Likewise, in Cynthia Kadohata's *Kira-Kira* (2004), when Katie's sister, Lynn, is diagnosed with lymphoma, her disease also goes through a diagnostic retranslation at home: "When Lynn returned from the hospital a couple days later, my mother insisted that she was basically fine. Apparently, Lynn's anemia was 'acting up' and she just needed more liver. . . . after I fed Lynn, I would give her iron pills" (129).

Bluebond-Langner found that many parents actively lied or tried hiding the severity, even the diagnosis, of disease from their children, yet the child patients understood far more than their parents realized. More importantly, she observed how profoundly children with leukemia internalized the taboo, discussing death with other children but keeping up a "mutual pretense" with parents that nothing was wrong. Not only did leukemic children in her study take responsibility for their parents' overburdened emotional state, but their pretense was partly motivated, ironically, to protect their parents. The children protected the desperate need their parents had of remaining protectors themselves, in spite of the fact that such pretense cost them therapeutic conversations as a family—opportunities for "open awareness" that might mitigate their own fears. Such lost opportunities are frequently regretted. In 2004, Ulrika Kreicbergs and colleagues surveyed 449 parents of terminally ill children in Sweden, discovering that "[n]one of the 147 parents who talked with their child about death regretted it. In contrast, 69 of 258 parents (27 percent) who did not talk with their child about death regretted not having done so" (1175).

And research supports the recognition of children's desire to be informed whenever possible, regardless of hardship. Gerison Lansdown has noted, in "Implementing Children's Rights and Health," "Consistently, the adults identified a need to withhold information from children in order to protect them. Equally consistently, the children took the view not only that they could cope with the information, but would resent being denied access to it. Indeed, they argued persuasively that exclusion would create more distress and anxiety" (286). David Small dramatizes this distress and anxiety in *Stitches* (2009), a graphic memoir covering the periods in his life (ages six, eleven, and fourteen) during which he was treated first with radiation for respiratory problems, and then later with two surgeries to remove a cancerous growth from around his vocal cords. Although he is fourteen for this second procedure, his parents keep the truth from him, protesting too much that all is well: "You look great! Doesn't he look great? And of course everything is fine. You probably can tell that the thing the, uh, the cyst is still in your neck," he's told between operations to remove it (168). He has lost his voice, and the illustrations heighten the reader's sense of his disempowered alienation as he is talked at, lied to, from frame to frame: "I told you, nothing is wrong. Now get some rest" (169). Small leaves no question in his images that he does not see the dishonesty surrounding him as protective; it is oppressive and frightening (see figure 5.1).

Such moments demonstrate how abusively protective "rights" can be invoked when trampling a child patient's right to participation. As a child, Small only discovered the truth about his disease from a letter he later found that had been written by his mother: "Dear Mama, David has been home two weeks now. Of course the boy does not know it was cancer" (204). Even naming her son has become taboo in the same sentence with "cancer." He reads, "The boy. The boy. The, boy, does, not. Know" (204). Once he confronts his parents with his new knowledge of the cancer they didn't expect him to survive (and their betrayal), they are angry and punishing toward him: "Well, the fact is, you did have cancer. . . . But you didn't need to know anything then . . . And you don't need to know about it now. That's FINAL!" (238). Eventually, David learns that his father felt guilt for possibly causing the cancer with the earlier, experimental radiation treatments he'd given his son, further indicating the extent to which lying to children about health risks only protects parents, not the children they are lying to (see figure 5.2).

What interests me is not simply the breaking of such silence, but how disconnected this silencing practice is from the consensus that now exists in medical practice and child-rights discourse. According to article 12 of the UN Convention on the Rights of the Child (CRC), children have a right to have their own say in general, and specifically in article 24, all parents AND children have the right to be medically "informed" (a term not taken lightly in the medical community, where consent must be informed), "with a view to abolishing traditional practices prejudicial to the health of children." Although the United States never ratified the CRC, these particular rights have been recognized, though not legally codified, for decades (Lewis and Lewis 1990, Beauchamp and Veatch 1996) by consensus though not evenly followed (Dickenson 1994; Shield and Baum 1994) in the medical community—it is the general public, and parents in particular, who've proven more difficult to convince.

Perhaps the best example of this potential divide between medical practice and public sentiment occurred in the UK, a CRC-ratifying nation, in the 1995 case of Jaymee Bowen, who was identified anonymously as "Child B" in order to maintain her ignorance of the severity of her three bouts with cancer (with two remissions), of which she remained unaware from the time she was first diagnosed at age six until a year before her death at age twelve. When the National Health Service (NHS) denied coverage for a costly procedure with

Figure 5.1. From Stitches: A Memoir, by David Small. Copyright ©2009 by David Small. Used by permission of W. W. Norton & Company, Inc. and Pippin Properties, Inc.

unlikely benefits for the sick child, her father, David, sued, and her case came to represent the horrors of cost-benefit analysis in allotting healthcare.

Jaymee Bowen's high-profile case reflects complications that also occur when you look at "cancer books" from a child-rights perspective. First, as a highly sensationalized case, it revealed the patheticizing tendencies of public discourse that have been highlighted in disability politics. Bylines dripped with inconsistent sentimentalizing: Jaymee, a "10-year-old widely recognized as mature" and "brave" was also called "little girl," "Little B," and "leukaemia girl" (Ham 65; Entwistle 1590; Midgley 1). The case fell into the same formulaic groove that trivializes suffering in cancer books—playing up the frightening reality of cost-benefit analysis in a situation that is unthinkable even to those of us thrown into making such decisions, the media focused on the NHS and doctors as villains who would let a child die simply because her treatment was too much of a financial gamble, when in fact the funds for her treatment might be more certain to save other children who'd received less treatment and were not at a terminal stage. Even more tellingly, by tapping "widespread reluctance

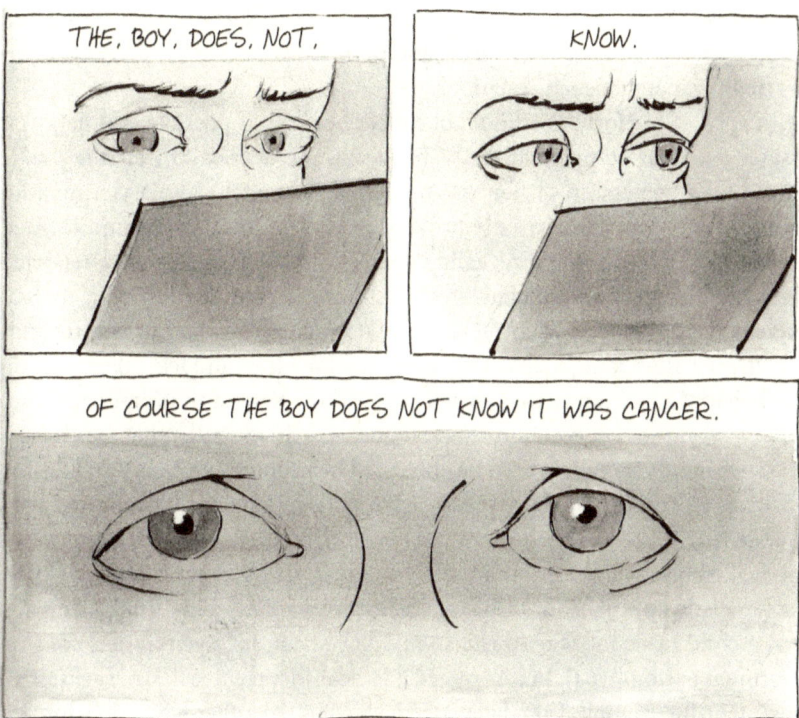

Figure 5.2. From Stitches: A Memoir, by David Small. Copyright ©2009 by David Small. Used by permission of W. W. Norton & Company, Inc. and Pippin Properties, Inc.

to accept that children sometimes die," the result was that "the question of whether the treatment was in the child's best interests was relatively neglected" (Entwistle 1590–91). So the issue of Jaymee's lack of say was completely ignored. In this sense, the case also revealed the power of protectionism to cloud better judgment or rights awareness, especially when limited by the oversimplifying tendencies of media sensationalism.

Bowen's case exposed this crack in reasoning. Chris Ham argues that in fact lack of informed consent explained why most pediatricians refused to continue Jaymee Bowen's treatment while a specialist in adult leukemia overlooked the issue and agreed with the father: "Being more accustomed to dealing with adult patients able to make decisions themselves, they were more willing to accept David Bowen's views as proxy for his daughter's" (65). In part this is because we still see the boundaries between parental rights to impose protective measures and child participation as very blurred, to the point that, as one doctor said of David Bowen, "He assumed that because she was his daughter she would have the same views as him. . . . And that was an assumption that a father is not entitled to make" (Ham 64).³ The slippage between caring and being responsible for one's offspring and possessing them as property becomes blurred for many in such situations.

In spite of the formulaic mold of cancer books, it is possible that fiction is a safer place for complete honesty. In the case of Jaymee Bowen, the public would take ownership of her as a figure—a "brave leukaemia victim" who heroically fought a supposedly broken medical system (as an uninformed nonparticipant). But some revealing details of her experience were reported once her identity was revealed—realities that speak to the futility of mutual pretense and to how much protectionism dominated the discourse surrounding Jaymee. Rampant paternalism dominated medical and legal decisions on her behalf. Chris Ham writes that "David Bowen sought to protect her from full knowledge of her condition and prognosis.... in the belief that the chances of a successful outcome would be enhanced by keeping her happy and feeling positive." According to Ham, the decision to keep Jaymee ignorant, and thus unable to give informed consent, was in disagreement with the opinions of medical professionals on the case. Ham writes that Bowen "adopted a truly paternalistic approach, but this troubled the paediatricians. Their view was that a child of Jaymee's maturity should have been involved in decisions on treatment options" (64). In retrospect, it is clear that Jaymee desired aggressive treatment, for example, from later statements like, "I'd rather have gone through more suffering to live than not go through anything and die" (Harrison). But at the time, the parent's wish to keep Jaymee ignorant was valued above the need to get her informed consent, so in spite of any lip service to participatory rights, consent by parental proxy trumped the demand for informed consent directly from the patient in question.

Like David Small, she found out the truth about her case (and implicitly the sin of omissions that had surrounded her) indirectly. And like so many children swept into the social demands of mutual pretense, Jaymee followed the cues of silence and didn't let on that she knew. Sarah Barclay reports, in language Hazel Grace Lancaster would deem appropriate to the "conventions of the genre," that Jaymee discovered the truth: "She was Child B, the little girl she had heard about once on the radio in her hospital room, the girl who was so sick that the doctors said there was no point in treating her anymore. To David Bowen's amazement, she told him she already knew—or at least that she had been virtually certain. Nurses at the Portland Hospital, who did not realise that she had heard the story on the radio, had brought her some of the Get Well cards that flooded in from all over the country." Jaymee explained, "I kind of figured it out because some of the cards put, 'To Child B, love from whomever,' and I'm thinking ... I must be Child B." Barclay reports, "But she never let slip her suspicions to the father trying so hard to protect her." Far from being a passive victim, Jaymee Bowen picked up on sophisticated social cues and respected the emotional needs of her father and other adults for her pretense of ignorance. So she observed the silence required.

Is this sin of omission, playing the role in the pretense, dishonesty? In actual experience, children are much more easily suspected of lying than adults. In his tellingly titled, *Why Kids Lie: How Parents Can Encourage Truthfulness* (1989), Paul Ekman provides a layered perspective on this issue. As his title implies, he takes as a given that kids will lie and approaches it as an inevitable problem that *adults* must strive to fix. From the beginning, he admits profound disappointment and surprise over an incident in which his teenaged son had a party while the parents were away and never told them about it. Ekman insists, "Concealing is no more justifiable, no more moral or proper than falsifying," and, "Our interviews with children found that most of them do recognize that concealing truth is a form of lying" (15). Nuancing this argument, however, is the inclusion of other chapters written by both Ekman's son, Tom, and his wife, Mary Ann Mason Ekman. Tom points out that lying is relative to power: "I think most kids are more reluctant to lie to their teachers than to their parents because teachers are harder to talk to if you get caught and, after all, the teacher is responsible for grading you, which gives him/her a lot of power" (108). The son seems much more aware of the power differential than his father, who has more power, but also speaks to the disincentives students have to lie to a teacher. His mother adds, "Perhaps the first thing that parents should consider when troubled about their children's lies is how prone they are to lying themselves" (118). Caring doesn't simply translate into comforting. This is the most important counterpoint to adult assumptions about child lying, and perhaps especially applies to the sins of omission Paul Ekman seems so concerned with. Letty Cottin Pogrebin provides two examples that help to disprove our misconceptions about how children and adults respond to child terminal illness. One is the testimony from the mother of Andrew Smith, an eight-year-old with brain cancer: "Kids were never negative or ugly toward him. One child asked him why his cheeks were so big, but by then we had taught him it was because of his medication so he could explain why. Our only negative experiences were with adults." In contrast, Andrew's mother reports numerous insensitivities on the part of adults (even hospital staff). When his steroids increased his appetite (a good thing, actually), one buffet customer threw in a little parent-blaming too, commenting, "How does anyone let their child get that fat?" (2013, 224). Another parent, of nine-year-old Jenny Asch, who died of a severe asthma attack, offers a partial explanation of adult insensitivities: "After she died some of our friends couldn't face us, probably because they had kids the same age. They reacted almost as if her death was catching. They didn't come to pay a condolence call, and in all the years since they've never said one word to me about Jenny, never even acknowledged her death. But her friends and classmates came every night, and they decided on their own to name the school's music room in her memory because she was very musical. They took up a collection and had a plaque made and created a ceremony for the presentation. That was the *best*" (220). While in these examples, adult fears and denial continue long after a child's death, the deceased's age peers seem to empathetically intuit not just how they need to grieve and honor their friend, but what her parents may find therapeutic as well.

John Green questions the misleading pretense behind the lies we tell about children after death as well. In *The Fault in Our Stars*, Hazel looks at the Facebook page of her boyfriend Gus's former girlfriend, which constructs a person shaped more by compensatory cancer narratives than individual truths. Gus explains, "The thing about dead people ... is you sound like a bastard if you don't romanticize them, but the truth is complicated, I guess. Like, you are familiar with the trope of the stoic and determined cancer victim who heroically fights her cancer with inhuman strength and never complains or stops smiling even at the very end.... But cancer kids are not statistically more likely to be awesome or compassionate or perseverant or whatever" (173–74). Resisting the formula, when Gus dies, Hazel honors his memory by reflecting truthfully on who he was and mocking the formula that disallows such truthfulness: "According to the conventions of the genre, Augustus Waters kept his sense of humor till the end, did not for a moment waiver in his courage, and his spirit soared like an indomitable eagle until the world itself could not contain his joyous soul.... But this was the truth, a pitiful boy who desperately wanted not to be pitiful, screaming and crying, poisoned by an infected G-tube that kept him alive, but not alive enough" (245). Even so, the power of public sentiment to override individualized grief proves too much. At his funeral, Hazel scraps the more honest eulogy she'd planned for one that would conform to the mutual pretense expected of those attending, but she privately regrets having to do so: "[E]veryone had to come up to me and tell me that I'd spoken beautifully, and that it was a lovely service, which was a lie. It was a funeral. It looked like any other funeral" (273). Her ultimate capitulation to conventions of public denial reminds the reader of how difficult it is to break culturally reinforced pretense even after the professed justification of protecting the child no longer applies. From the moral perspective of Green's novel, the pretense is a coercive lie.

Of course, total honesty is far more complicated than my analysis may acknowledge, and, like Hazel, Jaymee Bowen probably read her situation more in what wasn't said as well as the emotions expressed. Most persons, even very young ones, detect where fear and sorrow require great care and often silence. Brenda Comerford makes this abundantly clear in her "Parental Anticipatory Grief and Guidelines for Caregivers," on how to sensitively negotiate truth. Writing from the perspective of what she learned when her five-year-old was diagnosed, treated, and died after nineteen months of leukemia, Comerford stresses that how a parent communicates is just as important as what is said. She also clearly took her cues from her daughter rather than the other way around, from which she learned valuable lessons. On one hand, she stresses that both parents and doctors should "[a]nswer the child's questions as honestly as possible, because children do compare notes in clinic," and "[r]emember that children are much more aware than they are often thought to be. If they feel they are being lied to ... they will play along with the game" (155). But she qualifies boundaries: "Be careful not to use the term 'leukemia' in front of the child. Television is so explicit that the child may learn of his fatal disease in a traumatic way," making clear that understanding can be achieved more gently. Comerford followed the cues in Karen's own language for discussing how she made sense of the situation, referring to her illness as "bad blood" (148). This is not necessarily the same as the misleading mislabeling of "anemia" seen in *Kira-Kira*, or dismissing the possibility of death as in *Sadako*. It is a reminder that our language requires rational overrides that keep us from giving more information than is requested.

Comerford's example of following a child's linguistic cues is also extremely helpful in navigating honesty in the face of extreme hardship none of us is intuitively equipped to handle. And it enabled her to experience what Myra Bluebond-Langner has called "open awareness" with her child instead of letting mutual pretense silence necessary exchanges. One day, Comerford's daughter, Karen, came home from school brooding because "she said she knew she was going to die soon" from a classmate who'd overheard her parents' conversation: "'Let's talk about dying, Mom!'" (149). So they did. Karen also demonstrated a child's ability to sense and protect her parent's emotional vulnerability, reassuring her, "You have two other children when I go" (150). A similar moment is echoed in Green's *The Fault in Our Stars*, when Hazel ruminates about how her death will hurt those around her (like her mother, whom she's overheard dreading that when her daughter dies, "I won't be a mom anymore"). Hazel tells her, "I'm like a grenade, Mom. ... at some point I'm going to blow up and I would like to minimize the casualties" (99). The grenade simile (which we'll see repeated in a moment) testifies to the coercive power of silencing the ill with our sincerest cares.

Very few of the patients Myra Bluebond-Langner studied in the 1970s were able to break the pattern of imposed pretense to force "open awareness." And perhaps one of the few honest features about cancer books is how they so consistently conform to cheerful pretense. But fiction can also set up liberatory examples. Perhaps for the very reason that it was not written for a juvenile audience (although it has quite a crossover reading—even Picoult's son devoured it at age twelve), Jodi Picoult's *My Sister's Keeper* (2004) resists the sentimental dishonesty of the cancer-book formula by acknowledging children's attempts to force open awareness. Picoult manages to heighten her readers' awareness of most of the issues already discussed here—informed consent, consent by proxy, mutual pretense, and the subtler hazards of negotiating truthfulness when dealing with terminal disease in the young—pushing deeply into the impossibly gray territories imaginable.

Based loosely on the case of Anissa and Marissa Ayala (Jarman 217), Picoult's novel involves Kate, who has acute promyelocytic leukemia, and her little sister, Anna, a "savior sibling" genetically engineered as an allogeneic donor for Kate (Picoult 10). The primary conflict of the novel is not simply the formulaic focus of child against disease, but Anna's fight for medical emancipation and the challenges of doing so in order to break through parental protectionism into recognition of Anna's right to consent from a standpoint of informed volition. Like Green's novel, Picoult's does this by illustrating how thickly deterministic protectionism and mutual pretense can be. Like Green, Picoult investigates the subtle range of lies involved in the family's fight for survival and the individual child's struggle to have her own will recognized (in this case projected onto the sibling of the cancer patient but involving the hold their parents, doctors, and state have over their expressed wishes).

Picoult excavates mutual pretense in the family on the everyday level. For example, when asked by his wife, "How did Kate look to you?" Brian thinks to himself, "*Better than Anna did* ... but this was not what she was asking ... 'Kate looks great,' I lied, because this is what we do for each other" (44). Like many other literary parents discussed here, there are also moments of silencing child attempts at open awareness and moments in which the children express their awareness of taboos. While passing a cemetery, Kate's brother, Jesse, asks their mother, "[I]s that where Kate will go?" but his mother answers, "She's staying with us" (101). Anna is aware that she has internalized a complicated set of rules governing silence: "I'm afraid of saying too much" (375). At one point, even the word "die" becomes taboo, and as in Hazel's imagination (Green 99), the effect of the reality signified by it "explodes like a grenade" (Picoult 265). Even Au's description above describes the final phases of terminal leukemia as "blasting off" (246-48). This is a telling coincidence, indicating the vulnerability of bodies and threats of not following sentimental etiquette. In Green's novel, the grenade represents the ill child who embodies the taboo; in

Picoult's novel, it stands as an explosive analogy revealing the danger of breaking pretense—a forbidden yet questionable discursive rupture. The repetition of these figurations demonstrates multiple levels on which lies are imposed and then internalized under duress, burdening the young with the emotional protection of those who will survive them.

Some lies are inevitable as social and emotional lubrication. Dr. Michelle Au writes: "So many euphemisms we use in medicine. 'You're going to feel a little pinch' means, *I'm going to stick this gigantic needle into you now*. 'This is going to be a little uncomfortable' means, *This is going to hurt like a motherfucker*. 'There's a little bit of bleeding' means, *Don't freak out, but I think you might be bleeding to death*" (239–40). I think we all appreciate these euphemisms. But we also have a double standard about honesty and children that makes us slow to recognize grievous deceit. One example of this can be seen in *My Sister's Keeper*, when Kate's boyfriend dies. The family doesn't know for three days. Kate is "an emotional wreck" because she doesn't know why he hasn't called (320). When Sara (the mother) finds out that Taylor has in fact died from his cancer, she admits, "I don't tell Kate, not for a month," convincing herself that the lie is justified as it will help Kate remain positive (320–21). This lie is outrageous, and it might be the seal of doom for the character of Sara in terms of audience sympathy. But, surprisingly, it is a lie that some readers overlook (perhaps they agree with Sara's rationalization?). A reviewer for the Christian website TheThrivingFamily.com ranked the novel in terms of family appropriateness. "Lying" is one of the categories evaluated, but all the writer notes is that "Anna lies to a pawnshop owner about a necklace she is selling and hides the transaction from her parents. Jesse [brother] lies to Brian about quitting smoking. Campbell [attorney] lies about why he has a service dog." That's it. Nothing about the scores of bigger lies the parents tell or children's sins of omission required by pretense. Of course, I shouldn't have expected much from a website reviewer who refers to a novel as a "fiction book," but I think it speaks to how obliviously adults can maintain double standards of honesty with children.

Overwhelmed parents needing some escape into denial is not a justification for keeping kids ignorant of what affects them most. From the beginning of *My Sister's Keeper*, the question of who has the right to determine treatment (of either the cancer patient or her "perfect sibling match" donor) is framed in the body of Anna, who dramatically tells her attorney of her parents, "I want to sue them for the rights to my own body" (19). That Anna (and her sister Kate) need legal recourse to do this exposes the impossible conflict that can occur between parentally enforced protective rights and hard-won participatory rights to self-determination. Anna's participatory and protective rights have been violated with many painful and sometimes dangerous procedures to harvest and donate to her sister, whose protective rights are invoked as justification. Many readers initially see the sisters' mother, Sara, as the antagonist of the conflict, until it becomes clear that she really has no clear parental imperative: she is trying to keep all of her children alive, even though it means risking the health of her cancer-free daughter. Most importantly, the novel allows us to deeply consider the viewpoint of the child denied the right of consent or nonconsent. Savior sibling Anna's appointed GAL (*guardian ad litem*), Julia, reflects on what has been demanded of Anna, wondering if she'd do the same for her sister, Izzy: "What would *I* do, if I found out that Izzy needed a kidney, or part of my liver, or marrow? The answer isn't even questionable—I would ask how quickly we could go to the hospital and have it done. But then, it would have been *my* choice, *my* decision" (112–13). The question isn't whether Anna should donate so continuously to Kate, but whether or not she should be allowed to determine these measures herself.

Sara acknowledges to Anna, "I wonder if I lose perspective in being your mother," yet she tells the judge in chambers that "I believe I know better than Anna what is best for her" (405). So the classic distinction between "best interests" (which are decided by proxy—parents, doctors, GALs, and/or state) and the individual child's right to self-determination (participation through informed consent) is commonly elided in the public imagination, as in some cases, like that of Jaymee Bowen, where they appear to be in agreement only because the child has been kept purposely uninformed and excluded from the conversation. But Sara, like David Bowen, and no doubt most of us in their fictional and very real situations, does not necessarily have an ethical objectivity; as Sara suspects, she "loses perspective" of the broader picture. When Brian, Sara's husband and father of the sisters, tries to force more open awareness, he breaks the code of silence: "She is *dying*, Sara." The mother's response is emotionally believable and revealing of the possessive logic of caring: "But I love her" (265). Although unselfishly expressed love may have a palliative effect, it doesn't heal. Contrary to emotional logic, love doesn't grant authority either. And yet, it is a common appeal in determining best interests. Holly Brewer turns this logic around from a child's perspective: "If we include emotions, such as love, in our allocation of parents' custodial right, cannot children feel those too?" (687). Of course they can, but we would not even think about it, unless a kid tried to use that love as a claim to authority over the bodies of others.

The distinction between "best interests" and the weight of informed consent becomes clearer, however, in cases of informed *non*consent. In such cases, "best interests" trump decisions of minors who refuse treatment: "[T]he common law right to self-determination regarding one's own body and the constitutional right to privacy appear to guarantee a competent adult the right to refuse even life-saving medical treatment. In other words, the US Supreme Court has said that competent adults have the right to die rather than submit to unwanted medical intervention. The caveat here is that the individual making such a decision must be both adult and competent. Children are not presumed competent under U. S. law" (Walker, Brooks, and Wrightsman 141). For example, in the US case of Cassandra C, a seventeen-year-old with Hodgkin's lymphoma who preferred alternative therapy and refused chemotherapy, she was actually taken out of her mother's custody and eventually strapped to a bed to force her treatment (Harris). Unsuccessful in their legal suit against the state of Connecticut's imperative that chemo was in her best interests, Cassandra ran away after two days of treatment, but returned only to protect her mother from being jailed (C). Ms. C articulates the problem with our lip service to informed consent but default to external authorities when a minor disagrees with a more powerful party: "I was told I had a voice and was being heard, but I didn't feel like it" (C). Although, in the abstract, Cassandra's chemotherapy may have in fact been in her best interests, her ninety-two-day captivity demonstrates the power of emotional hierarchies to disguise the transference of burdensome "care" onto those we care about—a much subtler and more concretely consequential process than we often acknowledge.

In extreme cases, like those of Jaymee B. (noninformed consent by parental proxy for more aggressive therapy) and Cassandra C. (informed nonconsent to forced aggressive treatment), the only common factor involved is that in deciding best interests, medical opinion ultimately trumped both the patient's and the parent's expressed wishes. In the United States, citizens tend to confuse child rights with infringing on parental rights, but if children's medical participation were more culturally accommodated, Cassandra's rights might have been acknowledged, so her mother's (moot then) would also not have been violated. Children's fiction rarely contains such facts. "Cancer books" ultimately fit within emotional family dynamics, by challenging but capitulating to the status quo—imprinting homogenizing tropes like the pathetic victim, brave sufferer, and heroic supplicant to the medical will. These do little to illuminate public thinking about actual individual suffering and what we can learn from the individuals who experience it. Without such nuanced consideration, calculating the medical best interests of minors can entail wholesale dismissal of the perspective most in need of being informed and at least heard, resulting in shutting down the views of informed minors who refuse treatment, just because they are minors. And if "cancer books" dared to model more honesty, child readers might internalize and demand their right to participatory knowledge in situations where protective measures become oppositional.

The symbolic resonance of "protection" goes far beyond our avoidance of speaking too openly about child suffering and possible death. "Protection" is rarely as straight-forward as its utilitarian cousin, "safety." Instead it involves speculation about consequences further down the road of maturation. Will interventions now prevent trauma's after-effects later? In matters of preventive medicine, protection is, at least in the public imagination, open to great variance in interpretation. Eula Biss writes,

> When I search now for a synonym for *protect*, my thesaurus suggests, after *shield* and *shelter* and *secure*, one final option: *inoculate*. This was the question, when my son was born—would I inoculate him? As I understood it then, this was not a question of whether I would protect him so much as it was a question of whether inoculation was a risk worth taking. Would I enter into a gamble, like Thetis dipping the infant Achilles into the River Stix? (7)

Biss recalls the fairy tales she was read as a child, like "Tom Thumb" and "The Maiden with No Hands," in which parents "have a maddening habit of getting tricked into making bad gambles with their children's lives" (4). But she took away quite a different moral as a parent than she did as a child: "Immunity is a myth, these stories suggest, and no mortal can ever be made invulnerable. The truth of this was much easier for me to grasp before I became a mother" (5). The gambles we take are that much greater when we feel solely responsible for their impact on one who depends almost entirely upon us, and even worse when we don't support each other as a community in which we can interdependently take some responsibility for other people's children. Biss reports her sister's philosophical deduction of the quandary, "You don't own your body—that's not what we are, our bodies aren't independent. The health of our bodies always depends on choices other people are making" (124). In this equation, children should grow into reciprocal interdependence, not just able to rely on those outside of the nuclear family, but also be expected to in turn be responsible to them.

My home state, Kansas, was the first state to implement polio vaccination in 1957 for no other reason than a town's potent name: Protection. Beccy Tanner writes, "As part of the campaign, people soon found themselves doing quirky things like having an aerial photo taken of them standing in such a way that they spelled out the phrase, '100% Protection, Kansas.' They launched 400 weather balloons imprinted with 'We're all protected, are you?'" More consequentially, "In the years after Protection became the first town in America to be immunized against polio, the number of cases reported in Kansas dropped from a high of 1,718 in 1952 to zero by 1962" (A3). But "herd immunity" can't happen when parents increasingly close off the private worlds of family, making decisions based only upon what's best for the nucleus.

The legacy of privatizing families, islanding childhood, worshiping children individually but obscuring them as a political interest group has dire consequences. Pervasive higher sentiments of "selfless parenting" are not adequately practical in guaranteeing the safety and well-being of *all* children. The Physician's Oath, or "Declaration of Geneva, drafted in 1924 by the Save the Children International Union (SCIU), was the first official document to propose that children should be the first to receive relief in emergencies. After the Declaration of Geneva, 'children first' became a fundamental tenet in the struggle for children's rights" (Walker, Brooks, and Wrightsman 22). It would be adopted after World War II and echoes one of the most deeply held sentiments surrounding minors. As I hope I established in chapter 1, the idea of "children first" is hardly what it seems, further complicated by the fact that it is so ideologically embedded today we hardly recognize how oversimplified and untrue it can be. Prioritizing children as first to be rescued and first to be treated makes sense if followed in an emergency, meaning "before adults." But it becomes muddled in speculating about future isolated cases in which you might not agree on what the 'best interests' of a child are, especially within the skewed gloss of exceptionalism. From the perspective of children as a protected group (or basic math), it is clear not all can be first. When we look at minors as what Charlotte Perkins Gilman called a "permanent class," we can see that some children will be first, others last. And putting your own child always before others can be disastrous.

For an example that affects all children as part of this rotating class, not just those presently facing terminal illness, research may be needed to participate in finding safe and effective medical treatments (for more on therapeutic orphans see Coté et al. 1996). Consider this antivivisection league message from 1915: "Would you like to have your baby inoculated with consumption germs? Would you like to have your daughter given the most awful and vile disease known? Would you like your son to be inoculated with scarlet fever or poisonous pus? Would you like to have cancer grafted into your well breast so that it took root there?" (shown in Lederer 80). Surprisingly, this Anti-Vivisection Society poster reveals how much our civil disagreements today concerning vaccination against preventable disease are not so new at all. Appealing to parents and their children as individuals rather than the group is part of the problem, which Hara Estroff Marano identifies as a focusing fallacy in today's "hothouse approach to children's experience" through invasive parenting: "The cultivation of preciousness of one's offspring seems to breed in parents the conviction that everyone else in the culture, or at least the neighborhood, is as interested in and delighted by children, *specifically their children*, as they are. This is a well-recognized psychological phenomenon known as the focusing fallacy: parents inflate the importance of their kids" at the expense of other people's children (my emphasis, 254). The problem with such thinking is the separateness it exacerbates—further exceptionalizing children *from* the community rather than integrating them *within* it.

Stephanie Messenger's *Melanie's Marvelous Measles* (2012) unwittingly encapsulates these dangers: in a school where many children are not vaccinated, a child gets measles. An unvaccinated classmate is worried until her mother explains, "It is a common childhood disease. Children get spots on their body and they can feel very hot for a day or so." By the end of the book, Tina is excited to get them: "Maybe I'll be lucky enough to catch measles next time someone we know has them!" The overall message, "When you live by nature's laws . . . You thrive and survive!" is astoundingly ignorant of nature's so-called laws. And the book takes its own stab at the blame game as well when classmate Jared gets the measles and "Tina was not surprised really as she knew he ate so many sweets and chips every day." Jared's spotted face is seen illustrated with a slight grimace foregrounded by a revolting display of fast food, chips, cupcakes, cola, and a candy bar on his nightstand, as if these unhealthy foods are the real and only systemic cause of his illness. Aside from the deliberate, irresponsible misinformation, such lies completely misunderstand the point of inoculation—which is as much or more to protect other people's children, such as the immunocompromised leukemia patients discussed above who can't and should not get the vaccine, rather than just one's own exceptionalized darlings. Concerned parents have to wade through a lot of misinformation to decide for their children something that could simply be a matter of public trust (not to mention a little trust for the scientists who have worked for almost two centuries toward community immunity). Perhaps more frightening is that in spite of its ignorance, *Melanie's Marvelous Measles* offers a believable representation of contemporary parenting debates, and we're not just talking about young children here. Take as anecdotal evidence the case of Crystal McDonald's sixteen-year-old daughter during a California outbreak. When she and sixty-five other students had to stay out of school for two weeks because they weren't immunized, "she suggested simply getting a measles inoculation," but her mother strictly enforced her remaining unvaccinated, claiming: "I'd rather you miss an entire semester than you get the shot" (Healy and Paulson). Of course, Crystal probably carefully weighed her decision in the long term and so knew more about risks than her daughter, but she weighed them solely in that light, not considering the risks to other children—demonstrating just enough enlightened consumerism to be dangerously overconfident in her own judgment.

Markets for profit without adequate regulation make parenting decisions incredibly burdensome, eroding public trust and reproducing rampant private protectionism stemming from rational anxieties that are nonetheless exceedingly prone to manipulation. Those who know the political compromises made for profit in the United States and globalizing West, especially in the pharmaceutical and thus medical industry, have good reason to be skeptical. American ad campaigns for Gardasil expose the workings of emotional capitalism again—exploiting parental fears about future risks for cancer as motivation to inoculate children against HPV (human papillomavirus). In an analysis of Canada's similar campaign, Erin Connell and Alan Hunt describe how the "convergence of both medical and market interests thrusts responsibility on parents" by appealing to emotions through the "moralization of health" (63). By targeting a specific population (minors), such campaigns register as "health protection" but tend to hide their biopolitical agenda: to regulate girls' sexuality and/or reproductive healthcare, implicate boys in threats about cancer as well, and exploit parental anxieties about both (65). Unlike the vaccination for MMR, the HPV vaccination has not been tested enough yet to generate a clinical conclusion about its effectiveness, safety, or necessity. But what about the public service announcements that make them seem of equal importance? Or what if the family pediatrician recommends both as standard? That the weight of such decision making, blame, anxiety, and guilt is deflected back onto parents sometimes puts them in an impossible position.

If antivaccination activists were right, they would need to focus their protests on a larger scale (as some have, but most have not), but the privatization of children in nuclearized families erodes a sense of community interdependence, in which parents feel more comfortable making decisions for their own children oblivious to or deprioritizing consequences to others. Hara Estroff Marano puts it a bit more harshly: "Instead of summoning their energy to make a public push for institutional change, parents prefer to define a public world of hazard, privatize their vision to their own kids, and shift the burden ... wholly onto them. The more they privatize their fears and tighten their grip, the more fragile their kids become and the harder they make it for them to adapt to an ever-changing world. It's time for parents to back off. Safety is not a cure for uncertainty" (255). Such isolation, then, affects the public sphere without community awareness or solidarity. The magnitude of personal decisions that are ethically and existentially consequential to the group is simply mystified behind the supposedly impenetrable haven of the nuclear family.

But the history of inoculation and its detractors is long, varied, passionate, and fascinating. Indeed, it is a history in which the vulnerable or powerless—the enslaved, prisoners, and orphans—played an important role without consent. Often getting a sample of child subjects depended upon scientists and medical researchers experimenting on their own children or entire orphanages of children who, like the Tuskegee syphilis study, weren't even informed that they had been infected (Lederer 79, 83, 88, 102–3). Kanner, Langerman, and Grey, writing in the context of nursing as child advocacy, recount that the necessity of research for pediatric treatment has been complicated by the vulnerability of its subjects as well as a lack of priority, putting "children first" in a quite different sense: "Until the 1700s, children were considered chattels of their fathers; before this, physicians did not even care for children because physicians felt it was below their dignity.... The first [documented] test of immunizations used children and slaves as research subjects. In 1789, [Edward] Jenner inoculated his 10-month-old son, Edward, Jr., with the virus of a pox found on a pig" (16). This violation also happened to promise life-saving alternatives for future generations. M. T. Anderson mirrors this complicated and disturbing history of nonconsenting sacrifice in his novel set during the American Revolution, *The Astonishing Life of Octavian Nothing: Traitor to the Nation* (vol. 1: *The Pox Party*, 2006). Like the ads for HPV vaccine, the invitations to the "Pox Party" veil the event in sentimental language, in this case masking the College of Lucidity's racist research and revolution-quelling agenda: "Guests and their servants shall receive as it were the *Kiss of Life* upon the Arm," in order to protect against the threat, "Contagion may well stalk these fields" (184). This double reference to growing civil unrest and rumors among slaves that if they join the rebels they'll be freed turns out to be one of the "darker purposes" for "this gruesome fête," as quarantine will keep "their slaves weak, and fearful of running" (202). Anderson's novel makes explicit, in nauseatingly unforgettable detail, the suffering of those who die. One cannot mistake his point that the ends of such protections don't justify the means, but it does echo back a reflection upon the uncomfortable methods by which other people's children made medical advancements possible for future generations. Not all medical marvels have sprung from ethical practices.

The threat of contagion is powerful, not only because of the threat of fatality but also because, even where treatment is successful, we know that it can brutalize the body, just as small pox and plague once did, and cancer and its treatments still do. The pediatrician poet William Carlos Williams reminded his students (and reminds his readers) of this less romanticized but necessary dimension of medical treatment in *The Doctor Stories* (written from 1932–62).[4] His former student, Robert Coles, remembers Williams advising him in his choice of pediatric specialization: "I know you'll like the kids. They'll keep your spirits high. But can you go after them—grab them and hold them down and stick needles in them and be deaf to their noise?" (Williams viii). Our sentimentalized culture outside of the profession keeps such conversations semisecret, but in fact all of us, whether as former children or as parents, understand the restraint and/or temporary pain in certain medical procedures that a child has to tolerate before becoming completely socialized as a patient. In "The Use of Force," Williams recounts a particularly stubborn and frightened child who wouldn't submit to a throat culture:

> I have seen at least two children lying dead in bed of neglect in such cases, and feeling that I must get a diagnosis now or never I went at it again. But the worst of it was that I too had got beyond reason. I could have torn the child apart in my own fury and enjoyed it. It was a pleasure to attack her. My face was burning with it. The damned little brat must be protected against her own idiocy, one says to one's self at such times. Others must be protected against her. It is social necessity. (59)

Even the most everyday medical arts can insult our reticence about necessary pains in hopes of healing gains. But what we melodramatically disguise with sentimentality as a way of placating fear is that on a much smaller scale, medicine can hurt. Procedures and drugs can require suffering, side effects, gambles, and risks for the sake of safety and potential survival. William Carlos Williams documents the pediatric prerogative that hurting children is often necessary to heal them. Roald Dahl, whose seven-year-old daughter, Olivia, died from measles-encephalitis, put such measures in perspective in the 1980s, before the United States regressed in immunization success: "Apparently, you can't force a parent to stick their child with a needle, or even take the oral polio. But what the Americans did was absolutely delicious. They said that no child could go to school without a certificate of measles immunisation. A beautiful sort of blackmail. No immunisation, no school" (qtd. in Solomon 119). Decisions based on protectionist emotions (from sentimentality to fear) must be held in check by reason, collective debate, and public action. And sometimes this process will stab a bit.

Such necessity was well understood back when surgery was only performed by barbers and the occasional dentist—jobs for which a primary credential was the ability to inflict pain and calmly keep focus. And detachment has always been required. Like those involved in the unpopular decisions about Jaymee Bowen's treatment or vaccination policy, history is full of medical decisions for individuals being made within the ethical context of applying care by prioritizing the welfare of the community as a whole, a context that parents and family members cannot think of when one of their own is ill. This is, of course, why doctors do not treat their own family members for anything beyond minor complaints.

In the nineteenth century, aggressive treatment was called "heroic" medicine, capturing the idea of healing through hurting but also of serving the greater good rather than personal interests. This is one reason why *The Plague* (1947) by Albert Camus is sometimes used in ethics courses for medical students. Although many have perished by the height of conflict in the novel, ethical quandaries intensify around the painful death of one child that causes a crisis in doctrine for the priest and brings about many emotional and philosophical changes for those witnessing it: "[N]othing was more important on earth than a child's suffering, the horror it inspires in us, and the reasons we must find to account for it" (201). One character, Tarrou, expresses his own code of ethics, sounding a bit like the Hippocratic Oath: "What's natural is the microbe. All the rest—health, integrity, purity (if you like)—is a product of the human will, of a vigilance that must never falter. The good man, the man who infects hardly anyone, is the man who has the fewest lapses of attention. And it needs tremendous will-power, a never ending tension of the mind, to avoid such lapses" (229). The child's dramatic death is also relevant here for prompting discussions about the role of heroism in medical treatment. In the novel, there are several penetrating conversations between the journalist, Rambert, who has been quarantined in exile from his lover, and Dr. Rieux, whose impossible responsibility is to battle the plague, save as many as he can, and alleviate suffering. Rambert reflects on his experience in the Spanish Civil War: "I know now that man is capable of great deeds. But if he isn't capable of a great emotion, well, he leaves me cold" (149). Under quarantine, confined with multitudes dying from bubonic plague, the men having this conversation are all well aware that they are not simply talking about war—they are talking about fighting disease as well. As the pining lover in the piece, representing "love's egoism," Rambert is the emotional thinker, which leaves him skeptical of heroism: "[P]ersonally, I've seen enough of people who die for an idea. I don't believe in heroism; I know it's easy and I've learned it can be murderous. What interests me is living and dying for what one loves" (67, 149). Dr. Rieux counters with the simple but winning point of the argument, "Man isn't an idea, Rambert" (149).

This is the line which taught me, over thirty years ago when I first read it as a high school student, that fiction can be as honest, perhaps more honest, than we ever are in polite conversation. Long after, when I first published and since, I have protested that "*the child* does not exist," and yet I hope this pronouncement is understood in its affirmatory sense as well—not only *do* children exist, but none of them is simply a construct. Dr. Rieux understands that "the Man" of discourse and "our fellow man" are *different* constructs—one of abstract philosophy, the other nearer to our living, breathing neighbor who is as vulnerable to disease, oppression, and the cruelty of chance as we are ourselves. Camus does not let his reader forget that living, breathing person, no matter how imperfectly he has to rely upon language to do so. So I'm stealing his line: children are not an idea, either. They are worth fighting for. And that doesn't just mean defending vulnerable bodies. Children are material persons who require protections, but these must be balanced with participation that gives them opportunities for experience, competence, independence, accountability, and debate toward representing themselves where capable. The more these negotiations can take place in a public sphere, the better, as private political expression remains just that, private. To grow up within a full, supportive community with interdependent commitments will require open awareness, not just in the family or home, but in public spheres where all who care can have a voice. And we should all care.

Some cited throughout my discussion—Žižek, Coontz, Oaks, and Marano—have fittingly argued that none of the problems that plague us will be solved by private charity or individual efforts, instead requiring major systemic change. I passionately agree; we need cultural, community-level, and legal changes to reinforce protective *and* participatory rights wherever appropriate and necessary. And yet, this point seems to me to overlook the more immediate urgency we face in child advocacy. As Dr. Rieux says, "a man can't cure and know at the same time. So let's cure as quickly as we can. That's the more urgent job" (189). When you are looking at a nine-year-old who has constant tremors from past trauma, you aren't worrying about the system but about him; when you look at a child who has experienced so much hunger that she cannot stop shoveling the food she gets into her mouth until she vomits, you aren't going to wait for the revolution to help. Where children die of preventable disease, you can't simply hope that the world economy will shift toward fairer distribution of wealth.

"The child" of rights discourse is certainly an abstraction, but an actual child in crisis doesn't have time to wait for slow, deliberate structural change. This child is not an idea but a person—a person with great potential if granted proportionate recourse to social justice. By committing to our communities and to other people's children, we might not just help individuals but also build solidarity and forge public methods for effecting more lasting change.

Conclusion

A Last Note on the Nuclear Family

> "Can I find a balance
> between me and
> the box I call my family?
> I want equilibrium.
> I want subtle change."
> —Jessie Childress (age 16)

Many in the United States worry about exposing children to "broken homes" while too young. But divorce, remarriage, marriage resistance, fostering, adoption, or choosing family by cohabitating peacefully with nonbiological relations can "fix" lives too. Divorce doesn't break genuine parental-filial bonds, but violence, abuse, neglect, homophobia, rigid religiosity, lack of social support, poverty, food insecurity, and disease can. The hegemonic ideal of the nuclearized family, much like protectionism, is a result of an isolationism beset with inconsistent logic that, through merging sometimes conflicting interests essentializes the social, naturalizes the ideological. But nature isn't always right. Maggie Gallagher writes, "Marriage as a kin creator seeks to weave together moral relations and obligations out of the raw materials of human biology, to unite mothers and fathers, parents and children, love and sex, intimacy and economics: it confers social meaning on the accident of biology" (173).

Essentializing family as a biological certainty is no more sustainable than counting on social support alone. One is necessary for begetting children, the other for upbringing. Protections are required to keep children safe, but the right to participate and be heard on issues that affect their safety is necessary for applying protections justly. Human rights defined in terms of negatives (protection *from* exploitation, abuse, predation) are only humane with increasing counterbalances of input from the growing child on how and where they need to be applied. Love can be manipulative if we don't recognize its power, as in the tyranny of pretense, but when we love with self-awareness and reciprocal respect, we are more likely to serve "other people's children." In order to think outside of the box, we have to look at children not just as property of families, but also as citizens with public identities.

In this book, I have tried to contextualize children's rights to protection and participation within the historical development of middle-class nuclear families, and, of course, the fictions and dominant culture centered on them. If we can more clearly recognize the constraints of the model, we are more likely to be empathetic to the needs of the kinless or those within dysfunctional kinship units. Islanding children does not guarantee safety or all protections needed, especially within the legacy of parental and property rights. Jay Griffiths writes, "In the empire of the family, it has been too easy for adults to see a child as *Terra Parentis*, a dominion, a region of territorial expansion for the parent. In Rome, in the early days of empire, a father had *patria potestas*: absolute power of life and death over his children" (162). E. J. Graff adds that "Europe and its Western colonies followed the Romans' lead, taking for granted that a child's guardian was his or her father" (106). Instructions for religious and medical care "aimed their childrearing advice at the male patriarch—whether fathers or masters" because "a woman couldn't own property, and a child was, above all, productive property" (106–7). So mothers became religious and care-giving overseers, under patriarchal command, which eventually eclipsed "best interests" with the sentimental but not material supports of tender-years doctrine. Middle-class child rearing, managing productive property, eventually gave way to "selfless" parenting in the nineteenth century, sentimentalism in the twentieth, and "invasive" parenting in the twenty-first. Eva Illouz argues that within this emerging hegemonic ideal, capitalist development became inflected emotionally, especially with the influence of psychoanalytic theory: "[T]he nuclear family is the very point of origin of the self—the site within which and from which the story and history of the self could begin," but, "ironically, at the same time that the traditional foundations of marriage started to crumble, the family came back to haunt the self with a vengeance, but this time as a 'story' and as a way to 'emplot' the self. The family played a role that was all the more crucial for the constitution of new narratives of selfhood in that it was both the very origin of the self and that which the self had to be liberated from" (7). To be liberated from family-written "emplotments," especially those which do not fit, protect, or afford reciprocity, a child will need to participate as a member of the public.

I began this book with the voice of a fictional child becoming committed to child rights and will end with her as well. Emma (Emancipation) Sheridan, the eleven-year-old protagonist of Louise Fitzhugh's 1974 novel, *Nobody's Family Is Going to Change*, and her little brother Willie, begin discovering limitations within their upper-middle-class Manhattan family, due to the sexism and lookism of their authoritarian father, but also the nuclearized, thus isolating, family dynamic. For his dreams of being a dancer, Willie must find greater support from his extended family (their uncle), and Emma, who wants to be an attorney, which her father considers inappropriate for a female, has to find a public connection to other kids in her neighborhood who share an interest in children's rights: "Emma was drafting a Children's Charter. It was a Magna Charta, a Bill of Rights, a Constitution, and a Declaration of Independence rolled into one" (25, 26–27). She seeks solidarity in her neighborhood brigade of the Children's Army, with hopes that "they would really stick behind each kid and make it easier somehow to get through this business called childhood" (69). Through her participation with the group, Emma learns how much worse some children's family conflicts can be but also gains a broader sociostructural understanding of her situation, including an awareness that gender politics are just as much of a problem in the public sphere as they are in her private family life: "When it gets right down to it, the Children's Army is no different from any adult organization. Males were in control" (188). Emma is already familiar with such power structures and her lack of a voice within them.

But there is a key difference between her family and the Children's Army, which only children can join. And their focus is on children's issues, as a group functioning as a peer public, not as individuals disconnected by their private home lives and family roles. The stereotyped liberal, the leader of the group, Harrison Carter, explains the difference: "The Army is devoted, primarily, to the study of children's rights.... Naturally, pressing cases, which are the only kind we handle, are also helped, but the main purpose is not so much to help individuals as it is to impress upon the membership that children have no rights under our legal system" (185–86). Curiously, even though this group hints at readying for possible violence if necessary, the members draw a line at bucking the system of child protection. The group plans and stages interventions with parents who are treating their children unfairly. It is an effective move toward transparency, but Emma realizes that it probably doesn't actually change what goes on in the isolated privacy of the home once they leave: "I mean, do you really believe, like take a kid whose father is beating him up, the committee comes in and everything, and this guy, the father, says he'll change. Do you really believe he doesn't swat that kid the minute the committee leaves the house?" Her friend objects at first: "That's why, in bad cases like that, they get the kid removed" (215). So it appears that the Children's Army simply informs existing child protection services, something, I might add, anyone who works with child protection agencies would not consider so glibly. Emma will, in contrast, have to think outside of the box.

Emma gets a crash course in the radicalizing climate of her time and is a quick study, which Fitzhugh treats with humor. When shopping for the requisite box of cookies as the passcode for entering a meeting, Emma "pondered the boxes. Personally she preferred Mallomars, but what did revolutionaries eat? It would be awful to appear holding some kind of reactionary cookie that everyone had stopped eating years ago, like those pink puffs there looking a bit like Zsa Zsa Gabor, obviously capitalist cookies" (66). Fitzhugh shows, however, that the political point of the book is not to be taken lightly. Although sometimes indirectly, she strikes at some points I investigate closely in this book: privatized childhood, isolation, ownership, property, and shifting meanings of "kith and kin."

Harrison Carter, although often the object of the reader's scorn, packs a punch only made more dangerous by the buffering effect of humor, telling Emma, "I mean, you understand, don't you, that your father actually owns you, like a slave?" With a keener intuition of ethics than her lawyer father, and a sharp ability to argue with nuance, Emma "had thought of that, but not in exactly those terms," replying, "'He can't sell me, though'" (186). This might be the most radical scene I've had the delight of reading in children's literature, and it is certainly one of my favorites, because it may read as hyperbolically as those reactionary Mallomars, but it also happens to contain a historical truth that cuts through all the pop jargon and sweets: patriarchal Western countries, as we have seen, share a legacy that goes all the way back to Ancient Roman laws, like *patria potestas*, according to which not only are children explicitly the property of their fathers, but the primary check against abuse of power is a stipulation that they cannot sell their children into slavery.[1] Nonetheless, Emma is learning that, as Letty Cottin Pogrebin has pointed out, "[t]he defense of parental rights is linked to the defense of patriarchal power." The US swing toward isolating families and reaffirming parental autonomy just happens to regress toward patriarchal control: "The Family isn't a place where parents must love children, but where children must obey parents. The pro-family impulse isn't a nostalgic longing for a caring circle around the hearth, but a strategy against youthful insubordination and defiance. The awful truth is that this pro-family strategy touches a chord in millions of people who do not otherwise identify with ultra-right aims" (1983, 41). Political emotionalism powerfully co-opts a broader ideological range of supposedly autonomous middle-class citizens. Like the middle class, the nuclear family is a conservative social form that operates like a holding pattern, a sedimenting institution that recreates its own containment. If "nobody's family is going to change," the model it is based on will have to.

By first stripping it down to this most basic, unsentimental premise, Emma is able to build back up her own beliefs about justice, advocating nonviolence and equity, which ultimately retunes her group identity through the formation of a splinter group of the Children's Army called "the Changelings." When a member of the splinter group asks what "changeling" means in their context, acknowledging, "I thought it meant some kid in an Irish fairy tale, stolen away," she recasts their activism with this more positive message: "What I mean is, somebody who is young and somebody who changes. . . . I'm saying fathers don't change and mothers don't change. It's up to us to change" (Fitzhugh 214). And isn't that consistent with what it really means to be growing up? This is not the facile insight it may appear to be. Rather than waiting to be changed into a liberated person, Emma recommends defining and making the change for oneself. Consider the active voice used in the common idiom of "taking responsibility." Why, when applied to minors, does the phrase usually change to the passive form of being "given responsibilities," often a bit at a time like token chores, training wheels for future responsibilities? Emma's point is that a child can *take* responsibility; she might not be able to define the boundaries of freedom and mobility involved, the parameters, direction, and degree to which she takes it, but she can absolutely find rewarding responsibilities to take, perhaps even ones that provide greater independence. At dinner that night Emma's father rails as usual against her ambition, "Women lawyers are idiots! They're the laughing-stock of any group of lawyers. I think any woman who tries to be a lawyer is a damned fool!" but now she replies, "That is your problem, not mine" (221). And she is right. The first baby steps are a small but triumphant example of individuation on her own terms. Emma is protecting herself in the ways her parents fail to protect her, rejecting the "protections" that oppress her, through acceptance of the fact that it's ok to not be the person her parents are trying to mold (53, 120, 141). By selectively breaking family pretenses and parental projections, Emma models cherishing her own vision with transparency, boundaries, and open awareness (perhaps, like Victoria Rowell, "fathering" herself where necessary).

When the protections adults offer children are counterproductive to their actual needs, children can, do, and should protect themselves, rather than remaining isolated and appeased in the nucleus of capitalism's hush-money, hegemony, and amorphous middle-class institutions.

Notes

Introduction

1. This paragraph is from my review of *Human Rights in Children's Literature*, by Jonathan Todres and Sarah Higinbotham in *Children's Literature* 45 (2017) 239–44. An interdisciplinary project, it is a valuable resource for understanding how child readers can learn about rights from literature. Most important, it carefully integrates actual child readers' responses to literature.

2. Patricia Crain's *Reading Children: Literacy, Property, and the Dilemmas of Childhood in Nineteenth-Century America* (2016) provides an excellent example of how this method works and why it is imperative.

3. As a starting point, see Whitbeck and Hoyt, 7.

4. Yes, *Spiderman* fans, this familiar ring is further proof that one need only to read comic books to be a civilly literate human being!

Chapter 1

1. I'm not sure how those on shore were supposed to be able to see this particular display, but the gesture would become iconic. In a reader report, Lara Saguisag also pointed out that a different strain of protection rhetoric surrounded the nudity of Brooke Shields in the 1980 filmic adaption of the 1908 novel *The Blue Lagoon*, inspired by *Paul and Virginia*.

2. Notice that mention of "children" is dropped again or subsumed at best as a prop.

3. Just think of the most iconic shipwreck painting by Géricault showing half-submerged, half-eaten bodies clinging to a makeshift raft—that's the one.

4. The name "Richard Parker" became so iconic of youth in peril through oral transmission that Otilia Ribeiro, a young Brazilian female passing as male would borrow his moniker (after an altercation with him in 1884, when he caught her trying to stowaway on the *Mignonette* and ironically saved her life by throwing her off the yacht). In her journeys and impressive seamanship, she was known as Jack Straw, but Ribeiro also used the alias Ricardo Parker, perhaps emphasizing her appearance as a handsome youth (Simpson 44, 292–94). Such passings were a known enough occurrence to be reflected in a sea ballad entitled "The Female Cabin Boy," quoted in Simpson (1984, 292–93).

5. The trope (and *Mignonette* disaster specifically) is parodied in Monty Python's Flying Circus if you need comic relief from all of this child eating.

6. Perhaps this creating by stealing applies to Scliar's work as well. He's done his own share of borrowing from Hitchcock's *Lifeboat*.

7. Perhaps Pi's isolated containment feels like being consumed. Either way, this unusual variation on the theme will be relevant to my next chapter.

8. Neil Hanson explains that Richard Parker "lied about his age, claiming to be eighteen, when in fact he had only just turned seventeen" (39). Who knows how underaged some sailors were, even where laws applied.

9. The Donner party also had its implicit ethnic hierarchy. "Strangers to them all" were the apparently dispensable hired hands, Luis and Salvador, who are not given last names in my sources (Daniel James Brown 184–85).

10. Though I will rely on testimonies of minors throughout this book when possible, I am not presupposing their authenticity (a much thornier issue than I have room to debate here). Jessica Isaac aptly describes this interpretive difficulty in dealing specifically with the *Amistad* and Donner party accounts, explaining that they were "published because they contained eyewitness accounts of events of national importance. Their historical importance has also ensured that their manuscripts have survived, allowing an unusual window into the editing processes that preceded their publication.... [W]hile the contemporary understanding of conjoined rhetorical agency for children may have enabled adult editors and readers to believe that children's expressions became authentic and powerful thanks to adult intervention, the sponsors of these letters capitalized on the ideological weight of the child's voice as they edited these letters in support of their own ideological purposes" (9). This adult commissioning and meddling with children's testimonies is an intrinsic part of publication and preservation, and one that is difficult to measure in any accurate sense. My goal in using these sources is to identify fissures in protectionist rhetoric that not only leave some children robbed of any opportunity for participation, but also fail to protect them from harm. On the uncertain authenticity of child voices in publishing, see also Honeyman 2011.

11. For more on the common compensatory backlash in white apologist representations, Caroline Levander writes that "slave-ship narratives proceed to represent the numerous ways in which the nation's slave trade can capture the 'wrong' racial bodies—the ways in which it is flawed because it cannot always operate according to the precise logic of racial identity that differentiates black from white, African from American" (47).

12. Lawrance uses the term "orphan" for anyone cut off from relatives by death or even temporary abduction in order to emphasize the cruelty of involuntarily severing familial ties. This is a practical reminder that kinlessness can be temporary and unpredictable—all the more reason for girding child protection with rights to participation.

13. This device, by which paternal authority is exercised through letters or diary oversight is repeated enough to suggest it as a standard trope. Alcott's *Little Women* and Sendak's *Outside over There* (discussed in chapter 3) come to mind.

Chapter 2

1. Marx conveniently focused on Robinson's nonexploiting labors only—not the various slave labors he enforces (*Capital* 1:169–70).

2. See Marx, *Capital* 1:893–95, including footnotes.

3. Little Orphan Annie appears as one of these "hoboes" with the all-too-familiar bindle from May 11 through May 13, 1930 (3:74). On a more serious note, Thomas Minehan's *Boy and Girl Tramps of America* (1934) is an absolute treasure of scholarship, which I highly recommend to anyone interested in youths and hobo culture.

4. According to another anecdote, Gray had initially pitched the strip with a boy, but his editor claimed, "The kid looks like a pansy to me ... Put a skirt on him and we'll call it 'Little Orphan Annie'" (Smith 9).

5. There are many great examples of robinsonades that resist this false dilemma, focusing on females as either part or all of island populations. Two recent examples are Terry Pratchett's *Nation* (2008) and Libba Bray's *Beauty Queens* (2011), discussed later in this chapter. Jeannine Blackwell (1985) and Amy Hicks (2015) address the larger tradition of including females in the tradition.

6. I much prefer Susan Synarski's rendering of Lai Choi San in Sara Lorimer's *Booty: Girl Pirates on the High Seas* (60).

7. This is from a 1986 Report for the Independent Commission on International Humanitarian Issues by Susanne Agnelli (94).

8. That is, Rousseau would have approved of Brian and Mary's method of learning for boys, like his "Émile," not girls, like his "Sophie," but why dredge up all that foolishness here? What's important is that Mary, like the Miss Teen Dream contestants, can ruggedly triumph too.

9. Graham records many of his favorite readings, including Slocum's classic, Richard Henry Dana's *Two Years behind the Mast*, Richard Hughes's *High Wind in Jamaica*, Jacques-Henri Bernardin de Saint-Pierre's *Paul and Virginia* (which he relates to personally), and the Bible (22, 29, 36, 79, 93, 154, 162). Reading lists are common in the genre.

10. This sponsorship clearly favored Graham's voyage because of the novelty of someone so young attempting circumnavigation. According to Donald Holm, he was dubbed the "schoolboy sailor" by the media. It seems that *National Geographic* and "other sponsors" even paid for a replacement thirty-three-foot sloop christened *The Return of Dove* after *Dove* was "literally coming apart" and had to be sold in the West Indies (297, 303).

11. This sailing philosophy, in contrast to racing, can be better understood in Bernard Moitessier's *The Long Way* (1975). Laura's experience touring at stops is also well documented in the film *Maidentrip* (2013).

12. For a sense of how much competition for unassisted speed alters the experience, read Peter Nichols's fascinating *A Voyage for Madmen* (2001).

13. For one example of a foolishly risky and potentially deadly teen "adventure," see Tran.

Chapter 3

1. The excerpt is from *Mister Dog*, by Margaret Wise Brown, copyright 1952, renewed 1980 by Penguin Random House LLC. Used by permission of Golden Books, an imprint of Random House Children's Books, a division of Penguin Random House LLC. All rights reserved.

2. Kimberly D. Krawiec writes, "Throughout the world, in fact, baby selling is formally prohibited. And throughout the world, babies are sold each day" (41). Our denial of such transactions prevents improvements in the equity and welfare of participants while lining corrupt pockets: "Social pretense regarding the baby market is exhibited most clearly by the ban against baby selling.... this supposed ban merely prevents full compensation to certain

suppliers and does not (and is not designed to) prevent commercial transactions in children. Therein lies the harmful hypocrisy of baby-selling bans. Were Americans serious about their refusal to attach price tags to children, the law would ban all commercial transactions in babies, rather than merely restricting competition to baby market competitors" (52).

3. Letters from "Maria Rye Children" can be found at the Maria Rye Home Children database. Most are what you would expect—flattering appreciations toward Rye for providing them a "position" of dignified work—but one, concerning Agnes Rankin, who was nine when shipped, reveals that she had a seizure disorder and was abused to the point of her employers (Charles and Elizabeth Camidge) being tried for assault due to "misuse, cruelty, and ill treatment" in 1875.

4. Of note relevant to this and my last chapter is a "French law that forbade infants to travel on their ships" (Geller 172). This protection against liability more explicitly acknowledged both risk and extrafamilial responsibility toward the safety of the young.

5. On the underlying biases that complicate parental rights, Maggie Gallagher relates a similar hypothetical conundrum: "A nineteen-year-old single, pregnant black high school dropout walks into a government hospital in Harlem to deliver a baby. After the birth, a married, black, college-educated couple from Scarsdale shows up, offering to claim the baby and raise it as their own. To whom will the government hospital hand over the baby? Under current law, the answer is, of course, clear: the unmarried teenage high school dropout who gave birth is the mother and gets to keep her baby. But *why*?" (164). Her point is to question the conflicting logic we use in contested cases deciding custody or termination of parental rights: criteria used for "best interests" are social, but our laws will privilege biology wherever a viable claim. Gallagher argues that notions of family and parental rights are undergoing a profound shift, and "[w]hether liberal societies will find a conceptual grounding for taking seriously the biosocial experience of kinship in the world we are busily socially constructing remains an open question" (171, 173).

6. See chapter 2, note 4.

7. As the boat is reminiscent of my previous chapter, I searched to see this image more clearly. It also appears in *Upholsterer and Interior Decorator* 57 (1917): 69.

8. In the more recent readaptation starring Jamie Foxx, Annie and her super-rich father figure are updated and racially recast. He becomes a more nurturing father rather than distant benefactor. She becomes a foster child (with stereotyped foster mother, played by Cameron Diaz, who is just housing foster kids for the monthly check). Though harshly reviewed, this adaptation at least demonstrates that sugar daddies don't magically fix the emotional hardship of abandonment. In "daddy's" swanky bachelor pad, this Annie sleeps not in the enormous bed in her enormous room but by choice in the closet.

9. Bruce Smith writes, "Those who see the prototypes for Little Orphan Annie in Daddy Browning and Peaches are using faulty chronology. Annie and Daddy Warbucks were the best of friends in the funny papers by the time Peaches and Daddy Browning made the first page" (15), which makes me feel it necessary to point out that Browning's much publicized adoptions, his moniker as a "Cinderella man," and fairytale fatherhood in news coverage occurred during the years preceding *Little Orphan Annie*'s debut. These are the links that readers have probably seen over the years, not with Browning's 1926 marriage to Peaches, but in his "charitable" paternalism. It also is worth noting that Smith calls Annie and Warbucks "best of friends," revealing a bit of ambivalence in his own thinking about this odd duo.

10. Like many letter-writing comics fans, Updike aspired to be a cartoonist. More on this phenomenon in chapter 4.

11. Alluding to Michelle Alexander's popularizing of the coinage "the New Jim Crow" for our extreme, racially biased justice and prison system, Stephanie Clifford and Jessica Silver-Greenberg call the foster care system "Jane Crow" (*New York Times*, July 21, 2017). For more on the Jane Crow of foster care, see Dorothy Roberts (2002).

12. If so, in contrast to the opinions of neoconservatives, a job that is abysmally undercompensated.

13. Rowell's in-care childhood was also affected by racism. When her (white) biological mother became mentally ill and unable to parent, the extended (white) family disowned her biracial children while claiming her white children. Dorothy Rowell's biracial children were placed in different foster homes.

14. Most placements are rigidly restrictive geographically. Foster kids usually have to stay in "respite" care when their foster family travels out of state, unless planned very far in advance with much red tape to get permission. I have to get permission just to take my CASA kids anywhere in a car. The geographic flexibility that Rowell's caseworker and fosters arranged (often out-of-state) was remarkable.

15. Whitbeck and Hoyt explain that "traditional definitions distinguish between being a 'runaway,' 'throwaway,' or 'street youth.' 'Runaway' refers to someone who is away from home at least overnight without parental consent or knowledge. 'Throwaway' refers to a child's having been told that he or she may not return home or having been kicked out or locked out of the parents' house. 'Street youth' may be used to refer to runaways and nonrunaways. It usually refers to young people who hang out on the streets, and who may or may not have homes to return to at night" (4). The eliding of these terms is symptomatic of our common assumptions that all are derelict rather than abused and disowned. Francesca Lia Block makes this reality and our denial of it clear in her retelling of Little Red Riding Hood, "Wolf," in *The Rose and the Beast* (2000): "Same old boring boring story America can't stop telling itself. What is this sicko fascination? Every book and movie practically has to have a little, right? But why do you think all those runaways are on the streets tearing up their veins with junk and selling themselves so they can sleep in the gutter? What do you think the alternative was at home?" (103–4).

16. Interestingly, child liberation is also read in some contexts as spoiling. See Ehrensaft, 155–56.

17. This hardly seems credible in light of Rousseau's other excuses: "He had been forced to send his children to the foundling home by his own indifference and incapacity . . . by the monstrousness of her mother, and in a wild paranoid flight, by the premonition that, had he kept his children, he would have been trapped by his enemies into an incestuous muddle" (Kessen 156). A real *mensch*, that.

18. Adoptive father figures like Daddy Warbucks, Popeye, and *Gasoline Alley*'s Walt Wallet are also consistent with the backlash culture of the 1920s and 30s in which there were concerns that maternal centrality in the new privatized, nuclearized family would "sissify" boys. Consider them also in the context of Disney's father-centered films and the superhero-sidekick relationships that would soon pervade the genre.

19. Nevertheless, New Jersey would create a program based on the Finnish example in 2017. The New Jersey Baby Box Initiative guarantees a baby box and supplies to any new parent in the state who fills out the form and watches a short instructional video.

20. Because Pastor Lee has provided permanence for the more impaired babies abandoned at his church, disability rights play a huge role in this case as well and are worthy of more consideration than my digressions will allow.

21. Notable exceptions, perhaps because they are marketed to younger readers, are Eloise McGraw's *The Moorchild* (1996) and Francesca Lia Block's *The Waters and the Wild* (2009), both of which, to be believable, require negligible filial love from their main characters, who discover they are changelings and so successfully quest to return the human children they replaced.

22. With the exception of Iofur Raknison, the bear who wants his own doll-like daemon to assimilate with humans: he wants a transitional object who will reflect back his own subjectivity, subjugating a child to reflect his superior power.

23. For a literary exception, see Louise Fitzhugh's *Nobody's Family Is Going to Change* (1974), to be treated in my conclusion.

24. To be fair, Shusterman does have an aside on donation: "[I]f more people had been donors, unwinding never would have happened . . . but people like to keep what's theirs" (224). So, if you haven't already done so, please sign your license as a donor. For all you know this might serve "other people's children" someday without your having to lift anything but a pen today.

25. Gilman also indicates proportionality as an issue: "Children are part of humanity, and the largest part. . . . Any population which increases has a majority of children, our own being three-fifths. This large proportion of human beings constitutes a permanent class,—another fact we fail to consider because of our personal point of view" (118). Though children as a class are no longer a majority in the United States and many other countries, they certainly are in the global South. But the decreased proportion of minors in hyper-developed nations still contributes to oppression. In the United States, for example, states with high average ages (due to retired communities or dwindling small towns) tend to have more rights violations of youth. Florida is the worst, with Arizona a far second (completely unsubstantiated claim on my part relying solely on years of following news media, but I'll stand with it until I hear otherwise!).

26. Victoria Rowell does indicate, however, that such arrangements are particularly tempting for someone who has aged out of foster care, which is often as abrupt as jumping off a cliff from state guardianship without a safety net: "There was the necessity of physically removing myself from an entanglement with a man who fed, clothed, and housed me—like so many young girls who continue to enter compromising relationships after emancipation from foster care. We need to eat, and to have someone to hold, even if it's dangerous" (249).

Chapter 4

1. Of course, in spite of the poor-quality newsprint on which they were produced, comics owners and collectors frequently inscribed their copies on the covers or in margins, ink, pencil, or crayon. The cheapness of the product did not detract from the sense of ownership.

2. Neuroscientist V. S. Ramachandran goes as far as to suggest that our processing of image is faster than that of verbiage: "[T]he visual metaphor is probably understood by the right hemisphere long before the more literal-minded left hemisphere can spell out the reasons . . . [G]reat art sometimes succeeds by dissolving this barrier" (237).

3. For an excellent counter to such efforts authentically documenting Japanese experiences in concentration camps at the time, see Miné Okubo's *Citizen 13660*.

4. By the fall of 1942, some twenty thousand were enlisted in the metro area of Boston alone (Smith 50).

5. Richard Gid Powers writes, "Before, during, and after the Junior G-Man boom, the cereal manufacturers of America were arming and training youthful detectives, organizing them into posses, and sending them off in pursuit of imaginary desperados" (12). Post Toasties, for example, offered membership into the Junior Detective Corps under the authority of "Inspector Post," who includes this tip in his invitation letter: "Just so Inspector Post will know you are helping to keep your body strong and your mind alert (you know a detective must be strong and quick) he also asks that you send with the coupon two tops from Post Toasties boxes. Post Toasties, you know, is *full* of quick energy—just what a detective needs" (191).

6. In Powers, the letter is misattributed to a "Mark K.," but the facsimile in Bill Adler's *Kids' Letters to the F.B.I.* (1966) clearly reads "Mary K" (no pagination). Other favorites from this collection continue with similar themes: "Dear Sir, I would appreciate all the information you could send me about vice I don't know much about it. Thanks, Greg B. Detroit, Michigan" and "Dear Mr. Hoover, How can you make more money, as an F. B. I. agent or as a crook? Please give me an honest answer. Yours truly, Danny M. Brentwood, Calif." (no pagination).

7. Sometimes, of course, the family supported and even took part in or grudgingly approved of comics fandom. Many letters protesting against comics censorship in the Senate Subcommittee on Juvenile Delinquency archives are co-signed by parents or even written by them on behalf of their children.

8. For one example, you can do a simple search for "How to Spot a Jap" by Milton Caniff.

9. A later example of such reciprocity occurs in Phoebe Gloeckner's *The Diary of a Teenage Girl* (2002), in which she recounts an immediate letter exchange with comics artist Aline Kominsky in the summer of 1976: "I got a postcard from Aline Kominsky today. She said she never got a letter from a girl before, just from greasy fan-boys who think she's cute. Now I feel even more inspired to draw" (141).

10. These crusades and resulting purges in the comics industry are well covered (that is, with attention to the children's market) for an academic audience in Amy Kiste Nyberg's *Seal of Approval: The History of the Comics Code* and for a general audience in David Hajdu's *The Ten-Cent Plague: The Great Comic-Book Scare and How It Changed America*.

11. Stewart identifies himself as "a normal boy of sixteen years of age with average intelligence" and "co-editor of an amateur magazine devoted to the EC fan."

12. As scholars, this collecting constitutes archival work and preservation and is paramount with comic books. Those invested in the interactive potential of comics hopefully are also more likely to appreciate in their history the exercising of new consumer power, active readership, and participation in mass culture by young people. Children who consumed comics in the 1950s, some of whom protested in order to do so, are now in their sixties and seventies. We should hear more from them now, while we still can, and we should incorporate archival preservation and ethnographic voicing in our study of this unique field of readings that we adults are ever appropriating for our own consumption in the name of the young.

13. For an example of this historical embedding in daily comic strips, see the materialist analysis of Popeye strips from the 1920s and 30s in *Consuming Agency in Fairy Tales, Childlore, and Folkliterature* (Routledge 2010), 140–62.

14. The Comics Code was implemented as a self-regulating rubric within the industry to placate would-be censors in response to the anticomics crusades of the late 1940s and early 50s. It defined silver-age comics, stamped in the upper right-hand corner on the covers of approved comics. See also note 72.

15. This market was more gender balanced at this time than is often thought. In fact, "As early as 1946, a graph in *Newsdealer* magazine had shown that in the age groups eight to eleven years, and again at eighteen to thirty-four years, female comic-book readers outnumbered males" (Robbins 38).

16. The increase in television viewing among children also slowed the comics market for juvenile readers.

17. As mentioned before, most of these letters were written in response to the letter-writing campaign William Gaines, of EC comics, called for in a full-page ad in some EC titles in 1954 and quoted above. They, like the subcommittee hearings, were largely in response to horror and crime comics, but I think the awareness and agency it exhibits is indicative of the larger interactivity of the medium and industry at the time, and certainly this collective effort goes beyond the call, evidencing that kids were not simply parroting adult views (see Nyberg 118; Hajdu 251).

18. Matthew Pustz provides an excellent analysis of the letters-column tradition (166–68). Martin Barker adds the caveat that aspects of the letters columns are manipulated (biased selection, ghost-writing, 47). However, taken into account holistically with the many interactive pages and panels, one can see a genuine commitment to fostering fan communication and input that resulted in rhetorical reciprocity.

19. The full Comics Codes from 1948, 1954, and 1971 are available in Nyberg (165–74), but here are some relevant highlights from the one that may have affected Mayer (from 1954): "[W]henever possible good grammar shall be employed," and "Respect for parents ... shall be fostered" (166–68). Even tame rules like these could become restrictive, especially as Jackson and Arnold explain of the slightly later Harvey comics that "a key theme in Harvey Comics and in the generation gap of the 1960s and 1970s" was "parents not being able to understand their children. Children in the Harvey Comics always seem to be one-up on adults, exhibiting a higher vision. They show control, exhibit greater tolerance, and solve their own problems" (5).

20. The work of Sheldon Mayer, to many, represents some of the finer DC comics for children at a time of great struggle over age appropriateness and quality, as Seth contextualizes in his introduction to the John Stanley library: "Somehow I had gotten the idea that the humor comics of the '50s and '60s contained a lot of forgotten gems. This was completely erroneous. Besides *Sugar and Spike*, ACG's *Herbie* and some good *Nancy* reprints, I found out that the majority of old humour comics are terrible" (1).

21. Wording from personal interview: "My first mail!"

22. Much has been made of the thinly veiled sadomasochistic tendencies of Marston (penname Charles Moulton), the creator of Wonder Woman, but the earnest treatment of "captivation" as a part of normal development is explained in Moulton's *Emotions of Normal People* (292–301). Perhaps his title protests a bit too much?

23. Merrily Mayer also makes clear that as the original model for Sugar, she influenced her father's use of this theme by frequently springing her little brother from his playpen.

24. For the sake of thematic consistency, I've used the translation that Fredric Jameson uses (Erich Heller's loose translation in "Wittgenstein and Nietzsche" 152) as the epigraph to *The Prison-House of Language* (1972), even though Walter Kaufmann's translation of aphorism 522 from *The Will to Power* is as follows: "*We cease to think when we refuse to do so under the constraint of language*" (283).

25. Another consequence of serialization is that spellings are frequently inconsistent.

26. This strip was the inspiration for the title of Ethan Nicolle's *Chumble Spuzz*.

27. For more extensive coverage of this theme, please see *Elusive Childhood: Impossible Representations in Modern Fiction* (2005), 115–51.

28. Many famous accounts of such experiences (for example Sherman Alexie's and Italo Calvino's with *Superman*) could be cited here, but I'd like to go beyond this notion of visualcy to emphasize the actual sophistication of comics.

29. W. J. T. Mitchell debates the usefulness of the term "visual literacy," which I have long thought a necessary one to children's literature history and criticism because of the arc that spans from oralcy (preferable to the oxymoronic "oral literacy"), then traditional word literacy, and finally to film, television, and comics visualcy.

30. See W. J. T. Mitchell's *Blake's Composite Art: A Study of the Illuminated Poetry*. Princeton University Press, 1978.

31. Note that her interpretation is surprisingly complimentary to Sendak's own explanations quoted in chapter 3.

32. I'm taking historical liberties here, as this statement refers to the pictorial turn between 1910 and 1930—but the trend also continued and applies to the changes seen in the 1950s and again at the end of the twentieth century.

33. Artist-authors have the advantage of composing compositely. Alison Bechdel has explained and demonstrated that she "composes in images." But there have been some terrific illustrator-writer duos who create sublime moments of compositeness. For example, Quentin Blake and Roald Dahl have many simple points of contact between image and words that could not exist separately or carry any meaning (for a sample, see *Fantastic Mr. Fox*, 24–27).

34. This kind of self-reflexivity is an inherent part of the medium, as Winsor McCay amply demonstrated in the early part of the twentieth century. In fact, this cover, and others like it, has very McCaylike themes (the children are giants in a cityscape), reminiscent of *Little Nemo in Slumberland*.

Chapter 5

1. If this sounds extreme, consider what happens to your typical fairy-tale princess when she must transition to an adult social position or relationship. Like Bernardin's Virginia and all of those drowned and dripping ladies washed ashore, Sleeping Beauty and Snow White are the most extreme examples that come to my mind: somehow they have to die to be awakened by a (necrophiliac?) prince who will keep them in a coffin or accidentally awaken them to something other than girlhood, but is it "full adulthood" that a kiss awakens them to?

2. In fact, I can't help but wonder if the greater sales and longevity of the Gaes book comes from his survival, whereas Richmond eventually died from the disease.

3. I want to make clear that I am not disparaging Bowen's choices or trying to engage in parent blaming myself. As one who has experienced anticipatory grief, I'm most sympathetic. However, I did learn, with great regret, that indulging in one's need to grieve while the patient is still living does not ease their suffering a bit but simply alienates, and perhaps, significantly to my argument about protectionist sentiment, infantilizes the ill.

4. In addition to his private practice, William Carlos Williams administered care "as a school doctor and physician to the county orphanage, serving gratis" (133).

Conclusion

1. John Boswell writes, "To a modern reader, 'selling a child' suggests a questionable financial arrangement between natal parents and someone wishing to obtain a son or daughter, a transfer of authority rendered slightly distasteful by the intrusion of commerce. In the ancient world, selling a person meant making him or her a slave, the property of another person—irrevocably. It was not simply a change of guardianship but of personhood, and much Roman legislation ... was designed to prevent the wrongful enslavement of free citizens and their offspring. ... Even the *patria potestas* did not enable fathers to make slaves of freeborn offspring" (67). In fact, "children abandoned with the knowledge or consent of their fathers were automatically freed from his legal control" (325).

Works Cited

Adler, Bill. *Kids' Letters to the F.B.I.* Illus. Arnold Roth. Prentice-Hall, 1966.
Aebi, Tania, and Bernadette Brennan. *Maiden Voyage.* Simon and Schuster, 1989.
Agnelli, Susanna. *Street Children: A Growing Urban Tragedy.* Report for the Independent Commission on International Humanitarian Issues, Weidenfeld and Nicolson, 1986.
Ahmed, Sara. *Willful Subjects.* Duke University Press, 2014.
Alexander, Michelle. *The New Jim Crow: Mass Incarceration in the Age of Colorblindness.* New, 2010.
Alger, Bill. "Sugar's Daddy: Talking with Merrily Mayer Harris, Shelly Mayer's Daughter." http://www.twomourrows.com/comicbookartist/articles/11merrily.html.
Anderson, M. T. *The Astonishing Life of Octavian Nothing: Traitor to the Nation.* Vol. 1, *The Pox Party.* Candlewick, 2006.
Archard, David. *Children: Rights and Childhood.* Routledge, 1993.
Arendt, Hannah. "Reflections on Little Rock." *Dissent* 6, no. 1 (1959): 45–56.
Au, Michelle. *This Won't Hurt a Bit (and Other White Lies): My Education in Medicine and Motherhood.* Grand Central, 2013.
Avi. *The True Confessions of Charlotte Doyle.* Avon, 1992.
Barber, Benjamin. *Consumed: How Markets Corrupt Children, Infantilize Adults, and Swallow Citizens Whole.* W. W. Norton, 2007.
Barclay, Sarah. "Moving Story of the Girl Whose Battle for Life Has Until Now Been Protected by a Legal Cloak of Anonymity." *Daily Mail,* October 26, 1995. Web. January 2, 2015.
Barker, Martin. *Comics: Ideology, Power and the Critics.* New York: Manchester University Press, 1989.
Bassingame, John W., ed. *Slave Testimony: Two Centuries of Letters, Speeches, Interviews, and Autobiographies.* Louisiana University Press, 1977.
Beam, Cris. *To the End of June: The Intimate Life of American Foster Care.* Houghton Mifflin Harcourt, 2013.
Beauchamp, Tom L., and Robert M. Veatch. *Ethical Issues in Death and Dying.* 2nd ed. Prentice Hall, 1996.
Berger, James. "Falling Towers and Postmodern Wild Children: Oliver Sacks, Don DeLillo, and Turns against Language." *PMLA* 120, no. 2 (March 2005): 341–61.

Berlant, Lauren. *Cruel Optimism*. Duke University Press, 2011.
Bernardin de Saint-Pierre, Jacques-Henri. *Paul and Virginia*. 1788–89. Trans. John Donovan. Peter Owen, 2005.
Bernstein, Gaia, and Zvi Triger. "Over-Parenting." *University of California-Davis Law Review* 44, no. 4 (2011): 1221–79.
Biss, Eula. *On Immunity: An Inoculation*. Graywolf, 2014.
Bjork, Daniel W. *B. F. Skinner: A Life*. Basic Books, 1993.
Blackmore, David. *Blunders and Disasters at Sea*. Pen and Sword, 2004.
Blackwell, Jeannine. "An Island of Her Own: Heroines of the German Robinsonades from 1720 to 1800." *The German Quarterly* 58, no. 1 (1985): 5–26.
Block, Francesca Lia. *The Waters and the Wild*. HarperTeen, 2009.
Bloom, Paul. *How Children Learn the Meanings of Words*. MIT Press, 2000.
Bluebond-Langner, Myra. "I Know, Do You? A Study of Awareness, Communication, and Coping in Terminally Ill Children." In *Anticipatory Grief*, ed. Bernard Schoenberg et al. Columbia University Press, 1974, 171–86.
Bluebond-Langner, Myra. *The Private Worlds of Dying Children*. Princeton University Press, 1978.
Boswell, John. *The Kindness of Strangers: The Abandonment of Children in Western Europe from Late Antiquity to the Renaissance*. Pantheon, 1988.
Boyd, Danah. *It's Complicated: The Social Lives of Networked Teens*. Yale University Press, 2014.
Bray, Libba. *Beauty Queens*. Scholastic, 2011.
Brendtro, Larry, and Scott Larson. "The Resilience Code: Finding Greatness in Youth." *Reclaiming Children and Youth* 12. no. 4 (2004): 194–200.
Brent, Mary, and Caitlin Knutsson. *Chemo to the Rescue: A Children's Book about Leukemia*. AuthorHouse, 2008.
Brewer, Holly. *By Birth or Consent: Children, Law, and the Anglo-American Revolution in Authority*. University of North Carolina Press, 2005.
Brown, Daniel James. *The Indifferent Stars Above: The Harrowing Saga of the Donner Party*. HarperCollins, 2009.
Brown, Margaret Wise. *Mister Dog: The Dog Who Belonged to Himself*. Illus. Garth Williams. Random House Golden Book, 1952.
Buell, Marjorie Henderson (Marge). *Little Lulu on Parade*. David McKay, 1941.
Bunting, Eve. *SOS Titanic*. Houghton Mifflin Harcourt, 1996.
Burton, Virginia Lee. *Calico the Wonder Horse, or the Saga of Stewy Stinker*. Houghton Mifflin, 1941.
Burton, Virginia Lee. "Symphony in Comics." *Horn Book*. Vol. 17, 1941, 307–11.
Butler, Daniel Allen. *The Other Side of the Night*. CASEMATE, 2009.
Butler, Judith. *Precarious Life: The Powers of Mourning and Violence*. Verso, 2004.
Buzan, Deborah Skinner. "I Was Not a Lab Rat." *The Guardian*, March 12, 2004. www.theguardian.com.
C, Cassandra. "Cassandra's Chemo Fight: 'This Is My Life and My Body.'" *Hartford Courant*, January 8, 2015. Web. January 10, 2015.
Calvert, Karin. "Patterns of Childrearing in America." In *Beyond the Century of the Child: Cultural History and Developmental Psychology*, ed. Willem Koops and Michael Zuckerman. University of Pennsylvania Press, 2003.
Calvino, Italo. *Six Memos for the Next Millennium*. 1988. Random House, 1993.

Camus, Albert. *The Plague*. 1947. Trans. by Stuart Gilbert. Modern Library, 1948.
Caniff, Milton. *The Complete Terry and the Pirates, 1934–1936*. IDW, 2007.
Caniff, Milton. *Terry and the Pirates Shipwrecked on a Desert Island*. Whitman, 1938.
Carrier, David. *The Aesthetics of Comics*. Pennsylvania State University Press, 2000.
Cech, John. *Angels and Wild Things: The Archetypal Poetics of Maurice Sendak*. Pennsylvania State University Press, 1995.
Childress, Jessie. "New Honesty." In Franco, Betsy, and Nina Nickles. *Things I Have to Tell You: Poems and Writing by Teenage Girls*. Cambridge, MA: Candlewick, 2001. 12–13.
Chilman-Blair, Kim, and John Taddeo. *What's Up with Richard? Medikidz Explain Leukemia*. American Cancer Society, 2010.
Claflin, Carol J., and Oscar A. Barbarin. "Does 'Telling' Less Protect More? Relationships among Age, Information Disclosure, and What Children with Cancer See and Feel." *Journal of Pediatric Psychology* 16, no. 2 (1991): 169–91.
Clark, Cindy Dell. *In Sickness and Play: Children Coping with Chronic Illness*. Rutgers University Press, 2003.
Clifford, Stephanie, and Jessica Silver-Greenberg. "Foster Care as Punishment: The New Reality of 'Jane Crow.'" *New York Times*, July 21, 2017.
Coerr, Eleanor. *Sadako and the Thousand Paper Cranes*. Puffin, 1977.
Comerford, Brenda. "Parental Anticipatory Grief and Guidelines for Caregivers." *Anticipatory Grief* (1974): 147–57.
Connel, Erin, and Alan Hunt. "The HPV Vaccination Campaign: A Project of Moral Regulation in an Era of Biopolitics." *The Canadian Journal of Sociology/Cahiers canadiens de sociologie* 35, no. 1 (2010): 63–82.
Cook, Daniel Thomas. *The Commodification of Childhood: The Children's Clothing Industry and the Rise of the Child Consumer*. Duke University Press, 2004.
Coontz, Stephanie. *The Social Origins of Private Life*. Verso, 1988.
Coontz, Stephanie. *The Way We Never Were: American Families and the Nostalgia Trap*. 1992. Basic Books, 2016.
Coté, Charles J., Ralph E. Kauffman, Gloria J. Troendle, and George H. Lambert. "Is the 'Therapeutic Orphan' About to Be Adopted? *Pediatrics* 98, no. 1 (July 1996).
Couvreaux, Janis. "No, My Kids Didn't Wear Lifejackets for 10 Years at Sea." *Huff Post Blog*, January 15, 2016.
Crain, Patricia. *Reading Children: Literacy, Property, and the Dilemmas of Childhood in Nineteenth-Century America*. University of Pennsylvania, 2016.
Cross, Gary. *The Cute and the Cool: Wondrous Innocence and Modern American Children's Culture*. Oxford University Press, 2004.
Cunningham, Valentine. *Reading after Theory*. Blackwell, 2002.
Dahl, Roald. *Danny the Champion of the World*. 1975. Penguin, 1998.
Dahl, Roald. *Fantastic Mr. Fox*. 1970. Illus. by Quentin Blake. Puffin, 1998.
Daly, Martin, and Margo Wilson. *The Truth about Cinderella: A Darwinian View of Parental Love*. Yale University Press, 1998.
Dalrymple, Theodore. *Spoilt Rotten: The Toxic Cult of Sentimentality*. Gibson Square, 2011.
Dard, Charlotte-Adélaïde (née Picard). "The Sufferings of the Picard Family after the Shipwreck of the *Medusa*." Trans. Patrick Maxwell. *Medusa*. Leonaur, 2008. 203–315.
DC Comics. *Batman: The Brave and the Bold* 4 (June 2009).
Defoe, Daniel. *Robinson Crusoe*. 1719. (modernized edition). Broadview, 2014.
Dekker, Laura. *One Girl, One Dream*. 2013. HarperCollins, 2014.

Derbyshire, David. "How Children Lost the Right to Roam in Four Generations." http://www.dailymail.co.uk/news/article-462091/How-children-lost-right-roam-generations.html. Accessed June 3, 2017.

Diamond, Marion. *Emigration and Empire: The Life of Maria S. Rye*. Garland, 1999.

Dickenson, Donna. "Children's Informed Consent to Treatment: Is the Law an Ass?" *Journal of Medical Ethics* 20 (1994): 205–6, 222.

Donzelot, Jacques. *The Policing of Families*. Johns Hopkins University Press, 1979.

The Drop Box. Directed by Brian Ivie. Pine Creek Entertainment, 2015.

Eckholm, Erik. "Nebraska Revises Child Safe Haven Law," *New York Times*, November 21, 2008. www.nytimes.com.

Edinger, Monica. *Africa Is My Home: A Child of the* Amistad. Illus. Robert Byrd. Candlewick, 2013.

Ehrenreich, Barbara. "Welcome to Cancerland: A Mammogram Leads to a Cult of Pink Kitsch." *Harper's Magazine*. November 2011, 43–53.

Ehrensaft, Diane. *Spoiling Childhood: How Well-Meaning Parents Are Giving Children Too Much—But Not What They Need*. Guilford, 1997.

Eisen, Cliff, ed. *Mozart: A Life in Letters*. Trans. Stewart Spencer. Penguin, 2006.

Ekman, Paul. *Why Kids Lie: How Parents Can Encourage Truthfulness*. Penguin: New York, 1989.

Elinder, Mikael, and Oscar Erixson. "Gender, Social Norms, and Survival in Maritime Disasters." *Proceedings of the National Academy of Sciences of the United States of America* 109, no. 33. (August 14, 2012): 13220–24.

Engels, Frederick. *The Origin of the Family, Private Property, and the State*. 1884. International, 1993.

Entwistle, Vikki A., et al. "Media Coverage of the Child B Case." *British Medical Journal* 312.7046 (June 22 1996): 1587–91.

Epstein, Robert. *Teen 2.0: Saving Our Children and Families from the Torment of Adolescence*. Quill Driver Books, 2010.

Erickson, Megan. *Class War: The Privatization of Childhood*. Verso, 2015.

Farson, Richard. *Birthrights*. Macmillan, 1974.

Fass, Paula S. "The Child-Centered Family? New Rules in Postwar America." In *Reinventing Childhood after World War II*. Philadelphia: University of Pennsylvania Press, 2012. 1–18.

Fass, Paula S. *The End of American Childhood: A History of Parenting from Life on the Frontier to the Managed Child*. Princeton University Press, 2016.

Federici, Silvia. *Caliban and the Witch: Women, the Body, and Primitive Accumulation*. Autonomedia, 2004.

Fitzhugh, Louise. *Nobody's Family Is Going to Change*. Farrar, Strauss, and Giroux, 1974.

Foster, Kathleen A. *Shipwreck! Winslow Homer and* The Life Line. Philadelphia Museum of Art, 2012.

Frank, Arthur. *At the Will of the Body: Reflections on Illness*. Houghton Mifflin, 2002.

Frey, Bruno S., David A. Savage, and Benno Torgler. "Interaction of Natural Survival Instincts and Internalized Social Norms Exploring the Titanic and Lusitania Disasters." *Proceedings of the National Academy of Sciences of the United States of America* 107, no. 11 (March 16, 2010): 4862–65.

Fudge, Erica. *Animal*. ReaktionBooks, 2002.

Gaes, Jason. *My Book for Kids with Cansur: A Child's Autobiography of Hope*. Illustrated by Tim and Adam Gaes. Melius and Peterson, 1987.

Gallagher, Maggie. "Why Do Parents Have Rights? The Problem of Kinship in Liberal Thought." In *Baby Markets: Money and the New Politics of Creating Families*, ed. Michele Bratcher Goodwin. Cambridge University Press, 2010. 164–76.
Gardner, Jared. *Projections: Comics and the History of Twentieth-Century Storytelling.* Stanford University Press, 2012.
Gaynor, Kate. *The Famous Hat.* Illus. by Ruth Keating. Special Stories, 2008.
Geller, Judith B. *Titanic: Women and Children.* W. W. Norton, 1998.
Gelles, Richard J. "Children's Rights and Parents' Responsibilities." *Criminal Justice Ethics* 25 no. 2 (2006): 40–45.
Gilbert, James. *A Cycle of Outrage: America's Reaction to the Juvenile Delinquent in the 1950s.* Oxford University Press, 1986.
Gillis, John R. "The Islanding of Children—Reshaping the Mythical Landscapes of Childhood." In *Designing Modern Childhoods: History, Space, and the Material Culture of Children*, ed. Marta Gutman and Ning de Connick-Smith. Rutgers University Press, 2008. 316–30.
Gilman, Charlotte Perkins. *Concerning Children.* 1900. Rowman and Littlefield, 2003.
Gilroy, Paul. *The Black Atlantic: Modernity and Double Consciousness.* Harvard University Press, 1993.
Giroux, Henry A. *Disposable Youth: Racialized Memories and the Culture of Cruelty.* Routledge, 2012.
Gloeckner, Phoebe. *The Diary of a Teenage Girl: An Account in Words and Pictures.* Frog. 2002.
Golding, William. *Lord of the Flies.* 1954. Penguin, 2011.
Goldstein, Joseph, Anna Freud, and Albert J. Solnit. *Beyond the Best Interests of the Child.* 1973. Free, 1979.
Goodwin, Michele Bratcher, ed. "Introduction." In *Baby Markets: Money and the New Politics of Creating Families.* Cambridge University Press, 2010.
Graff, E. J. *What Is Marriage For? The Strange Social History of Our Most Intimate Institution.* Beacon, 2004.
Graham, Robin Lee, with Derek L. T. Gill. *Dove.* HarperPerennial, 1972.
Gray, Harold. *The Complete Little Orphan Annie, 1924–27.* Vol. 1, *Will Tomorrow Ever Come?* IDW, 2015.
Gray, Harold. *The Complete Little Orphan Annie, 1927–29.* Vol. 2, *The Darkest Hour Is Just before the Dawn.* IDW, 2008.
Gray, Harold. *The Complete Little Orphan Annie, 1929–31.* Vol. 3, *And a Blind Man Shall Lead Them.* IDW, 2009.
Gray, Harold. *The Complete Little Orphan Annie, 1943–1945.* Vol. 11, *Death Be Thy Name.* IDW, 2015.
Green, John. *The Fault in Our Stars.* Penguin, 2012.
Greenburg, Michael M. *Peaches and Daddy: A Story of the Roaring Twenties, the Birth of the Tabloid Media, and the Courtship that Captured the Heart and Imagination of the American Public.* Overlook, 2008.
Griffiths, Jay. *Kith: The Riddle of the Childscape.* Penguin, 2013.
Groff, Patrick. "Children's Literature Versus Wordless Books." *Top of the News* (April 1974): 294–303.
Grossberg, Lawrence. *Caught in the Crossfire: Kids, Politics, and America's Future.* Paradigm, 2005.

Grossberg, Michael. "Liberation and Caretaking: Fighting over Children's Rights in Postwar America." In *Reinventing Childhood after World War II*. University of Pennsylvania, 2012. 19–37.
Groth, Gary. "The Maurice Sendak Interview." *The Comics Journal* 302 (January 2013): 31–108.
Guggenheim, Martin. *What's Wrong with Children's Rights*. Harvard University Press, 2005.
Guttman, Allen. "The Progressive Era Appropriation of Children's Play." *The Journal of the History of Childhood and Youth* 3, no. 2 (2010): 147–51.
Habermas, Rebekka. "Parent-Child Relationships in the Nineteenth Century." *German History* 16 no. 1 (1998): 43–56.
Haejoang, Cho (Han). "National Subjects, Citizens and Refugees: Thoughts on the Politics of Survival, Violence and Mourning Following the *Sewol* Ferry Disaster in South Korea." In *New Worlds from Below: Informal Life Politics and Grassroots Action in Twenty-First Century Northeast Asia*. ANU, 2017. 167–96.
Hajdu, David. *The Ten-Cent Plague: The Great Comic-Book Scare and How It Changed America*. Farrar, Strauss, and Giroux, 2008.
Ham, Chris. "The Role of Doctors, Patients and Managers in Priority Setting Decisions: Lessons from the 'Child B' Case." *Health Expectations* 2 (1999): 61–18.
Hamilton, Virginia. *Bluish*. Scholastic, 1999.
Hanson, Neil. *The Custom of the Sea: A Shocking True Tale of Shipwreck, Murder, and the Last Taboo*. John Wiley and Sons, 1999.
Harris, Elizabeth. "Connecticut Teenager with Cancer Loses Court Fight to Refuse Chemotherapy." *The New York Times*, January 9, 2015. Web. January 10, 2015.
Harrison, Tracey, and Bill Mouland. "I Will Never Give Up Hope." *Daily Mail*, October 26, 1995. Web. January 2, 2015.
Hart, Roger. "Containing Children: Some Lessons on Planning for Play from New York City." *Environment and Urbanization* 14, no. 2 (2002): 135–48.
Harty, Joetta. "Imagining the Nation, Imagining an Empire: A Tour of Early Nineteenth-Century British Paracosms." In *Home and Away: The Place of the Child Writer*, ed. David Owen and Lesley Peterson. Cambridge Scholars Publishing, 2016. 96–121.
Harvey, Robert C. "Comedy at the Juncture of Word and Image: The Emergence of the Modern Magazine Gag Cartoon Reveals the Vital Blend." In *The Language of Comics: Word and Image*, ed. Robin Varnum and Christina T. Gibbons. University of Mississippi Press, 2001.
Harvey, Robert C. Ed. and introduction to *Milton Caniff: Conversations*. University of Mississippi Press, 2002.
Harvey, Robert C. *Meanwhile . . . A Biography of Milton Caniff, Creator of* Terry and the Pirates *and* Steve Canyon. Fantagraphic, 2007.
Hatfield, Charles. "Comic Art, Children's Literature, and the New Comics Studies." *The Lion and the Unicorn* 30 (2006): 360–82.
Hatfield, Charles. "Narrative vs. Non-narrative Demands, or Comic Art and Fragmentation in Aliki's *How a Book Is Made*." *Children's Literature Association Quarterly* 30, no. 1 (Spring 2005): 88–99.
Hatfield, Charles, and Craig Svonkin. "Why Comics Are and Are Not Picture Books: Introduction." *Children's Literature Association Quarterly* 37, no. 4 (Winter 2012): 429–35.
Healy, Jack, and Michael Paulson. "Vaccine Critics Turn Defensive over Measles." *New York Times*, January 30, 2015. Web. January 31, 2015.

Heer, Jeet. "Going to War with FDR." In *The Complete Little Orphan Annie*. Vol. 11, *Death Be Thy Name*, IDW 2015. 5–13.

Heller, Erich. "Wittgenstein and Nietzsche" *The Importance of Nietzsche: Ten Essays*. University of Chicago Press, 1988. 140–57.

Hicks, Amy. "Playing at Crusoe: Domestic Imperatives and Models of Motherhood in Robinson Crusoe-Inspired Toys and Novels for Girls." *Children's Literature in Education* 46 (2015): 110–26.

Holm, Donald. *The Circumnavigators: Small Boat Voyages of Modern Times*. Prentice-Hall, 1974.

Honeyman, Susan. *Elusive Childhood: Impossible Representations in Modern Fiction*. Ohio State University Press, 2005.

Honeyman, Susan. "Youth Voices in the War Diary Business." *International Research in Children's Literature* 4, no.1 (Summer): 73–86.

Illouz, Eva. *Cold Intimacies: The Making of Emotional Capitalism*. 2007. Polity, 2015.

Isaac, Jessica. "Compliant Circulation: Children's Writing, American Periodicals, and Public Culture, 1839–1882." Dissertation. University of Pittsburgh, 2015.

Isgro, Kirsten. "Unsanctioned (Bedroom) Commitments: The 2000 U. S. Census Discourse around Cohabitation and Single-Motherhood." In *Women and Children First: Feminism, Rhetoric, and Public Policy*, ed. Sharon M. Meagher and Patricie Diquinzio. State University of New York Press, 2005. 37–55.

Ishii, Takayuki. *One Thousand Paper Cranes: The Story of Sadako and the Children's Peace Statue*. Random House, 1997.

Jackson, Kathy Merlock, and Mark D. Arnold. "Baby-Boom Children and Harvey Comics after the Code: A Neighborhood of Little Girls and Boys." *ImageText* 3, no. 3 (2007).

Jacobs, Lorry. "Browning Tots Rival 'Alice in Wonderland'; Are Idolized by All Little Kiddies in the Land." *The Charleston Daily Mail*, June 20, 1920.

Jakobson, Roman. *Child Language Aphasia and Phonological Universals*. Harvard and MIT University Press, 1968.

Jameson, Fredric. *The Prison-House of Language: A Critical Account of Structuralism and Russian Formalism*. Princeton University Press, 1972.

Jarman, Michelle. "Disability on Trial: Complex Realities Staged for Courtroom Drama—the Case of Jodi Picoult." *Journal of Literary and Cultural Disability Studies* 6, no. 2 (2012): 209–25.

Joy, Melanie. *Why We Love Dogs, Eat Pigs, and Wear Cows: An Introduction to Carnism: The Belief System That Enables Us to Eat Some Animals and Not Others*. San Francisco: Conari, 2010.

Kadohata, Cynthia. *Kira-Kira*. Aladdin, 2004.

Kanner, Sheri, Susan Langerman, and Margaret Grey. "Ethical Considerations for a Child's Participation in Research" *Journal for Specialists in Pediatric Nursing* 9, no. 1 (January 2004): 15–23.

Kapur, Jyotsna. *Coining for Capital: Movies, Marketing, and the Transformation of Childhood*. Rutgers University Press, 2005.

Kessen, William. "Rousseau's Children." *Daedalus* 107, no. 3 (Summer 1978): 155–66.

Ketterer, David. "Yann Martel's *Life of Pi* and Poe's *Pym* (and 'Berenice')." *Poe Studies* 42, no. 1 (2009): 80–86.

Kidd, Kenneth. *Making American Boys: Boyology and the Feral Tale*. University of Minnesota Press, 2004.

Kidd, Kenneth. "Prizing Children's Literature: The Case of Newberry Gold." *Children's Literature* 35 (2007): 166–90.

King, Frank, and Peter Maresca. *Sundays with Walt & Skeezix: 1921 through 1934*. Palo Alto: Sunday Press Books, 2007.

King, Frank, Jeet Heer, Tim Samuelson, Allan Sekula, and Sally Stein. *Walt & Skeezix: 1921 & 1922*. Drawn and Quarterly, 2005.

King, Samantha. *Pink Ribbons, Inc.: Breast Cancer and the Politics of Philanthropy*. University of Minnesota Press, 2006.

Kings Comics, Starring Popeye 43 (November 1939).

Kingsley, Patrick. *The New Odyssey: The Story of the Twenty-First Century Refugee Crisis*. W. W. Norton, 2017.

Kipling, Rudyard. *The Writings in Prose and Verse of Rudyard Kipling*. Vol. 11, *Verses, 1889–1896*. Scribner, 1913.

Kipnis, Laura. *Against Love: A Polemic*. Random House, 2003.

Klein, Marty, and Nadine Strossen. *America's War on Sex: The Attack on Law, Lust and Liberty*. Praeger, 2006.

Kline, Stephen. *Out of the Garden: Toys, TV, and Children's Culture in the Age of Marketing*. Verso, 1993.

Koldau, Linda Maria. "*Titanic*: A Perfect Case for Cultural History." *The Nautilus* 3 (Spring 2012): 7–34.

Konner, Melvin. *The Evolution of Childhood: Relationships, Emotion, Mind*. Cambridge: Belknap Press of Harvard University Press, 2010.

Krawiec, Kimberly D. "Price and Pretense in the Baby Market." In *Baby Markets: Money and the New Politics of Creating Families*, ed. Michele Bratcher Goodwin. Cambridge University Press, 2010. 41–55.

Kreicbergs, Ulrika, et al. "Talking about Death with Children Who Have Severe Malignant Disease." *The New England Journal of Medicine* 351, no. 12 (September 16, 2004): 1175–86.

Kugler, Michael. "A Nebraska Boy's Comic Strip Narrative of World War II." *Journal of the History of Childhood and Youth* 10, no. 1 (2017): 7–19.

Lancy, David F. *The Anthropology of Childhood: Cherubs, Chattel, Changelings*. 2nd Ed. Cambridge University Press, 2015.

Lansdown, Gerison "Implementing Children's Rights and Health." *Archives of Disease in Childhood* 83 (2000): 286–88.

Laurgaard, Rachel K. *Patty Reed's Doll: The Story of the Donner Party*. 1956. Tomato Enterprises, 1989.

Lawrance, Benjamin N. *Amistad's Orphans: An Atlantic Story of Children, Slavery, and Smuggling*. Yale University Press, 2014.

Lawrence, D. H. "Ships in Bottles." In *The Complete Poems of D. H. Lawrence*. Wordsworth Poetry Editions, 1994. 454–55.

Lederer, Susan E. *Subjected to Science: Human Experimentation in America before the Second World War*. Baltimore: Johns Hopkins University Press, 1995.

Levander, Caroline. *Cradle of Liberty: Race, the Child, and National Belonging from Thomas Jefferson to W. E. B. DuBois*. Duke University Press, 2006.

Levine, Judith. *Harmful to Minors: The Perils of Protecting Children from Sex*. Thunder's Mouth, 2003.

Lévi-Strauss, Claude, and Jane M. Todd. *We Are All Cannibals and Other Essays*. Columbia University Press, 2016.

Lewis, Mary Ann, and Charles E. Lewis. "Consequences of Empowering Children to Care for Themselves." *Pediatrician* 17 (1990): 63–67.
Lilius, Aleko E. *I Sailed with Chinese Pirates*. 1930. Earnshaw Books, 2009.
Lo, Malinda. *Ash*. Hatchette, 2009.
Lo, Malinda. *Huntress*. Hatchette, 2011.
Lorimer, Sara. *Booty: Girl Pirates on the High Seas*. Illus. Susan Synarski. Chronicle Books, 2002.
Lutz, Tom. *Crying: The Natural and Cultural History of Tears*. W. W. Norton, 1999.
Ma, Sheng-Mei. *The Deathly Embrace: Orientalism and Asian American Identity*. University of Minnesota Press, 2000.
Mah, Adeline Yen. *Chinese Cinderella: The True Story of an Unwanted Daughter*. Random House, 1999.
Maidentrip. Jillian Schlesinger, Dir. Wild Shot films, 2013.
Males, Mike A. *Framing Youth: 10 Myths about the Next Generation*. Common Courage, 1999.
Males, Mike A. *Teenage Sex and Pregnancy: Modern Myths, Unsexy Realities*. Praeger, 2010.
Marano, Hara Estroff. *A Nation of Wimps: The High Cost of Invasive Parenting*. Broadway Books, 2008.
Marcus, Leonard. *Minders of Make Believe: Idealists, Entrepreneurs, and the Shaping of American Children's Literature*. Houghton Mifflin, 2008.
Marston, William Moulton. *Emotions of Normal People*. 1928. Thomas Lyster: Ormsmirk, Lancastershire, 1989.
Maria Rye Home Children Database. Letters from Maria Rye Children. Web. July 6, 2017.
Martel, Yann. *Life of Pi*. Houghton Mifflin, 2001.
Martin, Jesse. *Lionheart: A Journey of the Human Spirit*. Allen and Unwin, 2000.
Marx, Karl. *Capital: A Critique of Political Economy*. Vol. 1. 1867. Trans. Ben Fowkes. Penguin, 1990.
Mayer, Sheldon. "Adventures with the Air-Apples!" *Sugar and Spike* [New York: DC Comics] 20 (December 1958): n.p.
Mayer, Sheldon. "Baby-Talk Dictionary." *Sugar and Spike* [New York: DC Comics] 19 (October 1958): n.p.
Mayer, Sheldon. "Circus Parade Due in Town." *Sugar and Spike* [New York: DC Comics] 20 (December 1958): n.p.
Mayer, Sheldon. "Deep Sea Adventure." *Sugar and Spike* [New York: DC Comics] 19 (June–July 1964): n.p.
Mayer, Sheldon. "Dude Ranchers." *Sugar and Spike* [New York: DC Comics] 19 (October 1958): n.p.
Mayer, Sheldon. Lettercol. *Sugar and Spike* [New York: DC Comics] 8 (June–July 1957): n.p.
Mayer, Sheldon. Lettercol. *Sugar and Spike* [New York: DC Comics] 43 (October–November, 1962): n.p.
Mayer, Sheldon. Lettercol. *Sugar and Spike* [New York: DC Comics] 64 (April–May 1966): n.p.
Mayer, Sheldon. Lettercol. *Sugar and Spike* [New York: DC Comics] 67 (February–March 1967): n.p.
Mayer, Sheldon. "Look Who's Here Again!" *Sugar and Spike* [New York: DC Comics] 19 (October 1958): n.p.
Mayer, Sheldon. "Monkey Shines." *Sugar and Spike* [New York: DC Comics] 30 (August–September, 1960): n.p.

Mayer, Sheldon. "Poky Problem." *Sugar and Spike* [New York: DC Comics] 18 (September 1958): n.p.

Mayer, Sheldon. "Safety-Pin Scientist." *Sugar and Spike* [New York: DC Comics] 1 (April–May 1956): n.p.

Mayer, Sheldon. "Sugar's Problem." *Sugar and Spike* [New York: DC Comics] 25 (October–November 1959): n.p.

McDonald, Stephanie. *Opinion Divided on the Merits of South Korean Pastor's "Baby-Box."* SBS (Special Broadcasting Service of Australia). February 11, 2014. www.sbs.com.

McGraw, Eloise. *The Moorchild*. Aladdin, 1996.

McKee, Alexander. *Wreck of the Medusa: Mutiny, Murder, and Survival on the High Seas*. Skyhorse, 2007.

Meagher, Sharon M., and Patrice Diquinzo, eds. *Women and Children First: Feminism, Rhetoric, and Public Policy*. State University of New York Press, 2005.

Melville, Herman. *Moby-Dick, or the Whale*. 1851. Illus. Rockwell Kent. Random House, 1930.

Messenger, Stephanie. *Melanie's Marvelous Measles*. Illus. by Johan Van der Hoeff. Trafford, 2012.

Michals, Teresa. *Books for Children, Books for Adults: Age and the Novel from Defoe to James*. Cambridge University Press, 2014.

Midgley, Carol. "How Could You Let Me Die: Little B Tells of Her Fight for Life." *Daily Mirror*, October 26, 1995. Web. January 2, 2015.

Minehan, Thomas. *Boy and Girl Tramps of America*. Grosset and Dunlap, 1934.

Miskolcze, Robin. "Molly Brown and the *Titanic*: The Shipwrecked Woman in U.S. Culture." In *Shipwreck in Art and Literature: Images and Interpretations from Antiquity to the Present Day*, ed. Carl Thompson. Routledge, 2014. 171–86.

Miskolcze, Robin. *Women and Children First: Nineteenth-Century Sea Narratives and American Identity*. University of Nebraska, 2007.

Mitchell, W. J. T. *Blake's Composite Art: A Study of the Illuminated Poetry*. Princeton University Press, 1978.

Mitchell, W. J. T. *Picture Theory*. University of Chicago Press, 1994.

Mitchell, W. J. T. "Visual Literacy or Literary Visualcy?" In *Visual Literacy*, ed. James Elkins. Routledge, 2010. 11–29.

Moitessier, Bernard. *The Long Way*. Doubleday, 1975.

Morgenstern, John. "Children and Other Talking Animals." *The Lion and the Unicorn*. 24, no. 1 (January 2000): 110–27.

Moruzi, Kristine. "Charity, Affect, and Waif Novels." In *Affect, Emotion, and Children's Literature: Representation and Socialisation in Texts for Children and Young Adults*, ed. Kristine Moruzi, Michelle Smith, and Elizabeth Bullen. Routledge, 2018. 34–51.

Murphy, Virginia Reed. *Across the Plains in the Donner Party*. Ed. Karen Zeinart. SynergEbooks, 2016.

Nel, Philip. "Same Genus, Different Species? Comics and Picture Books" *Children's Literature Association Quarterly* 37 no. 4 (Winter 2012): 445–53.

Nichols, Peter. *A Voyage for Madmen*. HarperCollins, 2001.

Nickerson, Thomas. "The Boy's Story." In *The Loss of the Ship Essex, Sunk by a Whale*. Penguin, 2000. 83–183.

Nicolle, Ethan and Malachai. *Axe Cop*. Vol. 1. Dark Horse Books, 2010.

Nietzsche, Friedrich. *The Will to Power*. Trans. Walter Kaufmann and R. J. Hollingdale. Vintage Books, 1968.

Nodelman, Perry. *Words about Pictures: The Narrative Art of Children's Picture Books.* University of Georgia Press, 1988.
Nyberg, Amy Kiste. *Seal of Approval: The History of the Comics Code.* University Press of Mississippi, 1998.
Oaks, Laury. *Giving Up Baby: Safe Haven Laws, Motherhood, and Reproductive Justice.* New York University Press, 2015.
Okubo, Miné. *Citizen 13660.* Seattle: University of Washington Press, 1983.
Oliver, Neil. *Amazing Tales for Making Men out of Boys.* HarperCollins, 2009.
Ollestad, Norman. *Crazy for the Storm: A Memoir of Survival.* HarperCollins, 2009.
O'Malley, Andrew. *Children's Literature, Popular Culture and Robinson Crusoe.* New York: Palgrave Macmillan, 2012.
O'Neill, John. *Civic Capitalism: The State of Childhood.* University of Toronto Press, 2004.
op de Beeck, Nathalie. "On Comics-Style Picture Books and Picture-Bookish Comics." *Children's Literature Association Quarterly* 37, no. 4 (Winter 2012): 468–76.
op de Beeck, Nathalie. *Suspended Animation: Children's Picture Books and the Tale of Modernity.* University of Minnesota Press, 2010.
Orenstein, Catherine. *Little Red Riding Hood Uncloaked: Sex, Morality, and the Evolution of a Fairy Tale.* Basic Books, 2002.
O'Shannessy, Carmel. "Children's Production of Their Heritage Language and a New Mixed Language." In *Children's Language and Multilingualism: Indigenous Language Use at Home and School,* ed. Jane Simpson and Gillian Wigglesworth. Continuum, 2008. 261–82.
Oswell, David. *The Agency of Children: from Family to Global Human Rights.* Cambridge University Press, 2013.
Pasco, Duane, and Barbara Winther. *Life as Art.* University of Washington Press, 2012.
Paulsen, Gary. *Hatchet.* Bradbury, 1987.
Peachman, Rachel Rabkin. "Put Your Baby in a Box? Experts Advise Caution." *New York Times,* May 24, 2017. www.nytimes.com.
Perle, Liz. *Money, a Memoir: Women, Emotions, and Cash.* Picador, 2006.
Phelps, Donald. "The Peaceable Kingdom." Introduction to *Popeye: "Let's You and Him Fight."* Vol. 3. Fantagraphics, 2008.
Phillips, Adam. *On Kissing, Tickling, and Being Bored: Psychoanalytic Essays on the Unexamined Life.* Harvard University Press, 1993.
Phillips, Douglas W. *The Birkenhead Drill.* Vision Forum, 2002.
Picoult, Jodi. *My Sister's Keeper.* Washington Square, 2004.
Pinker, Steven. *The Stuff of Thought: Language as a Window into Human Nature.* Penguin, 2007.
Poe, Edgar Allan. *Narrative of Arthur Gordon Pym of Nantucket.* 1838. McAllister Editions, 2015.
Pogrebin, Letty Cottin. *Family Politics: Love and Power on an Intimate Frontier.* McGraw-Hill, 1983.
Pogrebin, Letty Cottin. *How to Be a Friend to a Friend Who's Sick.* Perseus, 2013.
Powers, Richard Gid. *G-Men: Hoover's FBI in American Popular Culture.* Southern Illinois University Press, 1983.
Pratchett, Terry. *Nation.* HarperCollins, 2008.
Prince, Debra Lindsey, and Esther M. Howard. "Children and Their Basic Needs." *Early Childhood Education Journal* 30, no. 1 (Fall 2002): 27–31.

Proctor, Philip. Email. 23 September 2015.
Pullman, Philip. *The Golden Compass*. 1995. Yearling, 2007.
Pullman, Philip. *The Golden Compass: The Graphic Novel*. Vol. 1. Illus. Clément Oubrerie. Trans. Annie Eaton. Alfred A. Knopf, 2015.
Pullman, Philip. *The Golden Compass: The Graphic Novel*. Vol. 2. Illus. Clément Oubrerie. Trans. Annie Eaton. Alfred A. Knopf, 2016.
Pustz, Matthew. *Comic Book Culture: Fan Boys and True Believers*. University of Mississippi Press, 1999.
Ramachandran, V. S. *The Tell-Tale Brain: A Neuroscientist's Quest for What Makes Us Human*. W. W. Norton, 2011.
Rarick, Ethan. *Desperate Passage: The Donner Party's Perilous Journey West*. Oxford University Press, 2008.
Read, Piers Paul. *Alive: The Story of the Andes Survivors*. Avon Books, 1974.
Rediker, Marcus. *The Amistad Rebellion: An Atlantic Odyssey of Slavery and Freedom*. Penguin, 2013.
Rediker, Marcus. *Between the Devil and the Deep Blue Sea: Merchant Seamen, Pirates, and the Anglo-American Maritime World, 1700–1750*. Cambridge University Press, 1987.
Richman, Amy L., Patrice M. Miller, and Margaret Johnson Solomon. "The Socialization of Infants in Suburban Boston." In *Parental Behavior in Diverse Societies*, ed. Robert A. LeVine, Patrice M. Miller, and Mary Maxwell West. Jossey-Bass, 1988. 65–74.
Richmond, Christina. *Chemo Girl: Saving the World One Treatment at a Time*. Jones and Bartlett, 1997.
Robbins, Trina. *From Girls to Grrrlz: A History of Women's Comics from Teens to Zines*. Chronicle Books, 1999.
Roberts, Dorothy. *Shattered Bonds: The Color of Child Welfare*. Perseus, 2002.
Roche, Timothy. "A Refuge for Throwaways." *Time*, February 13, 2000. Web.
Rodari, Gianni. *The Grammar of Fantasy: An Introduction to the Art of Inventing Stories*. 1973. Trans. Jack Zipes. Teachers and Writers Collaborative, 1996.
Rodgers, Mary. "Ladies First." *Free to Be . . . You and Me*. 1972. Arista, 1983.
Roseby, Rob. "Should Laura Dekker Be Allowed to Attempt to Sail Solo around the World?" *Journal of Pediatrics and Child Health* 46 (2010): 286–87.
Rousseau, Jean-Jacques. *Emile, or On Education*. 1762. Trans. Allan Bloom. Perseus, 1979.
Rowell, Victoria. *The Women Who Raised Me*. HarperCollins, 2007.
Royer, George, Beth Nettels, and William Aspray. "Active Readership: The Case of the American Comics Reader." In *Everyday Information: The Evolution of Information Seeking in America*. MIT Press, 2011: 277–303.
Rutherford, Markella B. *Adult Supervision Required: Private Freedoms and Public Restraints for Parents and Children*. Rutgers University Press, 2011.
Sánchez-Eppler, Karen. "In the Archives of Childhood." In *The Children's Table: Childhood Studies and the Humanities*, ed. Anna Mae Duane. University of Georgia Press, 2013a. 213–37.
Sánchez-Eppler, Karen. "Over a Century of Shipwrecks: American Child Readers and Robinson Crusoe." In *The Materials of Exchange between Britain and North East America*, ed. Daniel Maudlin and Robin Peel. Ashgate: 2013b. 117–42.
Sánchez-Eppler, Karen. "Then When We Clutch the Hardest: On the Death of a Child and the Replication of an Image." In *Sentimental Men: Masculinity and the Politics of Affect*

in American Culture, ed. Mary Chapman and Glenn Hendler. University of California Press, 1999. 64–85.
Schulz, Charles. *The Complete Peanuts 1950–1952*. Vol. 1. Fantagraphics, 2004.
Sealander, Judith. *The Failed Century of the Child: Governing America's Young in the Twentieth Century*. Cambridge University Press, 2003.
Segar, Elzie. *Popeye: "Let's You and Him Fight."* Vol. 3. Fantagraphics, 2008.
Segar, Elzie. *Popeye: "Plunder Island."* Vol. 4. Fantagraphics, 2009.
Segar, Elzie. *Popeye: "Wha's a Jeep?"* Vol. 5. Fantagraphics, 2011.
Sendak, Maurice. *Outside over There*. HarperCollins, 1981.
Sennett, Richard. *Families against the City: Middle Class Homes of Industrial Chicago, 1872–1890*. 1970. Harvard University Press, 1984.
Serchay, David S. "Comic Book Collectors: The Serials Librarians of the Home." *Serials Review* 24, no. 1 (1998): 57–71.
Seth, ed. *Thirteen Going on Eighteen*, by John Stanley. Drawn and Quarterly, 2010 reprint.
Shield, J. P. H., and J. D. Baum. "Children's Consent to Treatment." *British Medical Journal* 308 (May 7, 1994): 1182–83.
Shore, Bradd. "Is Language a Prisonhouse?" *Cultural Anthropology* 2, no. 1 (February 1987): 115–36.
Shusterman, Neal. *Unwind*. Simon and Schuster, 2007.
Simonton Black, Irma. "Don't Fence Me In!" *Redbook*, November 1952: 73.
Simpson, A. W. Brian. *Cannibalism and Common Law: The Story of the Tragic Last Voyage of the Mignonette and the Strange Legal Proceedings to Which It Gave Rise*. University of Chicago Press, 1984.
Simpson, A. W. Brian. "Cannibals at Common Law." *The Law School Record* 27 (Fall 1981): 3–10.
Skenazy, Lenore. *Free Range Kids: How to Raise Safe, Self-Reliant Children (without Going Nuts with Worry)*. Jossey-Bass, 2009.
Skinner, B. F. "Baby in a Box." *Cumulative Record*. Appleton-Century-Crofts. 1961. 419–26.
Slocum, Joshua. *Sailing Alone around the World*. 1900. Dover, 1956.
Small, David. *Stitches: A Memoir*. W. W. Norton, 2009.
Smith, Bruce. *The History of Little Orphan Annie*. Ballantine, 1982.
Snyder, Laurel. *Orphan Island*. Walden Pond, 2017.
Solomon, Tom. *Roald Dahl's Marvellous Medicine*. Liverpool University Press, 2016.
Spock, Benjamin. *The Common Sense Book of Baby and Child Care*. Duell, Sloan, and Pearce, 1946.
Starch, Daniel, and staff. *Kid Stuff Is Big Stuff a Primer of the Youth Market*. 1949. Records of the Senate Subcommittee on Juvenile Delinquency. National Archives, Washington, D.C.
Stephens, Mitchell. *The Rise of the Image, the Fall of the Word*. Oxford University Press, 1998.
Sulik, Gayle A. *Pink Ribbon Blues: How Breast Cancer Culture Undermines Women's Health*. Oxford University Press, 2011.
Sunderland, Abby, and Lynn Vincent. *Unsinkable: A Young Woman's Courageous Battle on the High Seas*. Thomas Nelson, 2011.
Tanner, Beccy. "Kansas Town Was First to Get Polio Protection." *The Wichita Eagle*, 30 March 2009, A3.
Taussig, Michael. "What Do Drawings Want?" *Culture, Theory and Critique* 50, nos. 2–3 (2009): 263–74.

Thompson, Carl, ed. *Shipwreck in Art and Literature: Images and Interpretations from Antiquity to the Present Day*. Routledge, 2014.

Thomson, Mathew. *Lost Freedom: The Landscape of the Child and the British Post-War Settlement*. Oxford University Press, 2013.

The Thriving Family.com. "My Sister's Keeper" (review). Web. November 9, 2014.

Tilley, Carol L. "Seducing the Innocent: Fredric Wertham and the Falsifications That Helped Condemn Critics." *Information and Culture* 47, no.4 (2012): 383–413.

Titlestad, Michael. "Wrecked in the Shallows: Yann Martel's *Life of Pi*." In *Shipwreck in Art and Literature: Images and Interpretations from Antiquity to the Present Day*, ed. Carl Thompson. Routledge, 2014. 204–17.

Todres, Jonathan, and Sarah Higinbotham. *Human Rights in Children's Literature: Imagination and the Narrative of Law*. Oxford University Press, 2016.

Todres, Jonathan, and Sarah Higinbotham. "A Person's a Person: Children's Rights in Children's Literature." *Columbia Human Rights Law Review* 45, no.1 (Fall 2013): 1–56.

Tournier, Michel. *Gilles and Jeanne*. 1985. Trans. Alan Sheridan. Minerva, 1987.

Tran, Mark. "Teenagers Found after 50 Days at Sea," *The Guardian*, November 25, 2010. Web.

Trites, Roberta S. *Disturbing the Universe: Power and Repression in Adolescent Literature*. University of Iowa Press, 2000.

Urban, Katharine, and Robert D. Wheeler, eds. *Guns against Gangsters*. Vol. 1, no. 3. Premium Group of Comics, 1949.

Vanderbilt, Tom. "How the Playpen Fell out of Favor." *Slate Magazine*, August 7, 2009.

Verne, Jules. *Dick Sand; or, A Captain at Fifteen*. George Munro, 1878.

Walker, Nancy E., Catherine M. Brooks, and Lawrence S. Wrightsman. *Children's Rights in the United States: In Search of a National Policy*. Sage, 1999.

Wall, Helena M. *Fierce Communion: Family and Community in Early America*. Harvard University Press, 1990.

Wall, John. *Children's Rights: Today's Global Challenge*. Rowman and Littlefield, 2017.

Wall, Nell Rose (née Kottal). Personal interview. July 14, 2012.

Watson, Jessica. *True Spirit*. Atria, 2010.

Watson, Victor, ed. *Talking Pictures: Pictorial Texts and Young Readers*. Hodder and Stoughton, 1996.

Watterson, Bill. *Calvin and Hobbes*, January 9, 1995.

Weilke-Mills, Courtney. *Imaginary Citizens: Child Readers and the Limits of American Independence*. John Hopkins University Press, 2013.

Wertham, Fredric. "The Comics . . . Very Funny." *Saturday Review of Literature* (May 29, 1948): 6–7, 27–29.

Wertham, Fredric. *Seduction of the Innocent*. Rinehart, 1954.

Whitbeck, Les. B., and Dan R. Hoyt. *Nowhere to Grow: Homeless and Runaway Adolescents and Their Families*. Walter de Gruyter, 1999.

Wigransky, David Pace. "Cain before Comics." *Saturday Review of Literature* (July 24, 1948): 19–20.

Willard, Jim. "'Sugar Daddy' Has a Sweet History." *Loveland Reporter-Herald*, February 21, 2013. http://www.reporterherald.com/portlet/article/html/fragments/print_article.jsp?articleId=22623737&siteId=47.

Williams, William Carlos. *The Doctor Stories*. 1932–1962. Ed. Robert Coles. New Directions, 1984.

Winnicott, D. W. "The Theory of the Parent-Infant Relationship." *International Journal of Psychoanalysis* 41 (1960): 585–95.
Woodhouse, Barbara Bennett.*Hidden in Plain Sight: The Tragedy of Children's Rights from Ben Franklin to Lionel Tate.* Princeton University Press, 2008.
Wright, Bradford W. *Comic Book Nation: The Transformation of Youth Culture in America.* Baltimore: Johns Hopkins University Press, 2001.
Wyss, Johann. *The Swiss Family Robinson.* 1812. Penguin 2007.
Young-Bruehl, Elisabeth. *Childism: Confronting Prejudice against Children.* Yale University Press, 2012.
Zeiher, Helga. "Shaping Daily Life in Urban Environments." *Children in the City: Home, Neighbourhood, and Community.* Routledge Falmer, 2003. 66–81.
Zelizer, Viviana A. *Economic Lives: How Culture Shapes the Economy.* Princeton University Press, 2011.
Zelizer, Viviana A. *Pricing the Priceless Child: The Changing Social Value of Children.* Basic Books, 1985.
Žižek, Slavoj. *First as Tragedy, Then as Farce.* Verso, 2009.

Index

Adult Supervision Required (Rutherford), 47, 149–50
Aebi, Tania, 68, 72
Africa Is My Home, Mar'gru, 38
Ahmed, Sara, 8, 107
Aldrich, C. Knight, 162
Alger, Bill, 146
Americans for a Society Free from Age Restrictions, 150
Amistad, 12, 37–39, 192n10; Colonel Stanton Pendleton, 37–38; Kag'ne, 37–38; Ka'le, 37–38; Mar'gru, 37–38, 78, 99; orphans, 86; Supreme Court, 37; Te'me, 37
Anderson, M. T., 180
Animal (Fudge), 150–51
Annie (Charnin), 83–84
Archard, David, 4, 6
Arendt, Hannah, 7
Arrival, The (Tan), 155
Ash (Lo), 102
Astonishing Life of Octavian Nothing: Traitor to the Nation, The (Anderson), 180
Au, Michelle, 163, 172–73
Avi, 42–43, 59
Axe Cop (Nicolle), 151

Baby Geniuses, 142
Barbarin, Oscar A., 162
Barclay, Sarah, 168–69

Barnardo, John Thomas, 77
"Baskets for Babies," Gigi Kelly, 114–15
Batman, 79
Batman: Brave and the Bold, The, 148
Beam, Cris, 89; "new Jane Crow," 87, 195n11
Beauty Queens (Bray), 60, 65, 193n5, 193n8; feminism, 61; infantilization, 62. See *Lord of the Flies*
Bend It Like Beckham, 115
Bender, Lauretta, 135
Berlant, Lauren, 8, 73
Bernadin de Saint-Pierre, Jacques-Henri. See *Paul and Virginia*
Bernstein, Gaia, 117
Birkenhead, 16–17; Marian Parkinson, 16
Birkenhead Drill, The (Phillips), 17, 27–28
Biss, Eula, 176
Bjork, Daniel W., 96
Black, Irma Simonton, *Redbook*, 148–49
Block, Francesca Lia, 195n15. See also *Waters and the Wild, The*
"Bluebeard," Gilles Garnier, 29
Bluebond-Langner, Myra, 162, 171. See also *Private Worlds of Dying Children, The*
Bluish (Hamilton), 160, 163
Booty: Girl Pirates on the High Seas (Lorimer), 57, 193n6
Boswell, John, 200n1. See *Kindness of Strangers*

Bowen, Jaymee, 166–70, 174–75, 181, 199n3. *See also* paternalism
Boyd, Danah, 116
Brady Bunch, The, 84
Bray, Libba, 63. See *Beauty Queens*
Brent, Mary, 162
Brewer, Holly, 174
Brig Caledonia, 32, 33
British Home Children, 77, 86
Brown, Daniel James, 29
Brown, Margaret Wise, 75
Brown, Molly, 24, 26
Browning, Edward West, 83, 194n9; "Cinderella man," 80; Daddy Browning, 80–81, 83–84. *See also* paternalism; sugar daddy
Bruce Wayne, 50
Bunting, Eve, 24
Burton, Virginia Lee, 153
Butler, Daniel Allen, 24
Butler, Judith, 5

Calico the Wonder Horse, or the Saga of Stewy Stinker (Burton), 153
Calvin and Hobbes, 151
Calvino, Italo, 153
Cameron, James, 26–27
Camus, Albert. See *Plague, The*
cannibalism, 28–35; China, 29
Caniff, Milton, 61. See also *Dickie Dare*; *Lai Choi San*; *Terry and the Pirates*
capitalism, 189; autonomy, 132; colonial, 41, 52; competitive, 12; consumer, 8, 61, 116; culture, 6, 157; Daddy Warbucks, 85; development, 185; Emma Sheridan, 187; emotional, 8, 179; fortune, 51; industrial, 8; society, 41
Captain Marvel, 131
Carpathia, 79
Carrier, David, 151, 153
Carroll, Lewis, and Alice, 151
CASA (court-appointed special advocate), 4, 78, 105, 195n14
Cassandra C, 175

Catcher in the Rye (Salinger), 129
Cech, John, 119
Charnin, Martin. See *Annie*
Chemo Girl: Saving the World One Treatment at a Time (Richmond), 162, 199n2
Chemo to the Rescue: A Children's Book about Leukemia (Brent and Knutsson), 162
Chicago Tribune, 148
Child Protective Services, 11
childhood studies, 5
child-rearing, 43
"Children and Other Talking Animals" (Morgenstern), 150
Childress, Jessie, 184
Chilman-Blair, Kim. See *What's Up with Richard*
Chinese Cinderella: The True Story of an Unwanted Daughter (Mah), 101–2. See Cinderella; fairy tales
Christianity, 100; chivalry, 17, 27; family appropriateness, 173; *The Huntress*, 103; Lai Choi San, 54; Maria Rye, 77; Mary Louise Spas, 81, 83; tales and tropes, 86, 102
Cinderella: *Ash*, 102; *Carpathia*, 79
circumnavigation, 68–73
Claflin, Carol J., 162
Clark, Cindy Dell, 159
Clark Kent, 50
Coerr, Eleanor, 160–63, 171
colonialism: British, 58; expansion, 51; robinsonade, 66
Comerford, Brenda, 171
comics: Code Authority, 141–43, 197n14, 198n19; reader participation, 14, 126–27, 132, 134–37, 139–47, 152
Connell, Erin, 179
consent, 4, 6, 8, 30, 70, 97, 105–6, 157, 165–68, 172–75, 180, 195n15, 200n1
conservative: evangelical waif novel, 78; privatization of citizenship, 73; resilience movement, 64. *See also* Gray, Harold
consumerism, 8, 131; enlightened, 178

Convention on the Rights of the Child, 10; articles 12 and 24, 165
Cook, Daniel Thomas, 8
Coontz, Stephanie, 7–8, 41, 66
court-appointed special advocate. *See* CASA
Couvreaux, Janis, 43
Crain, Patricia, 124–25, 191n2
Crazy for the Storm: A Memoir of Survival (Ollestad), 64–65
Cross, Gary, 8
Cruikshank, George, 77
cults: of manhood, 17; of masculinity, 24–25; of sentimentality, 114, 116, 118, 121
Cunningham, Valentine, 5

Dahl, Roald, 48, 181, 199n33
Dalrymple, Theodore, 101, 113–14, 118, 121
Daly, Marin, 101
Danny the Champion of the World (Dahl), 48
Dawes, Henry Edward, 18
DC comics, 140
Declaration of Geneva, 177
Defoe, Daniel, 62. *See Robinson Crusoe*
Dekker, Laura, 13, 68, 71–73; kith, 73; *Maidentrip*, 193n11
Detroit News Tribune, "Girl Bride Torn from Husband at Pistol Point," 25–26
Dick Sand; or, A Captain at Fifteen (Jules), 42–43
Dick Tracy, 125
Dickie Dare (Caniff), 58
Diquinzio, Patrice, 20
Dix, Dorothy, 87; Navratil case, 78–79, 92
Doctor Stories, The (Williams), 180–81
"Does 'Telling' Less Protect More?" (Barbarin and Claflin), 162
Doña Paz, 22
Donner party, 34, 192nn9–10; *Patty Reed's Doll*, 33
Donzelot, Jacques, 8
Dove (Graham), 68–69; *The Boy Who Sailed Around the World Alone*, 69
Doyle, Andrew, 78
Drop Box, The. See Lee, Jong-rak

EC campaign, 134–40; Ann Carnevale, 142; David Pace Wigransky, 143; Diane Sherry, 137; Elmont children, 144–45; Maurica Osborne, 136; petition, 142; Philip Proctor, 139
EC Comics, 129; "E.C. Fan-Addict Club Bulletin," 132; "Survey of E.C. Fan-Addict Club Letters," 134–40
Ehrenreich, Barbara, 158
Ehrensaft, Diane, 117
Ekman, Paul, 169
emancipation, 10, 90, 172, 196n26
empires: British, 16, 58; family, 185
Engels, Frederick, 6, 39
Essex, 29–35; ballad, 32; lots, 34
Euxine, 33

fairy tales: Adeline Yen Mah, 101; *Annie*, 86; "Bluebeard," 29; "eat or be eaten dilemma," 29; filicides, 101; "Hansel and Gretel," 135; intensive parenting, 117; "Jack and the Beanstalk," 135; "Little Red Riding Hood," 135; "The Maiden with No Hands," 176; Margaret Hays, 79; princesses, 199n1; "Tom Thumb," 176; "Ugly Duckling," 135; violence and fear, 135; womanhood, 67
familialism, 10, 74
Famous Hat, The (Gaynor), 162
Fault in Our Stars, The (Green), 160–61, 170–72
Fawcett Comics Group: *Captain Marvel*, 131; *Kid Stuff Is Big Stuff a Primer of the Youth Market*, 131, 133, 138; study on marketing, 135
Fiddler on the Roof, 115
Fitzhugh, Louise, 3, 186–88
Fleischer, Max, 93
focusing fallacy, 177
Foster, Kathleen, 18
Framing Youth: 10 Myths about the Next Generation (Males), 112
Francis Spaight, 32, 33
Frank, Arthur, 157

Frank, Josetta, 135
Free to Be ... You and Me (Rodgers), 26, 142
Free-Range parenting, 13, 115
Freud, Anna, 92
Freud, Sigmund, 63
Frye, Northrop, 153
Fudge, Erica, 150–51
funeral order, 16

Gaes, Jason, 162, 199n2
Gallagher, Maggie, 115, 184, 194n5
Gardner, Jared, 129
Gasoline Alley (King), 13, 113, 114, 115, 195n18
Gaynor, Kate, 162
Gelles, Richard J., 11
gender, 29; Annie, 84; binary, 27; breast cancer, 158; parenting equity, 113; politics, 186; prostate cancer, 58; terminal illness, 158; transcendence, 60. See also *Swiss Family Robinson*
George, 38; ballad, 32
Gil, Eliana, 87
Gilbert, James, 129
Gilles and Jeanne (Tournier), 99
Gillis, John, 49, 58
Gilman, Charlotte Perkins, 116, 177, 196n25
Gilroy, Paul, 36, 38
Giroux, Henry, 11
Godfrey, Joline, 76
Goethe, Johann Wolfgang von, 64
Golden Compass (Pullman), 13, 106–7, 118
Golding, William. See *Lord of the Flies*; robinsonade
Goldstein, Joseph, 92
Good Housekeeping, 82
Goodwin, Michele, 109
Graff, E. J., 185
Graham, Robin Lee, 16, 68–71, 73, 193nn9–10
Grampus, 31
Gray, Harold, 51, 81, 84, 193n4; conservative, 85, 90; nuclear family, 188. See *Little Orphan Annie*; *Robinson Crusoe*
Green, John. See *Fault in Our Stars, The*

Greenburg, Michael M., 80–81
Grey, Margaret, 180
Griffiths, Jay, 13, 41–42, 60, 66, 185
Groff, Patrick, 155
Grossberg, Michael, 6
Guardian ad litem (GAL), 10, 174
guardianship, 10, 66, 68, 75, 174, 185, 196
Guggenheim, Martin: child advocacy, 10–11; fostercare, 11; *What's Wrong with Children's Rights*, 9
Guiness Book of Records, 72
Gulliver's Travels (Swift), 90
Guns without Gangsters, 128
Guttman, Allen, 46
Gyurkó, Szilvia, 98

Habermas, Rebekka, 118
Ham, Chris, 167
Hamilton, Virginia, 160, 163
"Hansel and Gretel," 135
Hart, Roger, 149
Harty, Joetta, 58
Harvey, Robert C., 55, 153
Hatchet (Paulsen), 62, 64, 66–67
Hatfield, Charles, 142, 151–52, 155
healthcare, 6; mental, 128; National Health Service (UK), 165–66; universal, 9, 97
Hechinger, Scott, 88
helicopter parenting, 117
Hemy, Thomas, *Birkenhead*, 16
Henderson Buell, Marjorie (Margé), *Little Lulu*, 45, 46
Higinbotham, Sarah, 9, 191n1 (intro)
Hobbes, Thomas, 27
Home, 18
Homer, Winslow: *The Life Line*, 18; *Yachting Girl*, 18, 47
Hoover, Edgar J., 125–27
Human Rights in Children's Literature (Higinbotham and Todres), 191n1 (intro)
Hunt, Allen, 179
Hunt, Kaitlyn, 4
Huntress, The (Lo), 13, 103
Huston, John, 50

I Sailed with Chinese Pirates (Lilius), 54
Illouz, Eva, 8, 157–59
immunizations, 176–78, 180–82
"Implementing Children's Rights and Health" (Lansdown), 164
In the Heart of the Sea, 35. See also *Essex*
industrialization, 8, 12; factory, 86; modernization, 9; production, 11; Western countries, 118
infanticide, 100; Jaymee Bowen, 199n3. See also *Beauty Queens*
intensive parenting, 177–78; "Mozart effect," 117–18. See also fairy tales
Isgro, Kirsten, 73

"Jack and the Beanstalk," 135
Jameson, Fredric, 150
Joefield, Maisha, 88
Joy, Melanie, 35
juvenile delinquency: *Annie*, 85–86; crime, 125–26; crusade against comic books, 128, 130, 132–36, 141, 143, 146. See also Senate Subcommittee on Juvenile Delinquency

Kadohata, Cynthia, 160, 164, 171
Kanner, Sheri, 180
Kelly, Gigi, 114–15
Kidd, Kenneth, 155
Kindness of Strangers: The Abandonment of Children in Western Europe from Late Antiquity to the Renaissance, The (Boswell), 98–100, 104–6, 122
King, Frank. See *Gasoline Alley*
King, Samantha, 158
Kings Comics, 45, 93
Kipling, Rudyard, "Soldier an' Sailor Too," 17
Kira-Kira (Kadohata), 160, 164, 171
kith, 66–67, 77, 122; Fitzhugh, 187; *Nation*, 67; *One Girl, One Dream*, 73; *The Waters and the Wild*, 104
Kith: The Riddle of the Childscope (Griffiths), 60, 185. See also *Lord of the Flies*
Kline, Stephen, 141–43
Knutsson, Caitlin, 162

Koldau, Linda Maria, 21
Kottal, Nell Rose Wall. See *Sugar and Spike*
Kreicbergs, Ulrika, 164
Kugler, Michael, 127

"Ladies First" (Rodgers), 26
Ladies Home Journal, 94
Lai Choi San, 55; Aleko, 54; Caniff, 54–56; Dragon Lady, 54–57; Lilius, 54–56; Susan Synarski, 57, 193n6
Lancy, David F., 122
Langerman, Susan, 180
Lansdown, Gerison, 164
Lawrance, Benjamin N., 37, 192n12
Lawrence, D. H. (David Herbert), 45, 46
Lee, Jong-rak: "baby box," 97, 195nn19–20; *The Drop Box*, 97
Leukemia and Lymphoma Society, 158
Lévi-Strauss, Claude, 35
Life Line, The (Homer), 18
Life of Pi (Martel), 30–31, 192n7
Lilius, Aleko E., 54. See also *Lai Choi San*
Limon, Matthew, 3
Lindbergh, Charles, 119–21
Lionheart (Martin), 68
Little Orphan Annie (Gray), 13, 82, 126, 193n3; Annie, 49–50, 54, 80, 85–87, 90–91, 194n9; Daddy Warbucks, 50, 54, 80–81, 84–85, 88, 90–91, 194n9, 195n18; FDR, 84; Mrs. Bleating-Hart, 85–88; Mrs. Warbucks, 80; orphan mythology, 80, 89. See also fairy tales; paternalism; patriarchy
"Little Red Riding Hood," 135
Little Red Riding Hood Uncloaked (Orenstein), 29
Lo, Malinda, 13, 102, 103
Lord of the Flies (Golding), 59, 65, 149; *Beauty Queens*, 60–61; *Kith*, 60. See also robinsonade
Lorimer, Sara, 57, 193n6
Luce, Claire Booth, 90
Lutz, Tom, 27–28, 43

Ma, Sheng-Mei, 51
Mah, Adeline Yen, 101–2
Maiden Voyage (Aebi), 68
Males, Mike, 112
manhood: cult of, 17, 25; masculinity, 24–25; Popeye, 93
Marano, Hara Estroff, 117, 177–79, 183
Margé, 45, 46
Marston, William Moulton, 147–48, 198n22
Martel, Yann, *Life of Pi*, 30–31
Martin, Jesse, 68–70
Martin, Trayvon, 4
Marx, Karl, 47, 157, 192n1
Mary Lowell or the Desert Island (Sánchez-Eppler), 62–63; *Swiss Family Robinson*, 62. See also robinsonade
Mary Poppins, 142
Max and the Cats (Moacyr), 30
Mayer, Sheldon, 146–47, 198n20. See also *Sugar and Spike*
McGraw, Eloise. See *Moorchild, The*
Meagher, Sharon M., 20
Medikidz, 162–63
Medusa, 25, 28–29
Melanie's Marvelous Measles (Messenger), 178
Melville, Herman. See *Moby Dick*
Messenger, Stephanie, 178
Michals, Teresa, 40
Mickey Mouse, 152
Mignonette, 31–32, 191n4, 192n5
Miskolcze, Robin, 18
Mister Dog: The Dog Who Belonged to Himself (Brown), 75
Mitchell, W. J. T. (William John Thomas), 153, 155, 199n29
Moby Dick (Melville), 12, 39; Ishmael, 68
Mohammed, Achmed 4
Moorchild, The (McGraw), 13, 103–4, 196n21
Morgenstern, John. See "Children and Other Talking Animals"
Moruzi, Kristine, 78
Moses, 112

My Book for Kids with Cansur: A Child's Autobiography of Hope (Gaes), 162, 199n2
My Child! My Child! (Dawes), 18
My Sister's Keeper (Picoult), 160–61, 172–74; Anissa and Marissa Ayala, 172; savior sibling, 172, 174

Narrative of Arthur Gordon Pym of Nantucket (Poe), 30–31
Nation (Pratchett), 66–67, 69, 193n5. See also kith
National Archives (Washington, DC), 129–30, 132, 133, 134–40, 142, 144–46
National Health Service (NHS), 165–66. See also healthcare
"Nebraska Boy's Comic Strip Narrative of World War II" (Kugler), 127
Nel, Philip, 140
neonaticide, 122
New York Evening Journal, 79
NHS. See National Health Service
Nicolle, Malachai, 151
Nietzsche, Friedrich, 150
Nobody's Family Is Going to Change (Fitzhugh), Emancipation Sheridan (Emma), 3, 186–88. See also capitalism
Nodelman, Perry, 155

Oaks, Laury, 110–11, 183
O'Brien, Patrick, "The Sorrowful Fate of O'Brien," 32
Oedipus, 98
Ollestad, Norman, 64–65
O'Malley, Andrew, 51
One Girl, One Dream (Dekker), 68, 71
O'Neill, John, 11–12
op de Beeck, Nathalie, 140, 142, 153, 155
oppression, parental and societal, 61
Orenstein, Catherine, *Little Red Riding Hood Uncloaked*, 29
Origin of the Family, Private Property and the State (Engels), 39
Orphan Island (Snyder), 47

Our Gutter Children (Cruikshank), 77
Outside over There (Sendak), 118–21, 192n13; Charles Lindbergh kidnapping, 119–21; Mozart, 119, 154
Oxford English Dictionary, 91

"Parental Anticipatory Grief and Guidelines for Caregivers" (Comerford), 171
parentification, 120–21, 160
Parker, Richard ("Little Dickie"), 30–32, 191n4, 192n8
Parkinson, Marian, 16
Pasco, Duane, 128
paternalism: Daddy Browning and Warbucks, 81, 194n9; globalizing, 109; Jaymee Bowen, 168
patria potestas, 185, 187, 200n1
patriarchy: childrearing, 185; family command, 185, 187; *Little Orphan Annie*, 80, 85; Popeye, 91; power, 90, 187; private property, 100; provider, 12; *Pudd'nhead Wilson*, 105; Western countries, 187
Paul and Virginia (de Saint-Pierre), 18–21, 25, 62, 119, 191n1 (chap. 1), 193n9, 199n1
Paulsen, Gary. See *Hatchet*
Peachman, Rachel Rabkin, Finnbin, 97
Peanuts (Schulz), 151; Charlie Brown, 130, 131
Perham, Mike, 68–69
Phelps, Donald, 93
Phillips, Adam, 63
Phillips, Douglas, *The Birkenhead Drill*, 17, 27–28
Physician's Oath, 177
Picard Dard, Charlotte-Adélaïde, 13
Picoult, Jodi. See *My Sister's Keeper*
Plague, The (Camus), 182–83
Poe, Edgar Allan, *Narrative of Arthur Gordon Pym of Nantucket*, 30–31
Pogrebin, Letty Cottin, 169–70, 187–88
polio, 176
Popeye (Segar), 49, 95; "Little Swee'Pea," 93; Olive Oyl, 52–54, 92–93; Popeye, 51–54, 91–93, 110, 113, 195n18; "Popeye Shipwreck," 49; Swee'Pea, 54, 91–93, 110. *See also* masculinity; patriarchy
Pratchett, Terry. See *Nation*
pretense, 120–21, 158–59, 163–64, 171–73, 185, 188, 193n2
Private Worlds of Dying Children, The (Bluebond-Langner), 159–60, 163–64, 171–72
Proctor, Philip, 139
Pudd'nhead Wilson (Twain), 105. *See also* patriarchy
Pullman, Philip. See *Golden Compass*
Pustz, Matthew, 143

Quran, 104

Red Tree, The (Tan), 155
Redbook. *See* Black, Irma Simonton
Redding, Sarah, 3
Richman, Amy L., 94
Richmond, Christina, 162, 199n2
Rivera, Geraldo, 69
Robin Hood, 54
Robinson Crusoe (Defoe), 30, 39–41, 43, 49–50, 54, 192n1; children's editions, 51; Elzie Segar, 51–52; Harold Gray, 51; nuclear family, 66. *See also* Rousseau, Jean-Jacques
robinsonade, 6, 42, 45, 58, 193n5; adolescent risk, 63; female sexuality, 52; *Little Orphan Annie*, 49; *Lord of the Flies*, 59; *Mary Lowell or the Desert Island*, 62; Normandie Drake, 57; *Orphan Island*, 47; *Popeye*, 49, 52; "Popeye's Ark," 51; sentimentality, 49; *Swiss Family Robinson*, 51, 57; *Terry and the Pirates*, 49; women, 51. *See also* circumnavigation; colonialism
Rodari, Gianni, 152
Rodgers, Mary, "Ladies First," 26, 142
romance, 27
Romeo and Juliet, 115
Romulus and Remus, 98
Roosevelt, Franklin Delano. *See Little Orphan Annie*

Rousseau, Jean-Jacques, 193n8; children, 92, 98, 195n17; *Robinson Crusoe*, 63; trial, error, and risk, 47
Rowell, Victoria, 89–90, 121, 188, 195n13, 196n26
Rugrats, 142
Rutherford, Markella, 47, 149–50
Rye, Maria, 77–78, 194n3. See also Christianity

Sadako and the Thousand Paper Cranes (Coerr), 160–63, 171
safe havens, 110–12, 115, 122; Bastard Nation, 111; *Unwind*, 112
Sailing Alone Around the World (Slocum), 68
Sailing the Dream (Perham), 68
Saint-Géran, 17
Sánchez-Eppler, Karen, 5, 62–63, 157
Saturday Night Live: The Fault in Our Stars 2: The Ebola in Our Everything, 161
Save the Children International Union (SCIU), 177
Schulz, Charles, 130. See also *Peanuts*
Sclair, Moacyr, *Max and the Cats*, 30, 192n6
Seduction of the Innocent (Wertham), 128–29
Segar, Elzie, *Thimble Theatre*, 13, 50, 91. See also *Popeye*; *Robinson Crusoe*
"selfless" parenting, 91, 117–18, 177, 185
Senate Subcommittee on Juvenile Delinquency, 14, 129–40, 142, 197n7, 198n17
Sendak, Maurice, 119–20, 158–59, 199n31. See also *Outside over There*
Sennett, Richard, 8, 48
Series of Unfortunate Events, A, 142
"Ships in Bottles" (Lawrence), 46
Shusterman, Neal. See *Unwind*
Silverstein, Shel, 26
Simpson, A. W. Brian (Alfred William), 31–32, 191n
Skenazy, Izzy, 13
Skenazy, Lenore, 43, 62, 117
Skinner, B. F. (Burrhus Frederic): Air-Crib, 94–97; Daniel W. Bjork, 96

Skinner, Deborah Buzan, "I Was Not a Lab Rat," 96–97
Slocum, Joshua, 68, 193n9
Small, David. See *Stitches*
Smith, Tom, 43
Snyder, Laurel, *Orphan Island*, 47
"Soldier an' Sailor Too" (Kipling), 17
Solnit, Albert J., 92
SOS Titanic (Bunting), 24
Spock, Benjamin, 124, 149
Stephens, Mitchell, 152
Stitches (Small), 160, 164–68
Sugar and Spike (Mayer), 14, 141–43, 146–56, 198n20; *Batman*, 148; Nell Rose Kottal Wall, 146, 152–55
sugar daddy: Daddy Browning, 84–85; Daddy Warbucks, 80, 194n8; Victoria Rowell, 90, 121
Sulik, Gayle, 158
Sunderland, Abby, 68–69
Superman comics, 148
Supreme Court (US): *Amistad* orphans, 37; right to die, 175
Sutherland, Abby, 13
Svonkin, Craig, 142
Swift, Jonathan. See *Gulliver's Travels*
Swiss Family Robinson (Wyss), 17, 51; familialism, 52; gender norms, 62. See also *Mary Lowell or the Desert Island*; robinsonade

Taddeo, John, 162
Tan, Shaun, 155
Tanner, Beccy, 176–77
Teenage Sex and Pregnancy: Modern Myths, Unsexy Realities (Males), 112
tender-years doctrine, 77, 80, 82, 91, 185
Terry and the Pirates (Caniff), 49, 54–58, 59, 127–28, 130; *Terry and the Pirates Shipwrecked on a Desert Island*, 49
They're Saved! They're Saved! (Dawes), 18
Thimble Theatre (Segar), 13; *Popeye*, 50, 52–54, 93
"This Is Your F.B.I." (radio show), 125

This Won't Hurt a Bit (and Other White Lies) (Au), 163, 172–73
Thomas, Marlo, 26
Thomson, Matthew, 73
Three Mouseketeers, The, 153
Tilley, Carol, 128–29
Titanic, 16, 20–29; "Orphans of the Deep, Titanic Tots" (Michel and Edmond Navratil), 78–79. *See also* Dix, Dorothy
Titlestad, Michael, 30
Todres, Jonathan, 9, 191n1 (intro)
Tom Thumb tales, 99
Tournier, Michel, 99
Triger, Zvi, 117
True Confessions of Charlotte Doyle, The (Avi), 42–43, 59
True Spirit (Watson), 68
Truth about Cinderella: A Darwinian View of Parental Love, The (Daly and Wilson), 101
Tuskegee syphilis study, 180
Twain, Mark, 105

"Ugly Duckling, The," 135
United Nations: Convention on the Rights of the Child (CRC), 4, 6, 67, 165; Committee on the Rights of the Child, 98
Unsinkable (Sunderland), 68–69
Unwind (Shusterman), 108–9; "storking," 112–14, 118, 122, 196n24. *See also* safe havens
Uruguayan air force flight 571, 35–36, 63–64; "the Miracle of the Andes," 36
"Use of Force, The" (Williams), 181

Verne, Jules, *Dick Sand; or, A Captain at Fifteen*, 42–43

Walker, Nancy E., 4
Wall, Helena, 40, 48
Wall, John, 4
Waters and the Wild, The (Block), 103–4, 196n21. *See also* kith
Watson, J. B. (John Broadus), 147
Watson, Jessica, 68–72

Watson, Victor, 154
Weilke-Mills, Courtney, 8
Wertham, Fredric, 128–30, 134, 143; *Saturday Review of Literature*, 131
What's Up with Richard? Medikidz Explain Leukemia (Chilman-Blair and Taddeo), 162
What's Wrong with Children's Rights (Guggenheim), 9
Why Kids Lie: How Parents Can Encourage Truthfulness (Ekman), 169
Wiesner, David, 155
Wilhelm Gustoff, 21
Willems, Mo, 155
Williams, William Carlos, 180–81
Wilson, Margo, 101
Winnicott, D. W., 7
Wittgenstein, Ludwig, 150
women and children first (WCF), 16–17, 19–29, 33–34, 56–58, 71, 79, 97, 177–78
Women Who Raised Me, The (Rowell), 89–90, 121. *See also* sugar daddy
Wonder Woman (Marston), 147–48
Woodhouse, Barbara Bennett, 4
Wordsworth, William, 124, 150
World Sailing Speed Record Council, 68
Wright, Bradford, 125
Wyss, Johann, 62. *See also* robinsonade; *Swiss Family Robinson*

Yachting Girl (Homer), 18, 47
Yellow Kid, The, 80
Young-Bruehl, Elizabeth, 88

Zeiher, Hartmut, 49
Zeiher, Helga, 49
Zelizer, Viviana A., 8, 80–82
Žižek, Slavoj, 49, 84, 183

www.ingramcontent.com/pod-product-compliance
Lightning Source LLC
Chambersburg PA
CBHW030621230426
43661CB00053B/2093